3 2158 00020 7967

P9-DEL-903

DATE DUE			
JUL 2 3 1991			
DEC 1 0 1991			
DEC 0 8 1992			
OCT 2 9 2002			
10/06/14			

HARPER COLLEGE LIBRARY
1200 W. ALGONQUIN RD.
PALATINE, ILLINOIS 60067-7398

Contexts of Competence

Social and Cultural Considerations in
Communicative Language Teaching

TOPICS IN LANGUAGE AND LINGUISTICS

Series Editors
Thomas A. Sebeok and Albert Valdman
Indiana University, Bloomington, Indiana

CONTEXTS OF COMPETENCE
Social and Cultural Considerations in Communicative Language
Teaching
Margie Berns

THE DYNAMIC INTERLANGUAGE
Empirical Studies in Second Language Variation
Edited by Miriam R. Eisenstein

THE GRAMMAR OF DISCOURSE
Robert E. Longacre

ISSUES IN INTERNATIONAL BILINGUAL EDUCATION
The Role of the Vernacular
Edited by Beverly Hartford, Albert Valdman, and Charles R. Foster

LINGUISTICS AND LITERACY
Edited by William Frawley

LITERACY IN SCHOOL AND SOCIETY
Multidisciplinary Perspectives
Edited by Elisabetta Zuanelli Sonino

THE RELATION OF THEORETICAL AND
APPLIED LINGUISTICS
Edited by Olga Mišeska Tomić and Roger W. Shuy

Preface

The introduction of communicative competence as the goal of second and foreign language teaching has led to recognition of the role of context in language learning and use. As communicative competence is defined by the social and cultural contexts in which it is used, no single communicative competence can serve as the goal and model for all learners. This recognition has had an impact on program design and materials development. One significant change is that the choice of a teaching method is no longer the primary concern. Instead, the first step for the program designer is becoming familiar with the social and cultural features of the context of the language being taught. This includes a consideration of the uses speakers make of the language, their reasons for using it, and their attitudes toward it.

Contexts of Competence: Social and Cultural Considerations in Communicative Language Teaching explores the relationship between context and competence from a theoretical and practical perspective. Its audience is applied linguists in general and language teaching practitioners in particular. The overall aim of its five chapters is to provide a framework for consideration of various contexts of language learning and use and to guide the implementation and development of models of communicative language teaching that are responsive to the context-specific needs of learners. The approach to the design and evaluation of language teaching materials it presents also demonstrates that functional linguistics is well suited to second and foreign language teaching practice because of its emphasis on language as a means of social interaction and its recognition of the role of the social structure in determining language form and function.

Chapters 1 and 2 set up a theoretical background for an understanding of the nature of language use. Chapter 1 provides an historical and theoretical perspective on the significance of functional approaches for a variety of sociolinguistic and pedagogical issues, theoretical and applied, taken up in subsequent chapters. The chapter begins with a review of the Prague School and the British tradition, two functional approaches to linguistics which have contributed insights of the role of context in the use of language. These approaches have converged in the work of Michael Halliday, whose theory of language as social semiotic is taken up in the latter part of the chapter. Key concepts associated with each approach (for example, meaning, function, context of situation, functional sentence perspective, and meaning potential), as well as the aims and goals of linguists working within each approach, are discussed. The contributions of functional linguistics to language teaching are also considered. Chapter 2 explores three sociolinguistic notions that are closely linked with context—communicative competence, intelligibility, and model. The theoretical perspectives of Hymes and Halliday contribute to the framework for the discussion. An understanding of the interdependence of these notions is presented as an essential foundation for addressing a number of pedagogical concerns such as the identification of the goals and aims of language teaching, choice of materials and methodology, and the nature of evaluation and assessment. Drawing upon the theoretical foundation outlined in Chapters 1 and 2, Chapter 3 examines three distinct contexts of the use of English—India, West Germany, and Japan—and draws a "sociolinguistic profile" of each. The profiles, which describe the users of English in each setting, their attitudes toward it, the uses they make of it, the functions it serves, and the nature of the linguistic adaptation and innovation observable in their use of English, illustrate how the system of a language is firmly situated in a cultural and social system. Concerns of English language teaching in each of the contexts is also described. Chapter 4 reviews the origins of communicative language teaching and terminology associated with it (e.g., function, notion, and functional syllabus) and examines the theoretical underpinnings of interpretations that claim to be based on communicative principles. The focus is on selected interpretations made by methodologists and applied linguists from three countries whose work has been most influential in shaping the nature of communicative language teaching. The first to be described and discussed, from the United States, is Sandra Savignon's interactional approach; the second, from Great Britain, is Widdowson's discourse approach; and the third is that of Hans-Eberhard Piepho, from West Germany, whose approach is communication based. Each interpretation provides a basis for a definition of communicative language teaching that is useful as a starting point for curriculum and materials design. In Chapter 5, the issues and concerns introduced in earlier chapters are brought full circle. Principles of the Prague and British approaches to linguistics are defined as criteria for the assessment of communicative materials based on Savignon's, Piepho's, and Widdowson's approaches and designed for learners of English in Japan, West Germany, and India. Similarities and differences among the materials are discussed with reference to the notions of communicative competence, intelligibility, and model. The sociolinguistic profiles provide the context for understanding the source of the differences.

The examples presented and discussed throughout are taken from English language contexts and materials. However, this does not mean this is a book about English language teaching alone. The goals and outcomes it describes as well as the theoretical framework it provides are not language specific, but are applicable and relevant to the learning and use of all languages. The questions of "why language is as it is" in a particular context, who the users of the language are, what uses they make of it, and how they feel about this language are important for the teachers of any second or foreign language.

Basing program design upon the answers to these questions is becoming increasingly important. Worldwide there is greater interaction among members of different cultures and speakers of different languages and language varieties. This change creates the need for language teaching programs that develop learners' ability to express, interpret, and negotiate meaning in one or more languages. The more that is known about the relationship between context and communicative competence in particular social and cultural settings, the better prepared that teachers, materials writers, and program designers will be to respond and adapt to the communicative needs of learners in a variety of contexts and thus enable them to develop the communicative competence appropriate for interaction in those contexts.

Acknowledgments

The support, encouragement, and assistance of a number of students, colleagues, and friends have been invaluable in the completion of this book.

A professional debt of gratitude is owed those who read and responded to earlier versions of all or parts of the manuscript and who devoted time to discussing various issues addressed in this book with me. Their insights have contributed considerably to the spirit, substance, and form of the final product. They include Eyamba Bokamba, H. Douglas Brown, Christopher Candlin, Willis Edmondson, Kazumi Hatasa, Yukiko Hatasa, Juliane House-Edmondson, Claire Kramsch, Braj Kachru, Yamuna Kachru, Cecil Nelson, Ruth Petzold, N. S. Prabhu, Hildebrando Ruiz, Sandra Savignon, Tony Silva, S. N. Sridhar, Peter Strevens, J. L. M. Trim, Ladislav Zgusta, and the graduate students in my English as a Second Language seminar at Purdue University.

Thanks are also due to those who assisted me in countless technical tasks: Taunja Jarrett and Diana Woolen for their patience at spending seemingly endless hours at an antiquated word processor throughout the months of vision and revision; to Barbara Matthews for scrupulous attention to the numerous and time-consuming details of manuscript preparation; and to Russell Merzdorf for his talent and expertise in the production of a number of figures.

I also owe Eliot Werner, Andrea Martin, and Wendy Gravis of Plenum Press thanks and appreciation for their gracious and creative guidance throughout the process of transforming my manuscript into this book.

Margie Berns

West Lafayette, Indiana

Contents

Contexts of
Competence

CHAPTER 1

Functional Approaches to Linguistics

Functional approaches to linguistics have contributed considerably to an understanding of the relationship between contexts of language use and the communicative competence of speakers in those contexts. Insights into this relationship are well-represented by two linguistic traditions: the Prague School and the British tradition. As a representative of a functional approach, each is concerned with language as a tool which performs many tasks and with analysis in terms of the uses, or functions, that language serves. Each tradition has been particularly influential in the work of Michael Halliday, whose systemic-functional theory reflects a convergence of both approaches.[1] The Prague and British traditions can be distinguished from one another by the extent to which each explores the functional resources of a language and by the particular linguistic problems each focuses upon. The compatibility of their goals and aims and the complementary results of the efforts of scholars working within these traditions have led to a greater appreciation of the nature of language, of "why it is as it is." This chapter is a look at the goals and outcomes of the Prague School and the British tradition and their convergence into Halliday's functional approach. As such it provides an historical and theoretical perspective on the significance of functional approaches for a variety of theoretical and applied sociolinguistic and pedagogical issues taken up in subsequent chapters.

---

[1]Halliday has also been influenced by the Copenhagen School, particularly by the work of Hjelmslev. The present discussion is limited to the Prague and the British traditions because of their influence on Halliday's interpretation of function and variation, two features of language of particular significance for an exploration of language use in various contexts.

The Prague School

The approach to language study that has come to be known as the Prague School was founded in the mid-1920s in Prague at the initiative of Vilém Mathesius. It began with regular meetings of an informal organization of young scholars, known as the Prague Linguistic Circle, interested in a range of theoretical problems. Its early members included Nikolai Trubetzkoy, Roman Jakobson, Bohumil Trnka, and Bohuslav Havránek. Although participating scholars were scattered by the outbreak of the Second World War, this event did not interrupt their activities or their influence on a succeeding generation of Czech and Slovak linguists, both in Czechoslovakia and abroad.

The Prague School, as it is now known, can be described as "structuralist" and "functionalist" (Vachek 1966). *Structuralist* designates Prague School scholars' concern with the relationships between segments of language, which was conceived of as a hierarchically arranged whole. They insisted that no element of any language can be properly evaluated if viewed in isolation: its correct assessment can be obtained only if its relationship to all other elements coexisting in that same language system is established.

Functionalist applies to the Prague School in the sense that any item of language (e.g., sentence, word, morpheme, or phoneme) exists solely because it serves some purpose, or function. Function in the Prague School sense refers to the respective roles played by the various structural components in the use of the entire language. This functional perspective is identified with a particular view of language as:

> an instrument of communication and thought. In communication linguistic devices fulfil a certain function, have a certain task. No language element can be fully understood and evaluated unless its relations to the other elements are analyzed and unless its functions, especially its communicative function, are taken into consideration. (Menšíková 1972:44)

This view of language in terms of function has become the hallmark of the Prague School and explains why its approach is often referred to as "functionalism" (Chomsky 1977; Monaghan 1979) or "functional linguistics" (Sampson 1980). The functionalist perspective also distinguishes it from American structuralism, or descriptivism. While descriptivists were solely concerned with description of languages, the efforts of the Prague linguists, proceeding from a universally recognized view of language as a tool of communication, moved their analysis toward an explanation of the purpose of each feature of language. The Prague School linguists would use their ideas about the functions of different structures to explain structural differences between languages, such as the frequency of the passive construction in English as opposed to other languages. The descriptivists would not conceive of using such ideas in this way, since functional explanations make unavoidable use of such concepts as "the wish not to identify the actor explicitly" which are not observables and therefore are illegitimate by the descriptivists' behavioristic standards (Sampson 1980).

Early Prague School theorists focused primarily on showing the respective functions of the various structural components (internal functions) in the use of the entire language. The chief interest of many was the elaboration of morphology and phonology, and it is in the area of phonological theory that their impact is most strongly felt. A general result of their efforts to develop phonological theory was the establishment of the phoneme as one of the fundamental elements of linguistic theory as a whole and of scientific description and analysis of language in particular.

The work generally acknowledged as the most significant product of early Prague School scholarship is Trubetzkoy's *Grundzüge der Phonologie* (*Principles of Phonology*, 1939), which presents an analysis of the various functions that phonological analysis can serve. Trubetzkoy distinguished three phonological functions—the distinctive, delimitative, and the culminative—which ultimately enable the hearer to work out the sequence of words uttered by a speaker. The *distinctive* function keeps different words and sentences separate. In German, for example, the phoneme /j/ serves to distinguish *verjagen* 'to expel' from *versagen* 'to deny'. The *delimitative* function helps hearers locate word boundaries and thus segment utterances into meaningful units. The phoneme /j/ also serves this function in German by its appearance in morpheme-initial position only (*ver + jag + en*). The *culminative* function involves the role of stress. The English stress pattern of one main stress per word, for example, functions to signal to the hearer the number of words the signal must be segmented into. *Grenzsignale*, or boundary markers, is Trubetzkoy's term for these demarcators of syllable and word boundaries.

Prague linguists also worked at the sentence level. Mathesius' (1928, 1961) study of word order and its various functions led to what has come to be called Functional Sentence Perspective (FSP). By emphasizing the function of each sentence part over the form, FSP identifies the communicative and expressive necessities of speech as the starting point for analysis. FSP identifies the functional explanation of the way speakers tailor their statements to what the hearer already knows and to the context of the discourse built up to that point. According to Mathesius, the need to express this continuity means that a sentence commonly falls into two parts: the *theme*, which refers to something already known to the hearer, and the *rheme*, which is the new information relating to the theme. For example, in *Mary gave John a raise*, *Mary* is the theme and *gave John a raise* the rheme. This implies *Mary* has been the subject of the discourse and it is the act she performs, giving John a raise, that is new and of interest.

Although Prague School scholars are best known for their functional analyses of sounds and sentence structure, their concerns were not limited to these areas. They were also interested in functions of language which are external to the systems of sounds and sentences. For their description of language external functions they drew on the Austrian psychologist Karl Bühler's (1934) three-way analysis of utterances in terms of situational context: (1) the *referential function (Darstellungsfunktion)* is the purely communicative function, used to inform of the factual, objective content of extralingual reality; (2) *the expressive function (Kundgabefunktion)* characterizes individual speakers by such markers as gender, social class, or age which distinguish members of the same community from one another (i.e., it refers to personal characteristics of speed, rhythm, word, and phrase preferences); (3) *the conative function (Appelfunktion)* is used to influence the hearer in some way and is often signalled by sentence intonation. In American English this function can be signalled by the duration of a vowel. For example, lengthening the vowel in "give" in the utterance "I want you to put your hands in your pockets and give," used in an appeal made on behalf of a charity, fulfills this function (Sampson 1980).

Attention to language external functions is consistent with the Prague School's rejection of the view that language is a self-contained whole "hermetically separated from the extra-lingual reality" (Vachek 1966:7). In their view the main function of language is to react to and refer to this reality and to serve the needs and wants of the mutual understanding of individual members of a language community. Thus only by considering the internal and external purposes language serves is it possible to understand "why language is as it is."

The Neo-Prague School

Present-day representatives of Prague School Linguistics, for example, Josef Vachek (1964, 1976, 1985), Paul Garvin (1963, 1972), Jan Firbas (1964), František Daneš (1964), and Jacek Fisiak (1986) have been referred to as members of the "neo-Prague school." The fundamental elements of the neo-Prague approach are the same as those which characterized the early Prague group— focus on an explanation of why language is as it is and description of the functions language serves. The new generation of Prague School scholars both continues the work of the earlier generation and develops new areas of emphasis. Firbas (1972) has continued work on FSP. Investigation of issues related to machine translation has been one of Garvin's (1972) concerns. Daneš (1964) and Svoboda (1967) have provided analyses of the levels and systems of language that integrate FSP into the system of language as a whole and direct the study of FSP beyond the structure of the sentence and clause toward the structure of text, or discourse. Their work in particular influenced Halliday's early studies of the language system.

The Prague School and Language Teaching

Members of the Prague School have been consistently interested in the practical application of their theory to language teaching. Vilém Fried's (1972) collection of papers on this topic offers an overview of applications, a large number of which are concerned with methodology, for example, the classroom presentation of morphological features of technical English (Dubský 1972), principles of stylizing a dialogue (Camutaliová 1972), or the determination of sentence patterns to serve the practice of particular structural features (Barnet 1972). The pedagogical framework of their techniques and procedures is based on Harold Palmer's (1920) oral-aural method and the audio-lingual method derived from the association of American structuralism with behaviorism. However, these two methods have not been used to dictate what is to be taught; to do so would require ignoring an essential characteristic of the Prague School—the need for an understanding of the relationship of form to meaning and function (Camutaliová 1972).

As could be expected in an approach to methodology based on a functional view of language, attention is given to the ways in which forms actually function in the language being taught. Mathesius had proposed a contrastive method of analysis which was exploited in language teaching through contrasts of functions (e.g., word order) in the language being learned with the learners' native language (Vachek 1972). Teaching materials also address the functional differentiation within a language, for example, its literary styles, the style of the spoken language, its technical and scientific styles. Teaching to meet learners' need for specialization in the reading and writing of scientific and technical texts and understanding the functional style of these areas has also been addressed through a Prague approach (e.g., Beneš 1972). The same is true for the teaching of commercial English (Pytelka 1972).

Prague School linguists have claimed that the aim of language teaching is to enable the learner "to communicate in the foreign language" (Menšíková 1972:45). Their pedagogical applications, however, are not consistent with this claim. The contributions to Fried's volume focus on techniques and procedures that teachers can use in presenting information to learners and the nature of the information learners need to know about the language they are learning. The implications of teaching for communication have not been realized in techniques that engage learners in language use and that ultimately develop their communicative ability, techniques generally associated with language teaching approaches that have communication as their goal.

The British Tradition

Referred to by various names—Firthian linguistics (Davis 1973; Mitchell 1975; F. R. Palmer 1968), the London School (Langendoen 1968; Sampson 1980), and the British tradition (B. Kachru 1981a)—the linguistic approach associated with John Rupert Firth (1890-1960) is an independent variant of continental structural approaches.[2] Firth, historian-turned-linguist, was the holder of the first chair of linguistics in Great Britain (at the University of London) and had profound influence on developments in linguistic theory in Britain in the 1960s and 1970s. For a long time most linguists trained in Great Britain were direct students of Firth and worked within his philosophy of language.

The influence of the British tradition, the origins of which can be traced back to the work of Henry Sweet and Daniel Jones, has not been restricted to Great Britain. In Canada, for example, it has informed the study of register by Gregory and Carroll (1978) and Benson and Greaves (1973). In West Germany, where it is known as "British contextualism," it has been applied in Steiner's (1983) study of discourse and Geiger's (1979) description of a context-based model for the training of teachers of English as a foreign language. In the United States, where the British tradition has been overshadowed by the dominance of Chomskyan transformational linguistics, Braj Kachru (1977 and after) has drawn upon Firth's philosophy of language to inform a framework for descriptions of various sociocultural settings (e.g., India) of English language use.

Firth's Philosophy of Language

Firth's approach to language, more appropriately called a philosophy of language rather than a theory, is founded on the mutual dependency of language, culture, and society. Firth insisted upon seeing language primarily as a means used by people to function in society. His belief that language needs to be studied as part of the social process, or as a social phenomenon, was the basis for his insistence on what he termed the "sociological component" of linguistic studies. His investigations of language at every level—from the phonological to the contextual—bear evidence to the essential role of society in the under-

[2]Firth makes a careful distinction between *structural* (European approaches) and *structuralist* (American approaches) linguistics. The former examines the internal relations and functions of a language, while the latter assigns to the structure some kind of autonomy from the people who actually employ it and sees in language an arrangement of atomistic units that have some sort of independent existence. For Firth, structuralist perspectives "form only one part of one branch of what might properly be called structural linguistics" (1955 [1968]:44).

standing of language. The sociological component was particularly important in Firth's study of the notions of meaning and context.

Meaning

Firth defined *meaning* as function in context, a definition based on his view that meaning is not simply a matter of word-based semantics and is not to be regarded as a separate area of linguistics.[3] The central proposal of Firth's linguistic theory was "to split up the meaning or function into a series of component functions. Each function will be defined as the use of some language form or element in relation to some context" (1935 [1957b]:19). Meaning as a statement of the function of linguistic items in their context was regarded as the principle underlying all linguistic description.

Firth viewed meaning in much the same way as the Prague linguists. His distinction between formal and situational meaning corresponds to the Prague School's internal and external functions. *Formal meaning* refers to the relations between one formal item and another, for example, lexical items in collocation or syntactical relations between grammatical categories. *Situational meaning* refers to those relations between language items and nonverbal constituents of the situation. It includes phonological and phonetic features, lexical and grammatical features, even orthography. The latter is illustrated in a word with two spellings, such as *labor* (the American spelling) and *labour* (the British spelling). When the word *labour* is written *or* and not *our*, for example, it means "there's an American somewhere in the situation, either as author, reader, editor or publisher" (Catford 1969:254).

Mitchell's description of Firth's view of meaning highlights an innovative aspect of his philosophy, the notion of the discovery and statement of meaning: "He did not regard words or sentences as self-evident units of language, nor words as semantic units par excellence, lexical encapsulations of dictionary definitions . . . meaning was not a GIVEN for Firth, it was waiting to be discovered and stated" (1975:154-155). "Discovery" and "statement" are key concepts in the techniques Firth proposed for linguistic analysis.

As linguistic tasks, discovery and statement of meaning were to be made by means of a "hierarchy of techniques," which would describe the meaning of linguistic events in a range of specialized statements at the contextual, lexical, grammatical, and phonological levels (Firth 1950 [1957b]:183). At the phono-

---

[3]This view of semantics contrasts sharply with Bloomfield's view. For Bloomfield, in Firth's words, "semantics is the study of meaning; and also, the study of meaning is the study of grammar." For Firth, "nothing could be worse than this. It is precisely this confusion of formal grammar with contextual meaning that has been the downfall of all but the most intelligent students of language"(1935 [1957b]:15).

logical level, the statement of meaning is determined by the set of choices among phonemes available in a specific context. For example, in English, part of the meaning of the sound /t/ is its role among the choices available in the construction of a word-initial cluster of three consonants (such as that in *strap*). In contrast, the sound /b/ does not have this role as part of its meaning. At the lexical level, a statement of meaning is made in terms of such groupings as kinship terms, parts of the body, numerals, or proper names of people and places. Part of the meaning of *Chicago*, for instance, is its identification as a place name. At the grammatical level, the meaning is stated in terms of word and sentence classes and of the interrelation of these categories. The grammatical meaning of the word *drank*, for instance, includes its ability to be preceded by *you, they, Jane, Harry,* or *the dog* and followed by *milk, soda,* or *poison*, but not vice versa. At the contextual level, a statement of meaning is made in terms of the relationship between language and the various aspects of the situation, a relationship Firth referred to as the context of situation (which will be discussed below). The contextual meaning of an utterance includes the identity of the speaker and hearer, their relationship to one another and the effect of the utterance, that is, what happens after it is said.

Firth compared the levels of language to the colors of the rainbow and liked to use the analogy of the prism when explaining his approach to analysis of meaning at all levels. A summary of this analogy is provided by Berry:

> The analysis of language into its levels is like an experiment with white light. One sees a beam of light, holds up a prism, converts the white light into the colours of the spectrum, holds up another prism, converts the spectrum back into white light, and looks again at the beam of light with a new awareness of the colours that go to make it up. One reads or hears a piece of language, analyses it into levels, then rereads or rehears the language with a new awareness of its composition. (1975:48)

Berry also observes the usefulness of the spectrum analogy in preventing interpretation of the levels of language as rigidly distinct from one another because "they sometimes seem to shade into each other as do the colours of the rainbow" (1975:48).

Context and Context of Situation

Analysis of meaning into a range of levels is a productive means of gaining insight into language. Statements of meaning at the contextual level in particular have provided an understanding of the nature of language use. An appreciation of these insights, however, depends upon familiarity with Firth's use of the terms *context* and *context of situation*.

For Firth, context was more than the physical environment of a situation. Often it included the knowledge shared by participants in an interaction as well as the relevant objects that were present. This use of context was a significant step toward answering two related questions about language use and a native speaker's understanding of that use: (1) how is it that, in spite of a lack of perfect and consistent correlations between language and situation, the native speaker, given the text alone (e.g., a tape-recorded conversation), is often able, with a considerable degree of accuracy, to reconstruct the situation and (2) given the situation, how does a native speaker produce language which is appropriate? Concern with these issues underlies Firth's perception of what is "properly the province of linguistics: the study of what people say, what they hear, and in which contexts of situation and experience they do these things" (1930:150). Focus on these questions characterizes Firth's interest in the relationship between language and the various aspects of the situation in which it is used, a relationship he described as *context of situation*.

Firth borrowed the notion of context of situation from the anthropologist Bronislaw Malinowski (1923, 1935), who was his colleague for a time at the University of London. Malinowski considered the primary function of language to be its pragmatic function: language is a means of behaving. Thus, it is most appropriately studied as part of activity, as doing. In a two-volume description of fieldwork experiences in Polynesia engagingly titled *Coral Gardens and Their Magic*, he states that "the meaning of a single utterance . . . can be defined as the change produced by this sound in the behaviour of people" (cited in Dixon 1965:91).

Malinowski illustrated his pragmatic approach in his attempts to solve the problems of equivalence he encountered translating Trobriand Island texts into English. The translation task presented situations in which a view of language as merely the direct reflection of subject matter proved simplistic and inadequate. In studying the Islanders, Malinowski had observed that language used in connection with typical daily human activities derives its meaning from the context of the ongoing human activity, for example, fishing, hunting, cultivating, buying and selling, eating, greeting, or instructing a child. As the contexts change, the meanings of single items vary, depending upon

> the situation in which the words have been uttered. A phrase, a saying or a few sentences concerning famine may be found in a narrative, or in a magical formula, or in a proverbial saying. But they may also occur during a famine, forming an integral part of some of those essential transactions wherein human beings co-operate in order to help one another. The whole character of such words is different when they are uttered in earnest, or as a joke, or in a narrative of the distant past (cited in Dixon 1965:88).

To provide a framework for this phenomenon, he used the term *context of situation*. It was to embrace not only spoken words but facial expression, gesture, bodily activities, the whole group of people present during an exchange of utterances, and the part of the environment in which these people are engaged. This conception of and commitment to context means that the situation in which words are uttered cannot be passed over as irrelevant to the linguistic expression.[4]

Firth, who shared Malinowski's commitment to context, borrowed the term context of situation, but interpreted it more abstractly to refer to general situation types instead of the ongoing activity surrounding a particular utterance. Firth offered no classification of these contexts of situation, since he believed characterizations might differ: "Some might prefer to characterize situations by attempting a description of speech and language functions with reference to their effective observable results, and perhaps also with reference to a linguistically centred social analysis" (Firth 1957a [1968]:177).

As a means of establishing the features of these general situation types, or contexts of situation, Firth proposed a set of broad and general parameters to frame the analysis of language events in the social context:

1. The relevant features of participants, persons, personalities
   a. Verbal actions of participants
   b. Nonverbal actions of participants
2. The relevance of objects and nonverbal and nonpersonal events
3. The effect of the verbal action

Additional features considered relevant were the economic, religious, and social structures to which the participants belong; the type of discourse in which they are engaged (e.g., monologue or narrative); personal characteristics such as participants' age or sex; and the types of speech, such as flattery, cursing, praise, or blame (Firth 1957b [F. R. Palmer 1968]:178). Mitchell's (1957) study of the language of buying and selling in Cyrenaica illustrates the role of language in this typical situation and demonstrates the usefulness of the parameters Firth proposed for describing contexts of situation.

This specification of features is only an approximation of a context of situation, but "it is parallel with the grammatical rules, and is based on the repetitive routines of initiated persons in the society under description" (Firth 1950:182). The social roles of the initiated persons are determined by the social organization, and "the chief condition and means of that incorporation is learning to say what the other fellow expects us to say under the given circumstances" (Firth 1935 [1957b]:28). This is a result of the experience gained from childhood

---

[4]Another study which illustrates this view of context is Frake's (1964) description of "How to Ask for a Drink in Subanun."

on in the process of acculturation—we learn how to behave in speaking in the various roles we come to fulfill in our own life.

Language Variety and Restricted Languages

Firth rejected a monolithic view of language, believing that "unity is the last concept that should be applied to language" (Firth 1935 [1957b]:29). Early in the development of his philosophy of language he stressed that de Saussure's view of the unity of language is a misconception. If the goal of linguistic analysis is to understand language as a means of human behavior, recognition of the variety of language available to speakers is essential:

> The multiplicity of social roles we have to play as members of a race, nation, class, family, school, club, as sons, brothers, lovers, fathers, workers, churchgoers, golfers, newspaper readers, public speakers, involves also a certain degree of linguistic specialization. (Firth 1935:29)

Firth used the term *restricted language* to refer to the varieties of language related to the particular social roles, professional interests, or job-related activities in which individuals participate. The language varieties of the legal, scientific, or technical discourse, of women, men, children, or adolescents, are representative of restricted languages. In contemporary linguistic studies this notion is generally referred to as *register*.

Firth also acknowledged the role of language in broader pragmatic contexts. As a result of his experiences abroad, particularly in India, he observed firsthand the role of English as a tool for international communication and as a means of representing a particular way of life. This recognition underscores the key role of context in determining the varieties and functions of language. (A number of contexts and the varieties and functions associated with them are illustrated in Chapter 3.)

Firth's philosophy of language, the techniques he proposed for the analysis of meaning, his interpretation of the notion of context of situation, his rejection of the unity of language, and his insistence upon a sociological component in language study were substantial contributions to the British tradition of linguistics. Many of his ideas either have been developed further or have served as the basis of new directions in linguistic inquiry. Among the scholars who have followed Firth and have developed his philosophy of language, Michael Halliday is acknowledged as the most outstanding in taking Firth's ideas and developing them into more than a philosophy of language. Halliday's theory of language, commonly known as "systemic-functional" or simply "systemic" linguistics, serves as the framework for a number of linguists working throughout the world, especially in Europe, Great Britain, Canada, Australia, and the United States.

Halliday's Systemic-Functional Linguistics

Systemic-functional linguistics has been described as a way of thinking about language, and more specifically, as a way of asking questions about language as an object, about the nature and functions of language, and about what language is like and why (Halliday and Martin 1981). As its name implies, systemic-functional linguistics is concerned with the systems and functions of language. However, these notions are not studied independently of one another or of other aspects of language. They are part of a theory of language within the British tradition that views language in Firth's terms—as social behavior. In attributing importance to the sociological aspects of language, systemic-functional linguistics is particularly interested in investigating the role of social structure in determining human behavior in a given culture. Thus, the role of culture is related to the varieties of language the speakers use, the functions of language which serve the speakers, and the semantic systems that enable them to communicate with one another.

While it has been claimed that Halliday's systemic-functional linguistics has taken a form different from the work of Firth (Berry 1975; F.R. Palmer 1968), Firth's influence on Halliday is evident in the centrality of system to the theory, in the sociological orientation to the description of language varieties dependent on social situation, that is, social dialects and registers (Firth's restricted languages), and to the varying roles, or functions, language can serve. Due to his attention to the role of the social context in the expression and interpretation of speaker's meaning, Halliday has in fact been regarded as the developer of what Firth called "sociological linguistics" (Monaghan 1979). The Prague School also influenced Halliday, especially in the integration of the Functional Sentence Perspective into his theory of language and the formulation of the systems and levels of language.

Development of the Theory

Hallidayan linguistics has gone through a series of phases, beginning with focus on the grammatical level, as in "Categories of the Theory of Grammar" (1961) and "Notes on Transitivity and Theme in English" (1967, 1968). Much of Halliday's early work on transitivity and theme, modality and mood, and his later work with Hasan (Halliday and Hasan 1976) on cohesion are concerned with describing the textual function and elaborating on the lexicogrammatical system of language. The influence of Mathesius's FSP with its concepts of theme and rheme is considerable in these studies. Halliday was interested in FSP "because it is an integral part of the system of language, and therefore

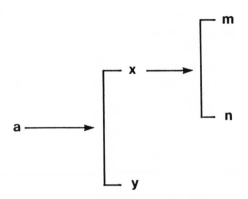

Figure 1. Schematic of a system.

essential to the understanding of the processes of speaking, listening, reading and writing" (Halliday 1970a [Kress 1976]:30).

Systemic grammar has been concerned primarily with the impact of the various choices speakers make in deciding to utter a particular sentence out of the infinitely numerous sentences that their language makes available. The goal is to establish a network of systems of relationships which will account for all the semantically relevant choices in a language as a whole.[5] In the 1970s, Halliday's development of systemic theory moved from concern with grammatical categories to the exploration of language development from a functional perspective. During this time emphasis on the semantic significance of systemic choice increased, and *system* emerged as the central category of the theory (Butler 1982). Language is conceived of as a system of systems. For Halliday, a *system* is defined as:

> a set of options with a condition of entry; that is, it is a range of alternatives which may be behavioural, semantic, grammatical etc., together with a specification of the environment in which selection must be made among these alternatives. It has the form 'If x, then either a or b or . . .' (1975:7)

An example of a system is represented in Figure 1. It reads as follows: There are two systems, x/y and m/n, the first having entry condition a; if a is chosen (over not choosing anything at all), then the choice is between x and y; the system m/n has entry condition x/y; if x is chosen over y, then either m or n has to be chosen, and so on (Halliday 1973).

Increasing emphasis on semantic significance is accompanied by increasing attention to the functional basis of the model and the establishment of three

[5]The selection of papers edited by Gunther Kress [1976] provides a useful summary of Halliday's systemic grammar and its development.

basic functional components of language, which Halliday labels "metafunctions." This phase of the theory can be characterized by a view of language (1) as social behavior, that is, as part of the social system, (2) as a system of options in meaning, labeled "meaning potential," and (3) as a network of multiple systems with mutually dependent formal and semantic systems of meaning potential and social structures.

Halliday's movement toward analysis of text and social context is represented in his 1978 collection of articles entitled *Language as Social Semiotic*. This volume, a summary of Halliday's thinking on the nature of language up to that point, is important as a presentation of his theory as a means of interpreting language and meaning within a sociocultural context. In its chapters, Halliday offers a schematic representation of language as social semiotic, a scheme which captures his view that language is explainable only as the realization of meanings that are inherent in the social system, or culture, and not "out there," separate from language. Halliday's subsequent publications are increasingly concerned with semiotics, particularly with a semiotics that brings together European functionalism, cultural analysis, social theory, and his theory of language as social semiotic (see e.g., Halliday and Hasan 1985; Threadgold, Grosz, Kress, and Halliday 1986).

Function

The central role of function, previously identified as characteristic of systemic-functional linguistics, has been interpreted in various ways and related to all levels of language. As has been shown, the Prague School contributed to the development of functional understanding of language at the sentence level through Mathesius's Functional Sentence Perspective (FSP). While the Prague School scholars and, to greater extent, Firth also addressed the communicative functions of language, it is Halliday's theory which has comprehensively investigated and developed situational as well as formal functions at a level between language and its social and cultural context.

One systemic-functional interpretation of function takes into account the speakers of a given language and what they can do with it. This interpretation operates at two levels of abstraction. The first level is that of particular uses of language—for example, to approve or disapprove; to express beliefs, opinions, or doubts; to include and exclude; to ask and answer questions; to express personal feelings; to greet. However, looking at uses of language in this sense is potentially misleading. If only this level is considered, the impression is given that such uses are easily identified and can be neatly listed and classified, a task that Firth had indicated would be a difficult one. Halliday puts this level of function into perspective:

It is obvious that language is used in a multitude of different ways, for a multitude of different purposes. It is not possible to enumerate them; nor is it necessary to try: there would be no way of preferring one list over another. These various ways of using language are sometimes referred to as "functions of language." But to say language has many "functions," in this sense, is to say no more than that people engage in a variety of social actions—that they do different things together. (1978:186-187)

The fact that language can serve a variety of purposes, Halliday maintains, is precisely because the language system, at a higher level of functional abstraction, is organized into metafunctions. They are a set of highly generalized, abstract functional components which comprise the semantic system. This system is a set of choices which represent the possibilities of what a speaker "can mean." The influence of the Prague School is evident in Halliday's formulation of the systems or levels of language. Although Firth had worked on a system-structure framework, Halliday turned to the Prague School for insight into this aspect of language because he found Firth's model insufficient "in the sense of explaining why language has the particular form and shape it has" (Halliday 1970a [Kress 1976]:26). Halliday borrowed Daneš's (1964) and Svoboda's (1968) notions of three "levels" or "systems" of language—semantic, grammatical, and organization/functional—as a basis for his definition of metafunctions. In identifying metafunctions, Halliday enriches the concept of function by introducing a more generalized level to underlie the so-called functions of language, which he sees as of relatively little importance to a linguistic description. The metafunctions form an interrelated set of three components of the linguistic system that are realized in every text a speaker creates: the interpersonal, the ideational, and the textual.

The *interpersonal function* represents the speakers' potential to establish and maintain social relationships and identifies and reinforces the speaker as an individual. Through this function speakers "intrude" into the situation in which they are participants. Whatever speakers do with language, they are also exploiting its potential for expressing content in terms of their own experience of the world and for giving structure to that experience. This potential is realized in the *ideational function*. It represents the meaning potential of speakers as observers of the situation. It serves for the expression of the speaker's experience of the processes, persons, objects, abstractions, qualities, states, and relations of the world around and inside them. The *textual function* determines the structural realizations of the ideational and interpersonal functions. This function, in Halliday's words, "is what enables the speaker or writer to construct 'texts' or connected passages of discourse that is situationally relevant; and enables the listener or reader to distinguish a text from a random set of sentences" (cited in Lyons 1970:143). Any linguistic unit is the simultaneous realization of the three functions. "Whatever we are using language for, we need to make some reference to the categories of our experience; we need to take on some role in the interpersonal situation; and we need to embody these in the form of text" (Halliday 1970a [Kress 1976]:29).

In the following text, created by a child and his father at play, each of the systems and simultaneous realizations of each metafunction are illustrated:

NIGEL [small wooden train in hand, approaching track laid along a plank sloping from chair to floor]: Here the railway line . . . but it not for the train to go on that.

FATHER: Isn't it?

NIGEL: Yes tis. . . . I wonder the train will carry the lorry [puts the train on lorry (sic)].

FATHER: I wonder.

NIGEL: Oh yes it will. . . . I don't want to send the train on this floor . . . you want to send the train on the railway line [runs it up plank onto chair] . . . but it doesn't go very well on the chair. . . . [makes train go round in circles] The train all round and round . . . it going all round and round . . . [tries to reach other train] have that train . . . have the blue train ('give it to me') [Father does so] . . . send the blue train down the railway line . . . [plank falls off chair] let me put the railway line on the chair ('you put the railway line on the chair!') [Father does so] . . . [looking at blue train] Daddy put sellotape on it ('previously') . . . there a very fierce lion in the train . . . Daddy go and see if the lion still there. . . . Have your engine ('give me my engine').

FATHER: Which engine? The little black engine?

NIGEL: Yes . . . Daddy go and find it for you . . . Daddy go and find the black engine for you. (Halliday 1978:115-116)

Each of the meaning systems and their realizations in this text are given in Figure 2. For example, in the interpersonal system the negative polarity for the demand *want* is realized in *don't want*. The person choice of speaker is realized in *I*. In the ideational system the expression of processes in the choice of location is realized in *on*; in the choice of participant structure of the process it is *give* for two participants and *have* for one. The textual system is realized in the cohesion choice of reference to situation through the demonstratives *this*, *that*, *the*, and *here*.

Meaning and "Meaning Potential"

For Halliday, like Firth, "The term semantic is not to be understood in the restricted sense of 'lexicosemantic'. . . . It refers to the totality of meaning in language" (1975:8-9). This totality of meaning consists of sets of semantic options, or systems, that correspond to the situation types available in a culture. These options, which are realized in the ideational, interpersonal, and textual functions (see Figure 2), are the meanings it is possible for the grammar of

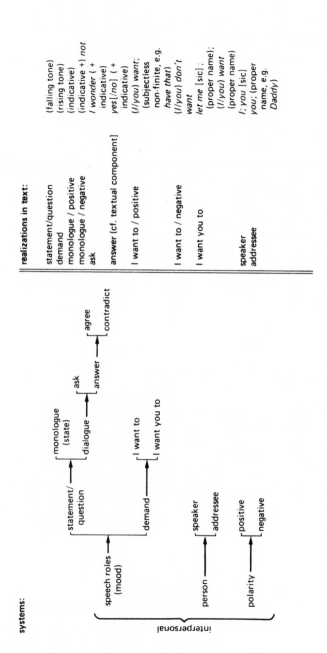

Figure 2. Realizations of metafunctions in text. Source: M. A. K. Halliday, 1978, *Language as Social Semiotic: the Social Interpretation of Language and Meaning*, Edward Arnold, pp. 118-120.

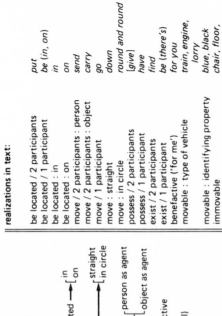

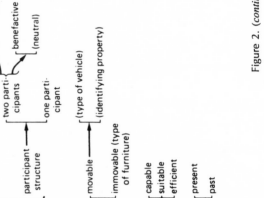

systems:

realizations in **text:**

be located / 2 participants	*put*
be located / 1 participant	*be (in, on)*
be located : in	*in*
be located : on	*on*
move / 2 participants : person	*send*
move / 2 participants : object	*carry*
move / 1 participant	*go*
move : straight	*down*
move : in circle	*round and round*
possess / 2 participants	*[give]*
possess / 1 participant	*have*
exist / 2 participants	*find*
benefactive ('for me')	*be (there's)*
	for you
movable : type of vehicle	*train, engine, lorry*
movable : identifying property	*blue, black*
immovable	*chair, floor, railway line*
	will
capable	*(be) for*
suitable	*(go) well*
efficient	
past	*(past tense)*
present	*(present tense)*

Figure 2. *(continued)*

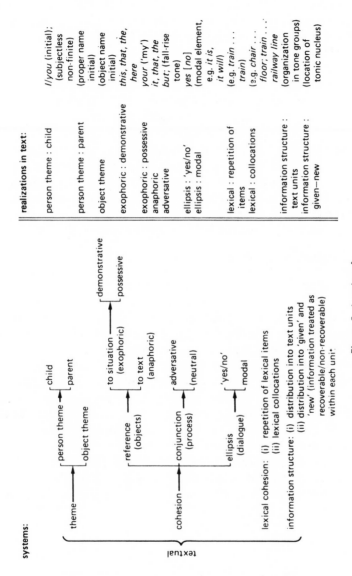

Figure 2. (*continued*)

the language to express. Halliday calls these semantic systems *meaning potential*.[6]

Meaning potential is one of a set of three potentials: the *behavior potential*, which includes, but is not restricted to, what a speaker can do with language as speaker/writer and hearer/reader, and the *lexicogrammatical potential*, what the speaker can say. The meaning potential, the "can mean," is the level of realization between the "can do" and the "can say." That is, the meaning potential is determined by the behavior potential of a culture or a group. It, in turn, determines the lexicogrammatical potential. Of the three potentials, meaning potential is the most important for Halliday because of its relationship to the culture. As he has stressed, "meaning potential is defined not in terms of the mind but in terms of the culture" (1973:52). He also asserts that the value system of a culture is encoded in the language behavior of the society's members and that as children learn language, they simultaneously acquire the meaning system of the culture. The development of a child's meaning potential, described as "learning how to mean," is taken up later in this chapter.

Context, Situation, and Language Variety

Firth's influence is evident in the connections Halliday makes between context, situation, and language varieties. For Halliday, "the contexts in which meanings are exchanged are not devoid of social value; a context of speech is itself a semiotic construct, having a form (deriving from the culture), that enables the participants to predict features of the prevailing register—and hence to understand one another as they go along" (1978:2). And "context plays a part in determining what we say; and what we say plays a part in determining the context. As we learn how to mean, we learn to predict each from the other" (1978:3). In this sense, context acts as an interface between the levels of culture (situation) and form (grammar, lexis) and is concerned with relationships between these levels and the situation.

Halliday, in investigating the interaction of language and the social system, developed the concept *register* (first used by Reid [1956]) to uncover the general principles governing variation by situation. He was interested in discovering

---

[6]This concept reflects Halliday's rejection of any dichotomy between doing (performance) and knowing (competence): "There is no difference between knowing a language and knowing how to use it" (1978:229). For him the two are inseparable. The potential is what is available to the speaker, what is known; choices are made from what is known for use of the language, for performing.

how it is possible for native speakers, drawing upon their knowledge of register, to predict a great deal about the language that will occur in a given situation, or a social context of use. These predictions through register are determined through three categories of features of the situation: what's going on, who's taking part, and what part language is playing, that is, whether it is spoken or written or in the form of a monologue, dialogue, letter, or newspaper report.[7] Halliday has organized these features into a framework and designated them as field, tenor, and mode, respectively.

Register refers to the obvious fact that the language we use (be it in speaking or writing) varies according to the type of situation in which speakers find themselves and the relevance of the particular parameters identified with the situation type. For example, concrete and immediate features of the environment may be more relevant in a situation in which young children's remarks bear direct pragmatic relation to the environment, as exemplified by the utterance *Some more*! to demand "more of that which I've been eating." The context of situation can also refer to abstract and remote features, as in a technical discussion among specialists, where "situation" could include the particular problem they are trying to solve and their own training and experiences. In this case, the immediate surrounding of objects and events would likely not be referred to (unless the object of their problem solving were a concrete object in front of them). Just as the immediate objects may not be relevant, the identity of the individuals in the situation may not be essential to predicting features of the discourse. For example, in "I love you" it is important that John is saying this to Mary, not to Jane. However, in "Would you please fill this prescription?" the role of "pharmacist" is important, but not the pharmacist's name.

Halliday's development of Firth's notion of restricted language and context of situation serves to clarify the explanatory power of context in describing language. The context influences what we say and what we say influences the context. This interpretation of context is central to Halliday's theory of language development as well as his theory of language.

Learning How to Mean

Halliday's goals in investigating language development are consistent with Malinowski's belief that "the study of meaning should start with observations on infant speech and the growth of linguistic expression within the context of culture" (1939:43). Halliday's observations of his son Nigel's language devel-

---

[7]Register is distinguished from dialect. The former is variation according to use and reflects the diversity of social processes; it is determined by what the speaker is doing. Dialect is variation according to user and reflects the social order in the sense of a hierarchy of social structure. It is determined by who the speaker is, not by what a speaker does.

opment from the age of nine to eighteen months provide substantial insight into the origin of language in a young child and into the role of a language in transmitting the norms of a culture and ultimately in mediating the child's behavior patterns.

As Nigel learned how to use the language system to make meanings, he simultaneously learned behavior that is relevant to the contexts of situation in which he is a participant. One example rich in its representation of the norms of the culture in which Nigel learned English is a set of instructions from his mother: "Leave that stick outside; stop teasing the cat; and go and wash your hands. It's time for tea" (1978:124). The cultural norms and values mediated through these words concern, among others, the boundaries dividing space (sticks don't belong inside), the continuity between the human and animal world (cats should not be teased), and the regular occurrence of cultural events (tea happens at a set time).

In studying child language development from a functional perspective, Halliday attempted to determine the linguistic functions through which children learn the language. Bernstein's (1964) work on the key linguistic contexts through which children learn the culture was useful in framing Halliday's analysis because of its compatibility with his views on language as an essential part of the process of cultural transmission from parent to child. While Bernstein's goal was the identification of the contexts through which children learn culture, Halliday's purpose was to discover the contexts of situation through which children build up a picture of the reality that is around and inside them.

Halliday found that at the beginning stages of language development meaning is related primarily to limited functions, or uses, of language. As the child broadens the uses made of language and takes on more social roles, the potential to mean increases and meaning becomes a more powerful feature of the realization of social acts. As language is developed and used, the child learns the potential within the language, develops a meaning potential for each function, and also learns roles in which this potential can be realized and even predicted. This process Halliday calls "learning how to mean."

The process (see lower portion of Figure 3) has three phases. Phase I, which begins at about nine months of age, is characterized by six social functions: the regulatory, the interactional, the imaginative, and the heuristic, which are derived from Bernstein, and the personal and the instrumental, which are Halliday's additions.

The *regulatory function* is the use of language to exert control over the behavior of others. It can also be called the "do as I tell you" function. The *interactional function* is used to establish and maintain contact with those who matter to the child. It is the "me and you" function. The *imaginative function* serves to create an environment of the child's own. This is known as the "let's

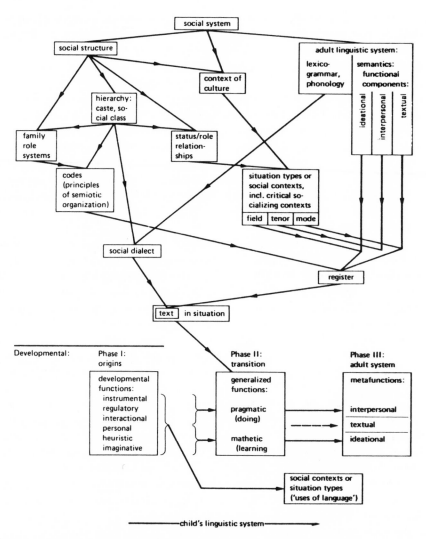

Figure 3. Schematic representation of language as social semiotic. Source: M. A. K. Halliday, 1978, *Language as Social Semiotic: the Social Interpretation of Language and Meaning*, Edward Arnold, p. 69.

pretend" function. The *heuristic function* is the use of language to explore the real-world environment. This is the "tell me why" function. The *personal function* is used by the child to express his own individuality and self-awareness. It is the "here I come" function. Finally, the *instrumental function* is the use of language to satisfy the child's own material needs, in terms of goods and services. It is the "I want" function.

The child does not make use of all six functions at once. The first to be used are the regulatory, instrumental, and interactional functions, which are synonymous with use of language in the child's system. Thus the content of the utterances is determined by the function, since the purposes are related to persons, objects and actions which are immediate. The child will refer only to things present and express a particular want or need to act upon those people who are present. At the same time, this environment is the child's context of situation. That is, if language is being used to regulate, the situation itself is one of regulation. The child eventually discovers that this language system is not adequate. Consequently, the personal, heuristic, and imaginative functions are added for their potential to "mean" about objects, persons, or events not immediate to the situation.

In Phase II, the child's language begins to take on more features of the adult linguistic system, namely, the lexicogrammatical, which is incorporated into the developing set of functions. The child's desire and need to learn about the immediate environment, as well as to share experiences, are realized through these functions which make it possible to talk about or demand objects not present, or to express liking, or approval of those objects. During this phase, the concept of function is modified, as the six functions (also uses) are replaced by two transitional functions: the *mathetic*, which is the "learning" function and subsumes the personal, heuristic, and imaginative uses of the previous phase, and the *pragmatic*, which is the "doing" function and replaces the regulatory, interactional, and instrumental functions. At the beginning of Phase II, the child uses either one or the other of these functions. However, as the child approaches the language system of the adult, the strict separation between them is abandoned, and eventually the two merge in every speech act, thus blending action and reflection.

Entry into Phase III, the adult language system, represents yet another interpretation in the concept of function. It is no longer synonymous with use, but becomes a more abstract concept representing the most general functions of the adult language system, the ideational and interpersonal. The adult system, through its reduction of the functions of the first phase into these two abstract functions, makes it possible for the speaker to talk about things not present. The content is no longer dependent upon its immediacy within the environment. The child's linguistic system, freed from situational constraints, makes it possible to talk about people and objects not present. In this phase, the textual function emerges and provides the form for the realization of the other two functions. This function brings with it the emergence of the language that the child will use and continue to develop for the rest of his or her life. The child has learned how to mean.

Models of Language and Language Development

Halliday's view of the language system as firmly situated within the entire social system, or context of culture, and the systematic nature of the relationship between the text, the linguistic system, and the situation is represented in Figure 3. The diagram serves as a concise summary of his models of language and language development.

Halliday's description of the relationships represented in the figure begins with text:

> Social interaction typically takes a linguistic form, which we call text. A text is the product of infinitely many simultaneous and successive choices in meaning, and is realized as lexicogrammatical structure, or "wording." The environment of the text is the context of situation, which is an instance of a social context, or *situation type*. The situation type is a semiotic construct which is structured in terms of *field, tenor* and *mode*: the text-generating activity, the role relationships of the participants, and the rhetorical modes they are adopting. These situational variables are related respectively to the *ideational, interpersonal* and *textual* components of the *semantic system*: meaning as content (the observer function of language), meaning as participation (the intruder function) and meaning as texture (the relevance function). They are related in the sense that each of the situational features typically calls forth a network of options from the corresponding semantic component; in this way the semiotic properties of a particular situation type, its structure in terms of field, tenor and mode, determine the semantic configuration or *register*—the meaning potential that is characteristic of the situation type in question, and is realized as what is known as a "speech variant". This process is regulated by the *code*, the semiotic grid or principles of the organization of social meaning that represent the particular subcultural angle on the social system. The subcultural variation is in its turn a product of the *social structure*, typically the social hierarchy acting through the distribution of family types having different familial role systems. A child, coming into the picture, interprets text-in-situation in terms of his generalized functional categories of *learning* (*mathetic*) and *doing* (*pragmatic*); from here by a further process of abstraction he constructs the functionally organized semantic system of the adult language. He has now gained access to the social semiotic; this is the context in which he himself will learn to mean, and in which all his subsequent meaning will take place. (1978:125)[8]

Halliday's systemic-functional linguistics has developed from a systemic grammar to a comprehensive theory of language and language development

---

[8]Halliday describes the relationship represented between the components of the system outlined in Figure 3 by the word pair determining/determined. He considers "determined" of greater importance because it denies the linguistic system as the sole determinant of meaning and recognizes other elements in the social system, among them context of situation, as codeterminants of meaning. Emphasis on "determined" and on the other components of the culture which are part of the social system contrasts with other schools of linguistics or philosophies of language which avoid considering the role of culture and the social system in shaping texts and, in the case of the latter, of determining the linguistic system itself.

which can account for a broad range of linguistic phenomena, including, but not limited to, language variation, meaning-making systems, language functions, and the origin of a language in a child. The Prague School and the British tradition have played significant roles in the development of Halliday's models. The influence of the Prague School was particularly important in contributing to Halliday's interpretation of the systems and levels of the semantic potential of language. From the British tradition, the work of Malinowski and Firth have been instrumental in shaping his interpretations of context and situation. The significance of Halliday's work is, in part, his development of these various notions and the comprehensive theory of language as social behavior of which they are an integral part. His work is also significant in its demonstration of the potential of a sociolinguistic perspective to language study and its necessity for answering the question of why language is as it is. Firth insisted upon a sociological component in linguistic studies and provided glimpses of its role in understanding the nature of language. Halliday has not only insisted upon it as a component, he has made it the very foundation of his theory and in so doing has provided much more than glimpses of the possibilities it offers—he has provided a panoramic view of the possibilities of culturally and socially informed studies of the nature of language learning and use.

The British Tradition and Language Teaching

Linguists working within the British tradition have had extensive experience in assessing the implications of a functional view of language for language teaching practice. This experience was in part directly related to the need for British linguists to respond to the demands for language teaching resulting from colonization. World War II also created demands for their expertise, a period in which Firth personally was involved in producing materials for and teaching in emergency intensive courses in a variety of languages.

Application of the British tradition continues in discussions and investigations of the role of English as an international language and as an institutionalized nonnative variety in a range of contexts (e.g., Chishimba 1985; B. Kachru 1982b, 1983; Lowenberg 1985; Nelson 1983, 1985; and L. Smith 1981, 1983). The implications of the reality of these varieties on English language teaching also have been elaborated on in these studies and in more comprehensive discussions (e.g., Strevens 1978, 1980). Firthian linguistics has also been applied to language teacher training (Geiger 1979, 1981), discourse analysis and English language teaching (Sinclair 1980; Widdowson 1978, 1979), and the development of materials for language for specific purpose courses (Allen and Widdowson 1974).

Halliday's particular approach to functional linguistics has been applied to language teaching with a variety of emphases. In the 1960s, scale-and-category grammar was offered as a linguistic basis for language teaching (Halliday, McIntosh, and Strevens 1964). This model was also applied in the development of a text for the study of stylistics (Benson and Greaves 1973). Ragan (1987) has explored the implications of a view of theory as use for the relation between text and context and language teaching. He suggests that the systemic-functional model inform teachers' understanding of text and thus the instance of language with which their learners come into contact and create.

The period in which Halliday was giving more weight to the concept of system and to the interpretation of language in terms of alternatives with systems networks roughly coincides with new orientations in the teaching of English. As the goals of learners increasingly were interpreted with respect to their purposes in the use of the language, a need evolved for a theoretical framework which could serve as a comprehensive basis for a use-based approach to language teaching. This framework, derived in part from Halliday's investigations of the sociosemantic aspects of language and language use and the concept of meaning potential, was applied to syllabus design (Munby 1978; Wilkins 1976) and to changes in methodology and materials development (Candlin 1976, 1981; Piepho 1974, 1979; Ventola 1983). A selection of these developments in language pedagogy will be discussed extensively in Chapters 4 and 5.

Functional linguistics is especially suited for application to second and foreign language teaching because of its emphasis on language as a means of social interaction and on the role of social structure in determining language form and function. Functional theories of language are also useful in the establishment of a framework for the analysis of concepts that are central to the development of language teaching approaches, syllabuses, and materials, for example, communicative competence, model, and intelligibility. This analysis, a necessary prerequisite to understanding the contexts in which languages are taught and learned, is undertaken in the next chapter.

CHAPTER 2

Communicative Competence, Intelligibility, and Model

First language development in a child does not take place in a social and cultural vacuum. This is also true for second and foreign language development. One crucial difference between first language development and second and foreign language development, however, is the options available in the classroom setting. These options are the pedagogical choices made concerning which model, whose intelligibility, and which communicative competence should be the learners' goal. The answers to these questions vary with the learners' purposes and with the speech community of which they want to become members. Thus, the questions are interrelated. The choice of a model depends on the identification of the communicative competence learners are to develop and the degree of mutual intelligibility with other speakers they are to achieve. An appreciation of the interdependence of these three notions and its consequences for pedagogy begins with a look at the issues and concerns, theoretical as well as applied, each represents.

Communicative Competence

In the early 1970s the term *communicative competence* emerged as an important theoretical construct in explorations of the relationship of language to society and culture. Scholars in Great Britain (Campbell and Wales 1970), West Germany (Habermas 1970, 1971), and the United States (Hymes 1971) introduced the term in a variety of interpretations. Although each interpretation has contributed to the indispensable role the concept has come to play in a number of disciplines, the American anthropologist Dell Hymes' use of the term, perhaps because it was a direct challenge to the prevailing linguistic theory of the time, has had the most significant impact on linguistics and language teaching in the United States.

29

Hymes's "communicative competence," a development and elaboration of Chomsky's notion of competence, is a reaction to two aspects of the Chomskyan view of language and linguistics. The first is restriction of the domain of linguistic inquiry to grammatical competence, that is, knowledge of grammatical rules. For Hymes, the linguist's task is not only the description of what a speaker knows about grammar but also an accounting "for the fact that a normal child acquires knowledge of sentences not only as grammatical but also as appropriate" (1971:5). This knowledge of appropriateness is knowledge of sociolinguistic rules and is separate from knowledge of grammatical rules.

Hymes also was concerned with language use as a meaning-making activity. No account of language can be considered descriptively adequate or complete until performance features of the very kind Chomsky excluded—"memory limitations, distractions, shifts of attention and interest, and errors (random or characteristic)" (1965:3)—were allowed for, because they can influence meaning. And since meaning is clear only in real language situations, idealized situations with an ideal speaker listener cannot provide insight into the nature of the sociolinguistic rules that comprise communicative competence. Only in an investigation of performance and of social interaction of all kinds, a procedure Hymes calls "ethnography of communication," can the nature of these rules be discovered. Hymes expresses his concern with the integration of linguistic theory with a more general theory of communication and culture: "social life shapes communicative competence and does so from infancy onward. Depending on gender, family, community and religion, children are raised in terms of one configuration of the use and meaning of language rather than another" (1980:vi).

Hymes's investigation of communicative competence and the parameters of appropriateness is in the spirit of Firth: "A piece of speech, a normal complete act of speech, is a pattern of group behavior in which two or more persons participate by means of common verbalizations of the common situational context, and of the experiential contexts of the participants" (Firth 1930:173). Appropriateness is determined by each speech community or, in Firth's term, a speech fellowship; it is defined by the shared social and cultural conventions of a particular group of speakers. Thus, there must be recognition of and allowance for different sets of culturally determined rules in describing and explaining language use.

Hymes and Halliday

Focus on language in use, the social dimension of language, and concern with language as a form of communication did not become a part of linguistic studies for the first time through Hymes. American linguistic research associated with the tradition of Sapir and Whorf and their interest in the relationship between language and thought represents attention to the pervasive influence of language on human life. British linguistics has a long tradition of viewing language as behavior and as related to its sociocultural context, a tradition Hymes acknowledges. Hymes has also noted that the Prague School and Firth are "noble exceptions" to the view of equating the speech community with the language of the members of the speech community, a perspective associated with transformational-generativism which rules out the heterogeneity of a speech community, diversity of role among speakers, and stylistic or social meaning.

Halliday has suggested that his approach to linguistic interaction is not unlike that of Hymes, particularly with regard to the notion of socially constrained meaning potential. Yet Halliday questions the need for the introduction of the term communicative competence, since it assumes (following Chomsky's notion of competence) that it is necessary to isolate this system of rules from its social context. Halliday does not believe this is how language should be conceived. "If we are concerned with 'what the speaker-hearer knows,' as distinct from what he can do, and we call this his 'competence', then competence is communicative competence; there is no other kind" (1978:92). Thus, for Halliday, it is unnecessary to speak of *communicative* competence; knowing how to use language is the same as knowing what one can do with language.

In spite of their differences, Hymes and Halliday share a view of the role of language in social life. Hymes's claim that "social life shapes a person's ability to use language appropriately from infancy onward" (1980:vi) is the assumption underlying Halliday's investigation of Nigel's language development. Halliday and Hymes also agree on the fundamental issue of society and behavior, which Hymes expresses as an "understanding of social life as something not given in advance and a priori, but as having an ineradicable aspect of being constituted by its participants in an ongoing evolving way" (1980:xiv).

Communicative Competences

If, as Hymes claims, social life shapes a person's ability to use language appropriately, that is, if the context determines a person's communicative competence, and if there is more than one social setting in which appropriateness in using a language can be shaped, the concept of communicative competence cannot be considered in monolithic terms. English, for example, as a result of contact with different cultural and social systems, has been adapted to the social life of the English-speaking communities in which it has come to function. This process of adaptation, or nativization, has been extended to notions of appropriateness in form and function.

Firth's interpretation of context of situation provides a theoretical orientation for describing the individual communicative competence of each speaker that has evolved in nonnative settings. The cultural setting and personal history of each participant in a speech situation determine what is appropriate within that setting. Nonnative English-speaking participants in a speech situation in India make choices of acceptable and appropriate forms and functions of English that an English speaker in the United States would not or cannot make because the options are not available or meaningful. For example, the expression "I bow my forehead" is an acceptable and appropriate form of greeting in Indian culture, but if used in American society, it would not have the same meaning as it has for Indian English speakers (if it would carry any meaning at all).

Context of situation, then, becomes essential to an understanding of communicative competence in general, because it leads to an appreciation of communicative competence "in specific." That is, only through inclusion of context of situation as a parameter for determining what communicative competence means do the pluralistic nature of a language and the independent existence and the dynamic creative processes of nonnative varieties come into focus.

Several studies of nonnative Englishes (e.g., Chishimba 1985; B. Kachru 1982b, 1983; Lowenberg 1985; Magura 1985) illustrate how different cultural settings of English language use have determined distinct communicative competences. Indian English, African English, and Indonesion English represent unique communicative competences with characteristic features and functions which are shared by members of the respective English speech communities and which those members are able to put into effect to express different aspects of their cultural identity. This pluralistic approach not only draws attention to the actual features of a language shared by a group of people and recognized as theirs through these common features, but also emphasizes that these same culture-bound features function to distinguish the varieties and subvarieties as distinct from one another.

Intelligibility

Intelligibility has been variously defined, with investigations of the concept typically based on two general interpretations: narrow (e.g., Bansal 1969; L. Smith and K. Rafiqzad 1979) and broad (e.g., Catford 1950; Nelson 1985; Olsson 1978; Voegelin and Harris 1951). This distinction rests upon whether "comprehending," which "involves a great deal more than intelligibility" (Smith and Rafiqzad 1979 [L. Smith 1983]:58), is considered in addition to phonetic features—the "noise" as Firth called it (1930:77).

Clarification of the confusion resulting from various interpretations of the concept has been offered by L. Smith and C. Nelson (1985). They identify three levels of understanding that are often referred to in the literature under the label of "intelligibility." Their terms for distinguishing each level are *intelligibility*, *comprehensibility*, and *interpretability*.

Intelligibility is related to pronunciation and to stress and rhythm differences. American English *con*troversy and *lab*oratory versus British English con*tro*versy and la*bor*atory are examples of this level.

Comprehensibility is related to word and utterance meaning. An instance of the word "troubleshooter" illustrates this level. In British and American English this term is generally used to refer to a person responsible for locating and eliminating the source of trouble in any flow of work; in Nigeria, however, it refers to a person who makes, rather than eliminates, trouble. Given these two meanings, one may ask how a native speaker unfamiliar with the Nigerian use of the term would understand a Nigerian newspaper headline that announces "the government will not tolerate any trouble shooters" (Adeyanju 1987).

Interpretability is related to meaning in terms of the question "What does a speaker (writer) mean *by* saying X" rather than "What does X mean?" (Leech 1983). To be able to answer this question the hearer/reader needs to be familiar with the social and cultural background of the creator of the text, for example, the norms and standards for behavior that determine what may be said, how it may be said, or whether something may be said at all. In other words, the hearer/reader needs to be familiar with the speaker's communicative competence. The relevance of interpretability can be observed in native-speaker reactions to texts in English written by nonnative speakers as rambling, incoherent, or replete with irrelevant material (Clyne 1981). Variations in discourse structure across cultures which have their source in different systems of values and beliefs are often the cause of such negative judgments.

As Smith and Nelson (1985) point out, crucial to the appreciation of nonnative varieties of English is the recognition that all three levels are important and that while intelligibility is a real concern, misunderstandings at the level of comprehensibility and interpretability are most serious in communication. Candlin's (1982) description of levels of discourse understanding highlights the significance of the level of interpretability in cross-cultural communication. In his two-part framework, intelligibility refers to the possible immediate cause of miscommunication, while interpretability is the deeper source, stemming from potentially conflicting systems of value and belief. However, degree of immediacy, Candlin stresses, should not be equated with the importance of one cause over the other. While unintelligible pronunciation can inhibit communication, there are means of repair available at this level, for example, repeating a word or phrase, spelling a word, writing a word or phrase down on paper, or pointing to the object referred to; uninterpretability, on the other hand, is less amenable to this type of on-the-spot repair. Cultural and social attitudes are more difficult to recognize as the source of miscommunication and more difficult to explain, since holders of social attitudes, values, and beliefs are not always able to recognize them as such, let alone articulate them.

Intelligibility and Context

The role of context in determining intelligibility is not a recent discovery. In a 1950 study of intelligibility, Catford stated that context "has an extremely important bearing on intelligibility" (1950:12). He defined context as "the situation as a whole in which any linguistic form which is being considered is set" (1950:13). "As a whole" refers to linguistic as well as situational context; the latter, which is of interest here, has four components similar to Firth's parameters of context of situation:

1. Speaker and hearer
2. Relative positions and actions at moment of utterance
3. Various objects in the surroundings and their relation to the speaker and hearer
4. The hearer's linguistic background and experience as well as educational and cultural background

Catford's specification of the features of the hearer's linguistic background and experience as well as educational and cultural background implies that an utterance may be judged unintelligible if it fails to meet all or any of the hearer's expectations regarding linguistic, educational, or cultural factors. In other words, intelligibility is dependent upon more than the "correct" pronunciation of sounds: it also involves the consideration of context of situation.

Nelson, like Catford, goes beyond the noise and formulates his interpretation of intelligibility as "the degree to which we are saying what we want to be saying, think we are saying, or ought to be saying; and . . . how we *interpret* what is being said to us, or what we are reading" (1985:3-4). To be intelligible, in Nelson's terms, is to be understood by an interlocutor at a given time in a given situation. This broad view of intelligibility includes comprehensibility and interpretability. It also brings in the components of the context of situation and the variability of intelligibility. The incorporation of variability is important because it acknowledges that what may be intelligible to one interlocutor may not be intelligible to another.

The role of the participants as a component for understanding the context of situation becomes salient in cross-cultural encounters. In understanding a text, the readers/hearers have tasks to perform; in creating the text, the speakers/writers desiring intelligibility must use language forms which are appropriate, that is, they must select the appropriate words, the morphological and syntactic devices, as well as appropriate sounds. The readers/hearers must identify the forms and associate them with appropriate elements in the situation. They must make a response to the utterance in accordance with the conventions of the speech community within which they are operating (Catford 1950:10).[1]

Systematic research by an international group of scholars and researchers provides insight into the cross-cultural parameters of interpretability. This research, associated with the Cross-Cultural Speech Act Realization Project, is focused on a comparison of interactions and the rules that govern the use of language in particular speech acts (e.g., apologies, directives, and compliments).[2] One of the project's goals is the establishment of the similarities and differences between native- and nonnative-speakers' patterns of use when making an apology or a request. Nessa Wolfson, a member of the project group, has pointed out that study of patterns of interaction in a given speech community provides evidence of cultural norms and values: "Beneath the surface structure of the linguistic forms and social etiquette involved in their use lies a gold-mine of information about the value systems of speakers" (1984:236).

A personal experience serves as illustration of the role of cultural values and norms in affecting interpretability. While in graduate school, I attended classes with students from a variety of cultural backgrounds. One student with whom I had a friendly relationship was Zambian. One day he greeted me with "Hello, Margie. How are you? Oh, I see you've put on weight," an utterance which, although syntactically well formed and intelligibile, struck me as inappropriate, since I had not been ill or in any other circumstances which would cause concern over weight loss and subsequent cause for remarking on weight gain. Why had he said this to me? It was not difficult to determine what the utterance "I see you've put on weight" meant in the sense of its reference, that is, that my friend had made the observation that I had gained a few pounds. However, it was less easy to determine what he meant *by* saying this. Did he mean to warn, to insult, or simply to describe? As an American English speaker I could have chosen any one of these, although none seemed likely given the situation (i.e., he is a friend, he has never insulted me before, and I had not been ill). When I asked what he had meant, my friend explained that he intended nothing more than to express his pleasure at my apparent good health and the prosperity it signified.

In the context of a greeting in Zambia, where a healthy, robust appearance is valued more highly than a lean, slender figure, my friend's observation would

[1]While Candlin's, Nelson's, and Catford's interpretations include L. Smith and C. Nelson's (1985) levels of comprehensibility and interpretability in the term intelligibility, this is not the sole source of their significance. They are important because they explore intelligibility as a sociolinguistic notion, as grounded in the structure of language and as finding its meaning and applicability in its use among participants in a speech event (Nelson 1985).

[2]See Wolfson (1984) for specific references.

have been recognized as appropriate to the situation by other Zambians. However, when said to an American, unfamiliar with Zambian norms of the greeting situation and with the cultural values reflected in these norms, miscommunication and a clash of conventional patterns resulted. Rather than being understood as a polite comment, it was initially interpreted as a rude and thoughtless one.

Appropriate choice of an item or feature for greeting is one example of sociocultural differences reflected in language. Indirectness of speaking is also realized differently from culture to culture. Chishimba (1985) offers examples of conventions for the creation of discourse in the African context in the following excerpt from Mulaisho's novel *Tongue of the Dumb*, set in southeast Zambia. In it, we see the realization of a very important norm of this context—indirectness of speaking. In a normal speech encounter, the participants begin with salutations, loaded in most cases with superfluous (by Western standards) words of respect, greeting, and exchange of opinion and impressions about the weather. Progressively, depending upon the topic and the relation of the participants, the discourse arrives at the focus of the conversation, with calculated pauses.

> "You come early," said Yuda when [the chief] entered the hut.
>
> "Yes, my son," replied the Chief.
>
> "Is it well at the house?" asked Yuda.
>
> "It is well. What about here; are you well, my son?"
>
> "I am well. A maimed man cannot expect to be as well as those who are lucky enough to have health," replied Yuda. You come to ask after my health, eh? It is as good as can be expected after being paraded round like rotten meat full of maggots which no one will touch."
>
> "But, my son, it was the white man's wish," said the Chief.
>
> "I know a thing or two, all the same. Lubinda has told me how much you did to protect me. You are a wonderful father of the village, aren't you! Naome!" he roared, "give the Chief some of that kacasu I have left . . ."
>
> "I have come about the visit of the Bwana Mkubwa," said (the Chief). (Mulaisho 1971:96-97)

As the anecdote and literary excerpt demonstrate, the acts speakers engage in are not constant across cultural boundaries. As Widdowson warns:

> Communicative functions are culture-specific in the same way as linguistic forms are language-specific. . . . What we call a complaint or a promise will not necessarily correspond directly with "categories of communicative function" in another culture. Asking for a drink in Subanun is not at all the same thing as asking for a drink in Britain. (1979:66)

Communication and the ability to participate successfully in discourse depend upon more than making and recognizing appropriate and intelligible noises. Knowledge of how to interpret the speaker's meaning is necessary if an individual is to find a text intelligible. Similarly, speakers and writers have to be able to express meaning through the linguistic and nonlinguistic conventions expected of them by their audience if they are to be both intelligible and interpretable. Thus, learning a language also means learning the patterns of structure that are expected for successful communication in the speech community of that language.

Interpretability and Contrastive Discourse Analysis

In including explicit reference to reading in an interpretation of intelligibility, Nelson, who has drawn on Olsson's (1978) work on intelligibility and written texts, provides a basis for considering written as well as spoken texts and the role of reader as well as writer in discussions of a speaker's intelligibility, comprehensibility, and interpretability. The importance of recognizing reading as a communicative act, or an act of interpretation, where intelligibility is a determinant of the success of the communication, is supported by recent work in contrastive discourse analysis (see, e.g., contributions to Kaplan 1983), which investigates the role of culture in the creation and interpretation of discourse and proposes to establish the nature of the differences between cultures and subcultures in the way texts are fashioned.

Constrastive discourse analysis and constrastive rhetoric are research areas which have developed around the investigation of discourse patterns and structures. Their purpose, ideally, is to relate the linguistic realization of a text to the cultural norms and meaning systems of the societies using the languages studied.

Attempts have been made to uncover the structures that writers impose upon the texts they are creating and the system of values and beliefs that are at the source of these structures. Attention to cross-cultural analyses of this type has increased in recent years, representing a broad range of languages. Interest in the notion of different patterns of text structure was first generated by Kaplan's (1966) study of paragraph organization of five major language groups.[3] In this study he describes what he considers to be dominant patterns of formal written discourse. While the models of paragraph structure he proposed reflect a cultural bias in favor of paragraph construction in American English, the models do serve as a significant attempt to deal with meaning at a level beyond the sentence (see Figure 4).

---

[3]While Kaplan's interpretation of the various cultures he investigated has been rightfully criticized for cultural bias, his findings have become a convenient point of departure for contrastive discourse studies. Kaplan's study has also proven significant because it underscores the inadequacy of sentence-level studies to account for all the distinguishing and meaningful features of a language. However, it also has limitations in this respect since Kaplan's focus was restricted to the paragraph level.

DOMINANT PATTERNS OF FORMAL WRITTEN DISCOURSE
IN MAJOR LANGUAGE GROUPS

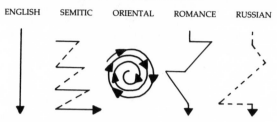

Figure 4. Cross-cultural patterns for paragraph organization. Source: Robert B. Kaplan, 1966, "Cultural Thought Patterns in Inter-Cultural Education," *Language Learning, 16,* p. 15. Reprinted by permission.

In addition to discovery of the specific features of the structures that shape texts, studies of texts in different languages and language varieties show that these structures are not universal but differ from culture to culture. While recognizing significant differences, Yamuna Kachru (1987) has proposed that all texts do share some structural features, such as those directly related to human thought patterns, for example, conventions governing what constitutes a beginning, middle, and end. This proposal led to subsequent investigation of the relationship between language and cognition based on the assumption that there is no difference in the underlying cognitive processes among various cultural groups. The assumption was supported by the study; the differences lie in the conventionalization of the appropriate rhetorical forms in different languages and cultures. The sociocultural norms of the community play a role in constructing and interpreting the texts.

The general principle underlying the analyses of these texts is that it is inaccurate to label one linguistic system and its attendant thought patterns as logical or illogical, since, as Halliday stresses, all linguistic systems are equally logical, although they may differ in their semantic organization:

> There is no reason to expect all ideologies to be modelled on the semiotic structure of Standard Average European; there are other modes of meaning in literature than the poetry and the drama of Renaissance Europe, and it will not be surprising to find differences in other genres also, including the various fields of intellectual activity. (Halliday 1978:77)

In research on the interpretation of texts, the structures or organizational patterns of text are known as schema (Rumelhart 1980), script (Beaugrande 1980), or frame (van Dijk 1972) and refer to an individual's attempts to impose a framework on a text in the act of interpretation. As Scollon and Scollon (1983) have found, if people approach communication with different frames there is a serious potential for miscommunication. If reader and writer do not share the same schema or are not familiar with each other's schema, incomplete or inaccurate interpretation of the text may result. Consequently, the reader may describe the text and its creator as unintelligible, although the formal features of the text are considered correct.

Y. Kachru (1983) uses a Hindi expository text to illustrate cultural norms of the language users. In a three-paragraph description of a well-known Hindi poet, the first paragraph is concerned with the person, his general talents as an administrator, general, scholar, and poet. The second paragraph is about the person as poet, the type of poems he wrote, and their features and content. The third paragraph is about his greatness as both poet and person, his qualities of scholarship and striving for perfection. In this paragraph, however, there is a reference in the second and fourth sentences to the person in the same terms as presented in the first paragraph, a reference which a Western reader would consider a digression. All other sentences in the third paragraph are restricted to a discussion of his greatness and link up directly with the second paragraph.[4]

It has been suggested that such digressions are more tolerable in Hindi than in English texts because "the sociocultural norms of the Hindi-speaking area [of India] impose a parallelism between artistic or professional greatness and personal greatness in the heroes it admires" (Y. Kachru 1983:63). Thus, it is equally important in this tradition of scholarship to point out the personal involvement as well as the intellectual involvement of the scholar, characteristics which are generally separated in the European tradition.

[4]The following is the excerpt upon which this discussion is based:

> Rahim (to give him his full name, Abdul Rahim Khan Khana) was one of the leading lights of Akbar's court. He excelled equally as a general, administrator, scholar and poet. He was so generous that it is difficult to say which were greater in him, the gifts of the head or of the heart. He was the son of Bairam Khan, who was Akbar's guardian in his period of minority, and he himself rendered meritorious service to the emperor in a variety of ways. On account of the eminent position that he held at the court and also of his personal greatness, he exerted a very great influence on the cultural life of his times. He continued to live in the reign of Jahangir, though he lost much of his influence and importance after the death of Akbar, who was his great friend and patron.
>
> Rahim is known primarily for his *dohas*, or couplets. These number more than seven hundred and have been compiled in a *Satsai*. Rahim's couplets are exquisite things. They do not only embody dessicated wisdom like the couplets of Vrinda, nor like the couplets of Bihari do they refer only to the erotic interests of life. They are a veritable treasure-house of human experience of the richest and noblest type. In them we find worldly wisdom ennobled by the innate goodness of the poet's heart. They are also remarkable for their artistic rounding-off, and in this they seem to anticipate the *dohas* of Bihari or Padmakar. Besides the couplets, Rahim wrote several other poems. His *Barvai Nayika Bhed* reveals not only his sensitiveness but also his dexterity in the handling of *barvai*, a metrical form preeminently suited to the genius of Avadhi. His other books are . . .

Digressions are also tolerated in the academic discourse of texts in German. Clyne's (1981) description of a North American reviewer's reactions to the English translation of Norbert Dittmar's *Soziolinquistik* as "chaotic" and showing "lack of focus and cohesiveness," "haphazardness of presentation," and "desultory organization" illustrates how a discourse structure with digressions can make a text difficult for a reader from a different context. In this case, Clyne explains, the text is an example of sociosemantic and pragmatic systems that privilege content over form in German academic discourse, which allows more digressive structures, known as *Exkurse* (literally *excursions*). The digressions, which cover various areas of the author's expertise and general knowledge, serve to convey the image of being learned and saying something scientifically significant. Repetition is often necessary to bring a reader back to the main or general point under discussion.

Frank (1988) has looked at a similar situation in the field of marketing, specifically, the method of direct-mail solicitation. Her study focuses on the effect of a direct-mail offer (sales letter to purchase a book) written by a speaker of a nonnative variety of English (Indian English) and sent to a native speaker (American). Frank contends that while native-speaker recipients of the offer may be able to comprehend the letter, they may not be persuaded to take advantage of the offer. This would happen, for example, if the discourse does not conform to expected shared norms of understanding, that is, if readers cannot apply conceptual frameworks which facilitate interpretation and enable them to draw appropriate pragmatic inferences with respect to the amount and type of information included in the letter or the style and tone of the offer. To illustrate, Frank cites the sentence "We come back upon the correspondence resting with the inclusion of your biographical note in the forthcoming volume of our "Bi-

---

Rahim's claims to greatness are manifold. He was a scholar and poet of catholic taste and wide interests. He counted among his friends talented men without any distinction between Hindus and Muslims, and likewise his works present a fine fusion of all that was best in Hindu and Muslim ways of thought. He was a scholar of Sanskrit and Persian besides being familiar with all the Hindi dialects that were culturally important, and we find in his poetry a blending of words and ideas taken from ancient Persian and Sanskrit poets and his own contemporaries. In this way the poet brings together within the framework of his poetic creation the old and the new and combines characteristically Hindu and Muslim ideas. Universality is his most important quality. Rahim's other title to greatness is that he believed in doing things well. Whatever he handled, he enriched and refined, and, therefore, it is difficult to find halting or unsatisfactory lines in his works. He tried his hands at a variety of metrical forms,. . . and wrote in Brajbhasa and Avadhi, and in every case he achieved astounding success. When everything is considered, the conclusion becomes irresistible that Rahim is one of the outstanding figures in the realm of Hindi literature (Ram Awadh Dwivedi: *A Critical Survey of Hindi Literature*, Delhi, Motilal Banarsi Dass, pp. 85-86).

ography International" and thank you much indeed for your esteemed cooperation in sending to us the same" (1988:28). For a non-Indic, western reader this sentence violates Grice's (1975) Maxim of Quantity: it is more informative than necessary, is not direct in presenting its point, has considerable stylistic ornamentation, and does not emphasize the information content. As a consequence, it may have an unintended effect. The reader may ask why the writer was not more succinct in expressing thanks for response to the initial correspondence.

Differences in text organization across cultures are not restricted to academic texts or commercial correspondence. Literary studies contain abundant examples of potential problems in interpretation due to a reader's unfamiliarity with cultural norms and the culture-bound discourse conventions of the author. These studies, like those of nonliterary texts, show to what extent meaning is extralinguistic. Studies of "contact literature," in particular, provide a resource for understanding the nature of the competence necessary for meaningful text interpretation. This literature is a body of creative writing in English which is significant stylistically and sociolinguistically; its texts are the product of multicultural and multilingual communities and therefore express a national identity and linguistic distinctiveness. Often these texts include a mixing of Western and non-Western resources at the lexical, syntactic, and discoursal levels. The work of South Asian authors writing in English is an example of a contact literature which describes contexts not traditionally associated with the English literature of Great Britian or the United States.

The work of the Indian author Raja Rao (1963) is an excellent example of the creative range of a writer using a second language to exploit and enlarge it for expressing the Indian experience. The following excerpt from *Kanthapura* provides an illustration of the Indian context at several linguistic levels:

> "Today," he says, "it will be the story of Siva and Parvati." And Parvati in penance becomes the country and Siva becomes heaven knows what! "Siva is the three-eyed," he says, "and Swaraj too is three-eyed: Self-purification, Hindu-Muslem unity, Khaddar." And then he talks of Damayanthi and Sakunthala and Yasodha and everywhere there is something about our country and something about Swaraj. Never had we heard Harikathas like this. And he can sing too, can Jayaramachar. He can keep us in tears for hours together. But the Harikatha he did, which I can never forget in this life and in all lives to come, is about the birth of Gandhiji. "What a title for a Harikatha!" cried out old Venkatalakshamma, the mother of the Postmaster. "It is neither about Rama nor Krishna!" - "But," said her son, who too has been to the city, "but, Mother, the Mahatma is a saint, a holy man." - "Holy man or lover of a widow, what does it matter to me? When I go to the temple I want to hear about Rama and Krishna and Mahadeva and not all this city nonsense," said she. And being an obedient son, he was silent. But the old woman came along that evening. She could never stay away from a Harikatha. And sitting beside us, how she wept!. . .
> (cited in Y. Kachru 1983)

The interpretation of this text by a reader not familiar with the Indian context requires knowledge of the lexical and contextual features of this text (e.g., knowledge of Siva and Parvati as Hindu gods, or of the significance of the references to Gandhi and the political climate of his time) which distinguish it culturally and historically from the body of literary texts generally identified as English literature.

A Cline of Intelligibility

Intelligibility, like communicative competence, cannot be seen as an absolute concept. To determine a speaker's intelligibility it is necessary to consider the purposes for which the language is used and to whom it is spoken. Americans cannot evaluate my Zambian friend's choice of topic to realize a function as incorrect or his speech as unintelligible unless they are able to consider the possibility that the cultural background of the speaker may be different from their own and may have some bearing on why he is saying what he is saying and what he means by saying it. The various examples of cross-cultural discourse considered above illustrate texts which are potentially unintelligible, or more precisely, open to misinterpretation when readers/speakers are not familiar with the sociocultural norms of the nonnative English speaker. A Zambian, to be intelligible in the American English context, would have to learn the appropriate means of expressing greeting behavior in a way interpretable to an American. In an international or nonnative English national context, it is necessary for the American to be familiar with the range of meanings and the various interpretations of meaning possible for an utterance. In doing so the American is increasing what Catford (1950:13) calls one's "threshold of intelligibility." Braj Kachru expresses this change thus: "an Englishman may have to 'de-Englishize' himself, and an American may have to 'de-Americanize' himself in order to understand these national varieties" (1983:238).

The concept *cline of intelligibility* has been proposed to describe a bilingual speaker's range of intelligibility (B. Kachru 1977). One end of the cline identifies mutual intelligibility among all speakers of the language. At the other extreme of the cline are speakers of a pidginized variety of English (e.g., Babu English for the context of India). This range of placement of speakers along a cline underscores the variability of language use; however, it is important to bear in mind that it is not possible to fix speakers at one point on the cline. The point at which they are located in a particular instance is determined by the interlocutors and other features of the context of situation. A speaker may use a pidginized variety for communication with pidgin English speakers and a standard, educated variety with Standard English speakers, uses which would situate this speaker at two different points on a cline of intelligibility.

Model

As the discussions of communicative competence and intelligibility indicate, the consideration of what it means to be a speaker of a particular language requires an appreciation of diversity across and within languages. The concept of model, like communicative competence and intelligibility, is also context dependent and thus must also be regarded in functional, or pragmatic, terms, that is, with respect to language use.

In pedagogical terms, the concept *model* implies a linguistic ideal which a learner and teacher keep in mind in the course of language instruction. The model represents a norm or standard for language use at all levels—from the phonological to the discoursal. Selection of a model is a key decision in language teaching. Often the terms *norm* and *standard* are used along with model to identify the "correct" and "acceptable" variety of the language chosen, which is based on that used by a segment of the educated population. Choice of a particular model depends upon the communicative competence learners are to develop and the speech community to whom they will be intelligible. A learner's progress is measured against the model: How closely does pronunciation approximate the desired norm? How well do written texts follow the conventions for text construction? How well is the learner able to interpret texts? Can the learner create texts that are intelligible, comprehensible and interpretable to other members of the speech community? Can the learner appropriately realize the functions needed in the contexts of the language?

The logical starting point for selection of a model is a consideration of (1) the uses the learners will make of the language and (2) the users who are members of the group in which learners will become members. Questions to be posed include: Which functions does the language serve? Who are the users? Will they use it in interaction with native speakers, other nonnative speakers, or both?

Although practical, this approach is not always the means for selection of a model. Attitudinal, social, and pedagogical factors also play a role in model choice. Learners may have a positive attitude toward a native-speaker variety because they perceive knowledge of it as bestowing prestige. They may prefer one native-speaker model over another for the same reasons. Some West Germans, for example, often have a preference for British English because the American variety is perceived as more informal or less "correct," or they find American pronunciation "vulgar." However, social factors may outweigh the attitudinal factors and lead other West Germans to prefer the American model because they want to be identified with the American image of being modern and up-to-date.

Attitudinal surveys done in nonnative contexts offer some insight into the question of an acceptable and appropriate model. In two separate studies,

Indians' attitudes toward their own variety of English were surveyed. When asked which variety they spoke, speakers identified their English as British English, although their pronunciation, use, and usage, while identifiable as English, did not strictly conform to British norms (B. Kachru 1983). When West Germans were asked in a pilot study of attitudes if some Germans spoke a variety of English other than a native variety, a number responded "yes." Yet, when asked to identify their variety of English these same respondents identified it with a native variety. They appeared to reject the validity of a nonnative model without recognizing that the features they consider "deviant" from a native norm may appear in their own use of English (Berns 1988a).

Suitability of a Model

Meaningful answers to the question of a suitable model require knowledge of the members of the local speech community, who they are and what their attitudes toward English are. It is also necessary to know the purposes for which the language will be used. Will the learner be interacting with others in an international setting, such as international commerce? Or will the work context be limited to administrative tasks within the speaker's culture? Will learners need to write, listen, and read as well as speak English? A native-speaker variety may be the best choice in some of these circumstances, while a local register-oriented variety may be more appropriate in other situations.

In specifying a pronunciation model of English for teaching purposes, two choices are generally acknowledged: American English and British English. Choice of either, which is often attitudinally based, usually implies the standard form of each variety. In the case of British English, Received Pronunciation (RP) has traditionally been the preferred model. Also known as BBC (British Broadcasting Corporation) English, educated English, and the Queen's English, RP is generally associated with British public (American private) schools. It has been estimated that only 3-5% of the English population speaks RP, a small percentage which represents those in the upper level of the social scale as measured by education, income, profession, or title. Its association with status and prestige explains one of the reasons for the learning of RP. Other reasons include its being widely understood as a result of its availability on radio and television around the world as well as in Britain. RP is also the most thoroughly described of accents (Gimson 1980; Jones 1956), a critical factor in the preparation of pedagogical materials.[5]

[5]RP has been challenged as the appropriate standard for British English speakers. Nearly 40 years ago, Abercrombie (1951:14-15) presented three arguments against setting it up as the norm for British English speakers:

While American and British varieties of English are acceptable as suitable models in their respective "home" contexts, are they appropriate as models in nonnative contexts? Should school children in rural Africa, for example, learn a variety of English based on a model used by American school children? Or should their English be one which ensures intelligibility with the members of their local speech community? In light of available formal and functional descriptions of nonnative varieties of English, it is evident that British and American English do not stand alone as possible standards and that norms can be identified for African, Asian, and Southeast Asian varieties of English (Bamgbose 1982; Bokamba 1982; B. Kachru 1983). Demands for mutual intelligibility between and among speakers of these varieties have resulted in the creation of acceptable levels of communicative competence and intelligibility, leading to the standardization of local, regional, national, and international varieties.

Model and Attitudes

The issue of attitudes is at the center of the question of which model. In former British colonies, where the prestige of RP speakers influenced the desire to learn and speak RP and the concomitant standard of English, a change in attitudes has led to the rejection of British English. In Nigeria, for example, the use of RP accent may produce negative reactions since many Nigerians will consider a Nigerian who speaks like a native speaker of English as affected and snobbish. Thus, the aim in the teaching of English is no longer to produce speakers of RP, but of Standard Nigerian English (Bamgbose 1971, 1982). Sey describes a similar attitude in Ghana, where an imitation of RP is "frowned upon as distasteful and pedantic" (1973:1). Hughes and Trudgill (1987) also point out that even in Great Britain RP speakers may be considered affected, particularly if their accent is "advanced RP", which is associated with the younger generation of speakers of highest social class and educated at the most prestigious public schools.

The choice of RP for English learners in West Germany has been questioned on the grounds that it is not appropriate as the accent for working- and middle-class school children growing up in West Germany's industrial region since it is the pronunciation associated with the British upper class, especially

1. Recognition of such a standard variety is "an anachronism in present-day democratic society."
2. It provides an "accent bar" reminiscent of the color bar.
3. It is also debatable whether RP represents "educated English" since RP speakers are outnumbered by educated individuals who do not speak RP.

graduates of the elite public schools. Further, while RP may be the model in school, the learners realize that pronunciation in English is a flexible phenomenon. This is a result of exposure to a wide variety of accents within West Germany through radio broadcasts of the BBC, Radio Luxembourg, the United States Armed Forces Network, as well as English language television broadcasting available through cable and satellite capabilities.

An additional argument against setting up RP as the model is the varying qualifications of teachers. Where the teachers are not native speakers (as in Europe), the teachers themselves do not have native-like pronunciation. And if they do, it may not be RP, since a number of teachers take advantage of study-abroad opportunities in Scotland, Wales, and all regions of England as well as in the United States. It may also be the case that native speakers teaching in the schools come from Australia, Canada, the United States, or New Zealand.

English departments at the university level in Europe may permit students to select either American English or British English as their model for speaking and writing, so long as they are consistent and do not mix them. This policy works only in theory, since students are exposed to more than one variety of English both in and outside the classroom, contact which can contribute to an English that is a distinct blend of British, American, and European elements.

The attitude of the learners toward the variety of language they are learning is also an important point to consider. Various learner reactions are related to Strevens's (1977) observation that the choice of which variety of a foreign language it is proper to teach is no longer always self-evident and is much influenced by the growth of national, ethnic, and regional feelings of identity. As a result, not all learners will want to sound like a native speaker. Some learners will in fact take pride in their regionally identifiable accent, as does T.T.B. Koh, Singapore's representative to the United Nations:

> When one is abroad, in a bus or train or aeroplane and when one overhears someone speaking, one can immediately say this is someone from Malaysia or Singapore. And I should hope that when I'm speaking abroad my countrymen will have no problem recognising that I am a Singaporean. (quoted in Tongue 1974:iv)

Unfortunately, not all learners share Koh's level of confidence and consciousness, as this excerpt from the journal of a Japanese student learning English illustrates. It describes the learner's desire to conform to the native speaker norms set before him and the conflict he experienced as a result of achieving them:

> I just don't know what to do right now. I might have been wrong since I began to learn English, I always tried to be better and wanted to be a good speaker. But it was *wrong, absolutely wrong!* When I got to California, I started imitating Americans and picked up the words that I heard. So, my English became just like Americans. I couldn't help it. I must have been funny to them, because I am a Japanese and have my own culture and background. I think I almost lost the most important thing

I should not have. I got California English including intonation, pronunciation, the way they act, which *are not* mine. I have to have *my own* English, be myself when I speak English. (quoted in Preston 1981:113: cited in Savignon 1983:113)

A Polymodel Approach

Recognition of the variation within and among Englishes requires an approach to models consistent with the existence of language varieties, an approach which B. Kachru identifies as "polymodel" and "based upon pragmatism and functional realism" (1982a:50).

While a polymodel approach seems most reasonable given the sociocultural dimensions of functional and formal diversity in speech communities requiring knowledge of English, it is not generally accepted by English teaching specialists. Clifford Prator in particular has spoken out against setting up local varieties as models, a practice he has reacted to very strongly because of its threat to mutual intelligibility among English speakers. He has advocated a monomodel approach in response to the opposite view which he considers "heretical":

> The heretical tenet I feel I must take exception to is the idea that it is best, in a country where English is not spoken natively but is widely used as the medium of instruction, to set up the local variety of English as the ultimate model to be imitated by those learning the language. (Prator 1968:459)

Prator maintains that the only suitable model is a native-speaker model. He argues that international mutual intelligibility can only be assured if all learners of English pattern their English after that of a native speaker. More recently, Randolph Quirk has expressed a view similar to Prator's in many respects. Quirk argues for the desirability of a global standard for English, claiming that "the relatively narrow range of purposes for which the non-native needs to use English is arguably well catered for by a single monochrome standard form that looks as good on paper as it sounds in speech" (1985:6). Studies of a variety of nonnative contexts (see Chapter 3) reveal substantial diversity in the functional range, use, and purposes Englishes serve globally. In many cases these uses and purposes are for intranational and local communication only. Both of these characteristics challenge Quirk's claim.

The question of the necessity for mutual intelligibility has been investigated in a variety of studies indicating that it is an unrealistic and unnecessary goal. L. Smith and K. Rafiqzad focused on differences between the intelligibility of educated native and nonnative speakers. The results of their study of 1,386 people in 11 Asian countries suggest that native-speaker English, in terms of phonology, does not appear to be more intelligible than nonnative phonology. Therefore, they state, "there seems to be no reason to insist that the performance target in the English classroom be a native speaker" (1979:57). In a later study,

L. Smith and J. Bisazza (1982) looked for significant differences in English language comprehensibility for native and nonnative users when they were exposed to three syntactically identical but phonologically different varieties of English. Over 200 subjects in seven countries were asked to listen to an American, an Indian, and a Japanese reading comparable texts. The researchers found that the extent of a listener's active exposure to a variety of English was a more reliable determinant of comprehensibility than nationality. Smith and Bisazza concluded that "the assumption that non-native students of English will be able to comprehend fluent non-native speakers if they understand native speakers is clearly not correct. They need exposure to both native and non-native varieties in order to improve understanding and communication" (1982:270).

The question of model, just as of intelligibility, cannot be restricted to matters of pronunciation. The identification of a norm for appropriate structures of written and spoken texts also must be sensitive to the existence of a variety of established, institutionalized patterns of discourse. If the teaching model, for example, is the local variety used in register-bound contexts, the norms and conventions of text structure created by the users of that variety will be realized in the construction of texts. The members of this group recognize these texts and their features as appropriate and acceptable in that context of situation, and the texts are considered intelligible and interpretable because their features are part of the communicative competence of the speech community.

If the selection of the model is not made on the basis of learners' needs for the language, the communicative competence and level of intelligibility achieved are likely to be inappropriate for these learners. A realistic determination of model must then include consideration of the actual forms and functions of the speech community with which learners will interact and the attitudes of members of that speech community toward the language and its speakers. A polymodel approach provides a means of addressing the question of "which model" from a perspective which does not regard the concept of model as absolute and which provides a basis for consideration of the diversity of the social and cultural context as fundamental to any informed and realistic choice of model for learners.

Communicative competence, intelligibility, and model are essential considerations in pedagogical decisions regarding the goals and objectives for language learning and teaching. These decisions, however, depend upon recognizing the interdependence of these concepts and their relationship to the sociocultural context in which a particular second or foreign language is being learned. In the following chapter, the relationship of these concepts to context is illustrated through an exploration of the nature of language learning and use in nonnative language settings.

CHAPTER 3

Sociolinguistic Profiles: India, West Germany, and Japan

The preceding chapters focused on the nature of functional approaches to language study and three sociolinguistic concepts—communicative competence, intelligibility, and model—and how they can be used to gain insight into language use and pedagogy in nonnative contexts. This chapter considers three particular contexts in which English is learned and used as a second or foreign language—India, West Germany, and Japan. These countries are particularly interesting for a look at nonnative contexts of language learning and use since each can be associated with a distinct nonnative variety: English in India is an institutionalized variety of English; Japanese English represents a performance variety. English in West Germany represents a variety of English which is best placed on a continuum between a performance and institutionalized variety.

The descriptions which emerge from a consideration of these unique settings and their Englishes are called *sociolinguistic profiles*, a term suggested by Charles Ferguson (1966) which has proven useful in characterizing the social and linguistic context of language-use situations. The sociolinguistic profiles offered here represent an exploration of processes of the nativization of English which are responsive to the diverse aspects of language and language use and the social and cultural parameters that influence the forms and functions of English in these settings.

In addition to nativization of formal features at the phonological, morphological, lexical, and discoursal levels, the processes of Indianization, West Germanization, and Japanization of English also occur with respect to functions of language. Accordingly, the sociolinguistic profiles will include an analysis of language use in each context. The categories for the analysis follow B. Kachru's (1981b) functional framework, which follows Bernstein (1971) in labeling the categories. Each category refers to a distinct use of language: the *regulative function* relates to the administrative and legal systems; the *instrumental function* is identified with the education system; the use of language across ethnic, religious, and social groups identifies the *interpersonal function*; the *imaginative/innovative function* represents the creative use of language in such areas as literature or advertising.

Formal and functional manifestations are not the only relevant issues to consider in drawing up a sociolinguistic profile. Attitudes of speakers toward a language have significant influence on the nativization of a language and need to be recognized as an integral part of the sociocultural reality of English in nonnative contexts. Attitudes also influence the tradition of English language teaching in each context which, in turn, has an impact on the proficiency level and kind of competence that learners in the classroom setting eventually achieve and develop. Thus, the formal, functional, attitudinal, and pedagogical dimensions are essential components of a sociolinguistic description that aims to identify the nature of the language variety associated with a particular context of use and to serve as a frame of reference for an understanding of how and why language "is as it is" in that context.

India

The role of English in India can be described in a variety of terms. From a pedagogical perspective it is viewed as a second language because it is acquired after the first language, or mother tongue. Serving as a norm for use and usage among Indian speakers, it is an institutionalized language; officially it has the constitutional status of "associate official language." The terms "second" and "institutionalized" alone, however, are not adequate for an understanding of the pragmatics of English in the sociolcultural context of India. Needed is an approach that brings the implications of these terms together and looks at the complexity and diversity of the uses and purposes associated with each term.[1]

Attitudes toward English

In India, English is associated with elitist, professional, and administrative power and authority. Its symbolic status can be traced to the period of colonial

---

[1]While the complex and diverse nature of English in India and its sociolinguistic parameters are the focus of this section, this discusion is not exhaustive. Extensive documentation of the development of Indian English is available in a number of publications. One authority on Indian English, Braj Kachru, has documented the development of this unique variety and has contributed to a description of its formal and functional manifestations. Much of the data presented in this discussion is drawn from his 1983 publication, *The Indianization of English: The English Language in India* (Delhi: Oxford), which also includes an extensive bibliography of relevant publications and sources of linguistic data.

rule when English was formally established as the official and academic language of India, replacing Sanskrit, Persian, and the vernaculars. Replacement of indigenous languages was achieved by the imposition of British and Western educational systems and values and by the Indian bourgeoisie's need to get along with the British. Acceptance of a Western-style education was an important signifier of position in the new social structure. Ultimately, English became associated with prestige and status and acquired a privileged position in most walks of life. Individuals who were bilingual in English and another language were regarded as members of a superior class.

By the time the British left India in 1947, English had become an indispensable tool for higher education and intellectual discourse and had been appropriated as a productive power in dealing with the colonizers and in gaining access to Western knowledge and technology. Although it was no longer as favored a medium of instruction in the schools as it had been under the Raj, use of English continued for official as well as unofficial purposes after independence. Due to lack of widespread acceptance of Hindi as the national language, especially in the southern states, the use of English as an associate official language persisted even beyond the deadline for its removal in January 1965.

In bilingual situations when social position is associated with knowing a prestige language, it is common for individuals to attempt to conceal their lack of competence in it. The multilingual context of India, where English language use continues to be a status marker, is no exception. In a pilot study of English language use in India, Ghosh and Datta (1983) found that Indians were not always accurate when asked about their need for or their proficiency in English. Although their work required considerably more written than spoken use, many wanted more teaching in the spoken use of language. Several self-rated their competence much higher than the interviewers rated it. The researchers attribute this behavior as a response to the status associated with proficiency in English. Admitting little need for or little competence in the language, they assert, would result in being stigmatized as socially and culturally inferior.

A sense of inferiority can also be observed among parents with children in primary and secondary school. Parents say it is the quality of education at public schools, where English is the medium of instruction, that makes them superior to the vernacular-medium schools. In a study of parents' attitudes toward English- and non-English-medium schools, Jha (1979) found that most of the educated people surveyed preferred to send their children to an English-medium school. Nonliterates also considered English-medium schools superior to the vernacular schools. Among the parents surveyed, the quality of the education their children received was not the criterion used as the basis for the choice; rather, it was the belief that education in English is related to a higher standard of living, better jobs, and prestige.

The Users and Uses

The use of English in India is not restricted to a single social or economic class. However, amount of use varies. It has been estimated that English is used extensively by approximately 5% of the population, which comprises the entire leadership of India's economic, industrial, professional, political, and social life. A large proportion of these users are concentrated in the largest cities, where English is the common language. In some families, English may even be the language used at home among family members. These users represent the English-knowing elite who can afford to send their children to privately supported English-medium schools. Although they may have fewer occasions for use of English than the elite, travel guides, letter carriers, and shop-keepers also use English to some extent. Civil servants and teachers of English use English to a greater degree. While it may not be the home language, it is necessary among these users for business, professional, and legal transactions.

In terms of its functional range, English serves well-established and significant purposes for its users. Education, law, government administration, interpersonal communication, and literature are areas in which English is utilized for special functions within Indian society.

The Regulative Function

As the associate official language in India, English serves the regulative function in the areas of the law and administration. Although there have been efforts to introduce the use of regional languages in higher and lower courts, English is still used extensively in the legal system, at least at the higher levels. The Indian Bar Council claims this is necessary to insure "national integration" and "all India" standards. For administrative purposes, different languages are used at various levels. However, English is the dominant language at higher levels and is used more than any other language in advertising and publications by central and state governments.

It is through texts written in English that information about the various parts of India and information distributed by the national government throughout India is made accessible. Thus, as an intranational "link language," English serves as the primary unifying force in a country of more than 1,652 mother tongues and 15 languages recognized as major by the Constitution.

The Instrumental Function

English is the medium of instruction in the schools of 23 states and union territories. At the tertiary level, it is the medium of instruction in 19 universities and holds a dominant position in 83 universities.[2] It is the main medium of learning at the postgraduate level. Textbooks printed in English are standard in the educational system at the tertiary level and are considered essential for access to advanced technological and scientific information, which is primarily available from English language sources outside India. Where English is not the medium of instruction, the "library language" function of English is stressed (Verma 1987:421).

The Interpersonal Function

The interpersonal function is related to the use of English as an international and intranational link language. Knowledge of an internationally intelligible variety of English enables Indians to participate in intellectual and political discourse with other nonnative as well as native English speakers. It is generally the case that educated speakers using English have the same cultural background but do not necessarily share linguistic backgrounds. Thus, knowledge of an intranationally intelligible variety enables communication between regions and states with nonmutually intelligible indigenous languages or dialects.

The Imaginative/Innovative Function

The imaginative/innovative function is characterized by the use of English in creative contexts. Literature in English by Indian authors is one example of their creativity in the use of the colonizers' language to represent Indian culture, society, and typical contexts. The history of creative writing in English by nonnative users goes back 200 years, but it is in the last 40 or 50 years that this literature has matured and come to be regarded as a national literature (Iyengar 1962; B. Kachru 1982c). Themes and plots are concerned with the ways of life and people of India, and as a result Indian English literature has become increasingly important as a means of expressing Indian culture. Significant factors in its acceptance are the growth of bilingualism in English, which has brought about an increase in the size of its potential audience and the increase through creative writing of the representation of English in registers other than the legal and administrative. Sridhar refers to this change as the "de-bureaucratization of English," which is the result of "the increasing confidence with which non-native writers came to handle the language in registers other than the legal and administrative" (1982:291-292).

[2]*The Commonwealth Universities Yearbook 1988* (London: Association of Commonwealth Universities) reports 178 universities in India as of 1987.

Linguistic Innovation and Adaptation

Nativization has been sufficiently extensive to establish Indian English as a variety alongside American, British, Canadian, New Zealand, and Australian English. Appropriation of English began in the 19th century as a gradual but steady process of "Indianization" at all linguistic levels, that is, phonetic, grammatical, lexical, and semantic. Speakers' production of "deviations" from native forms identify their unique variety. One distinctive feature of Indian English, as spoken in the Hindi region, is the insertion of a high vowel before clusters such as *sk, st, sp*, resulting in [Ipsik]. Deviations in stress, rhythm, and intonation are more striking features and contribute significantly to its distinctiveness as a new English. Syllable-timing in Indian languages as opposed to the stress-timing of English results in a rhythm based on long and short syllables instead of stressed and unstressed syllables. The differences can be traced to characteristics of Indian languages, which are transferred to English.

Examples of nativization at the grammatical level include omission of the reflexive pronoun, use of transitive verbs in place of intransitive verbs and vice versa, use of *isn't it* as an invariant tag in tag questions, and high frequency of reduplication of nouns and verbs as well as other items from other word classes. At the lexical level nativization can be observed in processes applied to items transferred from Indian languages. Hybridization identifies the formation of a lexical item which comprises two or more elements, at least one of which is from English (e.g., *lahti-charge, Babu-English*). Collocational differences also contribute to the Indianness of English. *To break rest, America-returned*, and *bangled-widow* are illustrations of lexical innovations. The extension of the semantic features of a lexical item illustrates nativization at the semantic level. For example, *boy* is used to refer to a male who performs the domestic services of "bearer" or a waiter.

Nativization processes can also be observed in the work of creative writers who employ them as a means of expressing culture in literature. Not only are culturally specific lexical items used to refer to indigenous concepts and objects, but, in addition to these formal features, patterns related to the social context of India are represented. Valentine (1985) illustrates, for example, how gender-specific rules of speech among Hindi speakers, such as nonuse of proper names and use of kinship indicators and deference markers meaningful in the context of India, are carried over into texts by creative writers. This transference of linguistic behavior from Hindi to Indian English contributes toward a text that can convey underlying indicators of attitude, sex-role stereotyping, and evaluative perceptions of one gender by another.

Communicative Competence and the Cline of Englishes

Indian English, like other Englishes, is not a homogeneous language. There is no single standard or norm to which speakers conform. Therefore, communicative competence in this variety has to be identified with respect to the individual user and the uses made of the language. Up to this point, the features of Indian English that have been addressed are those of the "standard" or the "educated" variety, yet, as discussed above, English is also used by bilinguals who are minimally proficient. Their competence is restricted to items relevant to their employment, for example, postman, "bearer," or travel guide. The labels "Babu-English," butler English" or "kitchen English" have been used to distinguish their competence from that of professionals or Indian English writers. Just as proficiency levels differ, so do speakers' needs. For example, not every speaker will need English for the four functions described above. Nor will they need it for speaking as well as writing.

Because there are varieties within a variety, observable differences in proficiency levels, and diverse reasons for using English, it is necessary to speak of competence in the plural, that is, in terms of communicative competences. The concept of a cline (B. Kachru 1965) makes the relationship of these competences clearer and aids in appreciating the range of proficiency found among Indian English speakers. With three measuring points—the zero point, the midpoint, and the ambilingual point—it is possible to situate the users. Postmen, travel guides, and "bearers" can be placed just above the zero point; they may use English occasionally, but would not be considered proficient. A large number of Indian civil servants and teachers who learned English as their major subject at university represent the midpoint; they are able to use it effectively in such fields as the law, administration, and science. Speakers who can be placed near the ambilingual point are highly proficient and are intelligible not only to other Indians but also to educated native speakers outside India; they are able to communicate with an international audience. Political leaders such as Gandhi and Nehru or the literary figures of Narayan and Rao are examples of speakers who would be situated at this point on the cline.

English Language Teaching

Variation in use among the 23 million or so speakers of English can also be understood in terms of educational parameters. Chief among these parameters is the rationale for teaching English, the language teaching tradition, actual teaching practices, and new approaches to language teaching.

After independence, English was looked upon as "a mark of slavery" and no longer favored as the medium of instruction in schools. It could be taught, however, as a second or foreign language in schools which did not continue its use as the medium. Today, since education and educational policy are controlled by the states, there are marked regional differences in the educational policies and in the role of English in each state. For example, in 23 states and union territories it is the medium of instruction, while it is a second, third, or optional language elsewhere.

However, there is an attempt at a national language policy for India, which is known as the "three language policy." This policy was approved by Parliament, incorporated into the National Policy on Education in 1968, and was endorsed by all the states and union territories (except two). English is given more time, weight, and attention than any other language, including the first language, which is probably related to its role in higher education (Chaturvedi and Mohale 1976). The teaching of the mother tongue or regional language begins in the first standard (age 6) and continues for 10 years. The second language, the official language of the union (Hindi) or the associate official language (English), is a compulsory subject for six years from the fifth standard (age 10) to the tenth standard (age 15). In classes eight (age 13) to ten (age 15) all students are required to study three languages, the third being a modern Indian or foreign language that is not a mother tongue, regional, official, or associate language and not the language used as medium of instruction.

All universities, graduate colleges, and junior colleges have separate departments for the teaching of English. At the tertiary level, language study in either the mother tongue or English is known as "compulsory additional," which means that students have to take an examination in one of these languages, but do not have to pass it for graduation.

Among adult learners, good employment and social recognition provide immediate motivation for becoming proficient in English. One result of the increasing demand for proficiency is its use in on-the-job training programs. While it is true that English is required for government employment (i.e., the regulative function), it is necessary to know more than one needs for the duties associated with the position itself in order to be successful in job interviews, many of which are conducted in English. Spoken English is often required for the interview, while written English may be all that is essential for the position itself. This difference between the requirement and the actual use of English on the job reveals an inconsistency similar to that found in Ghosh and Datta's survey.

In many cases, placement in a position that will bring both money and status (e.g., work with the Indian Administrative Service, bank officers' jobs, or college teaching) are the ultimate motivation for obtaining a university education. The chances for obtaining one of these positions are enhanced by the kind of advanced training and extensive experience in English gained by attending an English medium university. Knowledge of English is also essential for those who want to explore employment possibilities outside their geographical region.

Traditional approaches and methodology in English language teaching stress literary and formal content and rote learning. The texts used at both primary and secondary levels are often essays and poetry, written more than 60 years ago, and selected on the basis of their "high moral content" (Ghosh and Datta 1983). This is the consequence of setting outmoded cultural aims and literary appreciation with its attendant promotion of Western literature and Christian culture as top priority and of ignoring the role of English as a South Asian contact language.

There is a movement away from these aims and priorities. The nature of language teaching is in a state of transition from traditional approaches toward views that are more responsive to the needs of Indian society and learners of English. Just as the English language has been adapted to suit the needs of its Indian users, schools are finding means of adapting their approaches to the social realities of English users and use in India. The British Council has been instrumental in introducing new approaches to English language teaching. The Central Institute of English and Foreign Languages, set up in Hyderabad in 1958, has taken a leading role in training teachers and defining the goals of language teaching and thus has contributed to significant changes in the teaching of English.

West Germany

The role of English in West Germany can be described as a performance variety and as a foreign language. These terms distinguish it from the role of English in India in significant ways. The term *foreign language* reflects the pedagogical status of English as a language which is learned formally, outside of the native context and with reference to a native-speaker model. This status implies that the main learning objective is providing learners direct access to native speakers and their cultures. The term *performance variety* refers to its role for its users. This label implies that the users rely upon a native rather than nativized model as the acceptable standard and norm to approximate. Although performance status has been claimed for English by Görlach and Schröder (1985), who maintain that the English spoken by West Germans and taught in the schools is solely determined by an external norm, the following sociolinguistic profile suggests that the English used in and outside the classroom can be described as German English and that performance standards need to be adjusted accordingly. This position challenges the long-standing view that

English is a foreign, not a second, language in this particular European social and cultural context.

As with the description of English in India, attitudinal, functional, and pedagogical perspectives will be reviewed to determine the sociolinguistic profile. The issue of its status as a foreign or second language and as a performance or institutionalized variety will also be addressed in the discussion of English language teaching.

Attitudes toward English

Germans' attitudes toward English have changed over years of contact between Germans and English speakers. These attitudes have influenced the extent to which English has an impact on the West German language or culture. Prior to the 19th century, influence from English was limited to that of literary movements and the British system of government. In other domains during that period, French was the language of diplomacy and fashion and German was the language of science and scholarship. In the 19th century a few English words were introduced from Britain, an influence more strongly apparent in such northern commercial centers as Hamburg than elsewhere. World War I marks the beginning of the displacement of French and German in science and scholarship by English, particularly British English. This change also marks the shift from French to English as the first foreign language in the education system. The outcome of World War II supported the transition that had been introduced some 20 years earlier, but with a new accent. With an Allied victory, American English was introduced into Europe in greater proximity and through large numbers of native speakers wearing the uniforms of military personnel. The American variety soon took the place of British English among the Germans and began to spread among the general population.

Different reasons can be cited for continuing expansion in the use of American English. The network of cultural institutions known as the "Amerikahäuser" contributes by providing a meeting place and dissemination point for literature, popular publications, and information about American social and political institutions. Not least significant is the role played by films, television, and radio. The media is recognized as playing a particularly decisive role in the fifties and sixties in the spread of new items and in aiding their establishment in the speech of the general public within only a few days. This rate of spread is in sharp contrast to the time of Goethe and Schiller, when it often took years before a new word came into general use. Simple exposure to the media, however, is not sufficient to account for the postwar fascination of many West Germans with things American, both material and linguistic.

The attitude of the Germans themselves after the war, in tandem with increased contact with American English, played a substantial role in the spread of English. Politically, West Germany adopted a supranational point of view and was consciously more open to the world at large. The outgrowth of this outlook was an increase in the use of English words and expressions, a trend distressing to purists in both West Germany and Britain. In 1960 the *London Times*, referring to West Germany's postwar condition, proclaimed: "The language also seems to have suffered defeat."

Interest in America, its culture and its language, was particularly marked in the 1960s. Such words as *hit parade, know-how, do-it-yourself,* and *babysitter* were adopted, not only for the actual concepts or objects they referred to but also as symbols of American values, attitudes, and modernity. The desire to identify with this modern society is captured in Görlach and Schröder's (1985) illustration of a German school child's postwar distinction between "good" and "bad" English. The "progressive, useful English" heard on the radio in the afternoon after school was "good"; what one had to learn at school in the morning was "bad."

Although attitudes toward American culture may be changing as a result of increasingly negative estimations of American foreign and economic policies, the use of the language does not appear to be losing its prestige value, which penetrates even the highest levels of government. The *Sunday Times*, for example, has reported that West Germany's chancellor, Helmut Kohl, is known to pepper his speeches with "Germlish" by using *der Housing-Boom* instead of *der Aufschwung in Wohnungsbau.* The West German weekly newsmagazine *Der Spiegel* has attributed Mr. Kohl's choice of English to his desire to appear as sophisticated and cosmopolitan as his predecessor, Helmut Schmidt, who is fluent in English (Moynahan 1983).

In addition to its prestige function, English plays a substantial pragmatic role in the fields of science and technology. Concerns about the extent of its use have been expressed by the director of the Duden dictionary editorial office, who regards the increasing publication of research results in English or the presentation of them outside of Europe before doing so in West Germany as "a tragedy" for the scientific register of German (*Süddeutsche Zeitung*, February 3, 1983). There is also fear that at the frontiers of knowledge the exclusive use of English means there are no generally recognized and unambiguous technical terms available in German. Denison (1981) reports that a further consequence of conducting scientific debates in English is a growing embarrassment among some scholars at their inability to use their native language in their area of specialization when they are called upon to do so.

The Users and Uses

In terms of functional allocation, English is more limited in West Germany than it is in India. Only three categories of function are represented in the sociolinguistic context of English in this setting—the instrumental, interpersonal, and imaginative/innovative.

The Instrumental Function

Usually related to the status of a language as a medium of instruction, the instrumental function is interpreted more broadly for the West German context to include the role of English in the public school curriculum. Although the educational system requires the teaching of foreign languages, German remains the medium of instruction in elementary and secondary schools (except in a small number of private international schools). At the university level, however, it is possible that English is the medium of instruction in English Department seminars if the faculty feel comfortable using English. However, this is rarely the case since these individuals use it primarily as a research tool.

The instrumental function can also be described by its place in the school curriculum. English is the first foreign language in nearly all schools. Grade 5 is generally the starting point, although experimental programs for third graders also have been available in the State of Hesse (Gompf 1986). Taught to all children for six years, instruction after grade 10 is dependent upon the learners' future plans for education and employment, which are related to the instrumental and interpersonal functions. After grade 10, some learners go on to a college preparatory program, others to apprenticeships, while still others begin training in technical institutes. Advanced instruction traditionally has been reserved for those planning to go on to the university; however instruction is becoming more common at technical institutes, where English is taught as a means of communication and learning. This orientation contrasts with that of the college preparatory school *(Gymnasium)* which teaches English as a cultural object, focusing on the language and literature of Great Britain and the United States.

The prominence of English in the school curriculum also is reflected in the number of English teachers graduated each year. Depending upon an individual state's system of higher education, teachers are prepared at a *Pädagogische Hochschule* (teaching college) or in the *Seminar für Didaktik* (teacher preparation program) of university English departments. In the 1985-86 academic year, English teachers were among the 24,455 of the 1,367,369 students enrolled at the tertiary level who majored in British/American Studies. These numbers indicate the popularity of English over Romance languages, for example, which showed an enrollment of only 19,874 during the same period (*Statistisches Bundesamt, Wiesbaden* 1987).

The Interpersonal Function

The interpersonal function is realized in two senses. One is its use as a symbol of prestige and modernity, as illustrated by the use of English by public figures and by the media. The other is its use as a link language between speakers of various national and regional languages in the pluralistic context of Europe.

International meetings are one particular setting for this function, where peculiarly European uses of tenses and lexical items have been observed. For example, when used in the European context, English *eventual* is used to mean *possible* and English *actual* is used to mean *topical*, showing transference from European languages (e.g., German *eventuell* and *aktuell*). Especially interesting about this phenomenon is the adaptation that has been observed among native speakers who find themselves using such features as a communicative strategy when talking with nonnative users (Ferguson 1982).

English also fulfills the interpersonal function on the job market. The chances for good employment motivate many adults to learn English, especially those at the technical level, in secretarial and clerical positions, and at some levels of industry and management. In German corporations, in particular, English is used in many situations for a variety of reasons. S. Smith (1987) points out that a large percentage of the business of a typical large firm (e.g., Siemens GmbH or Schering AG) both at home and abroad involves dealing with foreigners. Much of this business is conducted in various languages, with English the single most important. Individual employees frequently find English necessary for advancement, and many positions simply cannot be filled by an employee who cannot communicate in it. To meet the corporations' needs for qualified employees who are proficient, many firms offer in-house courses.

The classified ads page of a West German newspaper with national distribution, such as *Die Zeit*, illustrates the market value of knowledge of English (Berns 1988b). Advertisers in both the "positions sought" and the "positions offered" columns include proficiency in English as a qualification. Among those seeking positions is a journalist with "perfect" knowledge of English, a mechanical engineer with several years experience of technical English, and a social worker with "good" knowledge of English. Among the positions offered is a sales position for an engineer with a "good" knowledge of English (in addition to a willingness to travel throughout Europe) and a position in a pharmaceutical firm for a products manager with a mastery of the English language.

Exactly what is meant by "mastery" or "good" and "perfect" knowledge is not specified, but it is evident that high salaries and prestige positions are related to some knowledge of and ability to use English. There are also less prestigious positions for which English can be essential, especially in the tourist industry. Individuals in this area find it helpful in serving the 9 million people who come to West Germany as tourists from all over the world each year.

The ability to use English is not restricted, then, to any one level of society. Proficiency varies with the actual competence associated with uses made of it at each level and for each function. Users represent a cline of proficiency which ranges from the speaker able to interact on the international level to the individual whose knowledge is restricted to a set of lexical items which are mixed with German. At a midpoint on the cline is the user whose use is limited to one mode, for example, a physicist who can draft research reports but is unable to speak conversationally on a nontechnical subject.

The Imaginative/Innovative Function

In the sociolinguistic profile of India, the imaginative/creative function was linked to literature in English written by Indians with themes and plots concerned with India, its culture, and its people. West Germany cannot claim its own literature in English, but imagination and creativity is evident in nonliterary spoken and written texts. Through such linguistic processes as borrowing, abbreviation, and hybridization, West Germans nativize English to suit their unique sociolinguistic needs. A number of innovations resulting from these processes are illustrated in the next section.

Linguistic Innovation and Adaptation

Görlach and Schröder have claimed that "there is no 'nativization' of English in Europe" and that "one can have no doubt that all countries in Europe (outside of Britain and Ireland)" fall into the English as a foreign language category, with "the teaching and usage norms being derived from outside the respective countries" of Europe (1985:227). The nature of English language use in West Germany and the adaptations German speakers have made at the phonetic, lexical, semantic, and functional levels do not support this claim. Contact with English and the prestige associated with it have had subsequent impact on language use and usage, as has been the case in other regions where English is used (e.g., South and Southeast Asia, Africa). Unique patterns of functional allocation are one manifestation of this language contact situation. Extensive lexical borrowing also has been a productive process.

There are an estimated 80,000 lexical items among borrowings in German. The words listed in Table 1, only a fraction of this number, illustrate the nature and extent of borrowing into the nontechnical register. The list, included in the

Table 1. English Words Familiar to German Learners

Action	Disc jockey	LP	Roast beef
Baby	Disco	Made in Germany	Roller skates
Baby sitter	Do-it-yourself	Make-up	Sandwich
Bar	Drink	Manager	Scotland Yard
Basketball	Fair	Match	Service
Beefsteak	Fan	Matchbox car	Sheriff
Blue jeans	Farm	Milk shake	Shop
Body building	Festival	Miss	Shopping center
Boiler	Fifty-fifty	Mister	Shorts
Boots	Fit	Mixer	Show
Boss	Foul	Motel	Single
Box	Gag	Music box	Soft ice
Boy	Gangster	No	Song
Bubble gum	Gentleman	Non-stop	Spray
Butler	Girl	Off/on	Star
Camping	Golf	O.K.	Steak
Caravan	Grapefruit	Oldie	Stewardess
Center	Hairspray	Party	Story
Chewing gum	Hit	Pipeline	Supermarket
City	Hobby	Playboy	Swimming pool
Clever	Interview	Player	T-shirt
Clown	Jeep	Pony	Team
Colt	Jet	Pop	Teenager
Comic	Job	Popcorn	Test
Computer	Ketchup	Pop song	Toast
Corned beef	Killer	Pullover	Toaster
Cornflakes	Lady	Quiz	Western
Cotton	Lift	Ranch	Whisky
Country music	Lord	Reporter	Yes
Cowboy			

Source: H. E. Piepho *et al.*, 1987. *Contacts 5: Basic Course*. Kamp. p. 5.

opening pages of an English language teaching text for West German public schools, is intended to demonstrate to first-year learners just how much English they already "know."

Linguistic motivation has been sought for the borrowing of English words. It has been suggested that the borrowing of monosyllabic words in particular is a response to a modern need or desire for short words. Another explanation offers that the English words are phonologically less complex and therefore easier to pronounce than an existing equivalent in German. Such a case would be the choice of *jet* over *Düsenjäger*, or *pilot* over *Flugzeugführer*, or the sports term *foul* over *regelwidrig* (Moser 1974; Priebsch and Collinson 1966). These suggestions are dubious, however, in light of the evidence supporting more powerful factors in the borrowing process, for example, the need to name new inventions, products, and concepts, the pressure for more precise terminology in such fields as medicine, chemistry, or computer science, or the desire to display familiarity with a foreign language and thus enhance one's social status. Such communicative strategies afford the individual and group an expanded range of linguistic means to achieve a variety of social ends without necessarily becoming completely bilingual.

In their use of English words, German speakers have nativized the borrowings. In response to linguistic and cultural forces, they have "de-Americanized" or "de-Anglicized" these lexical items through a variety of linguistic and cultural processes.

Nativization in spelling or orthography of borrowed items is generally limited to capitalization of nouns or the insertion of a hyphen (e.g., *Swimming-Pool*, *Hit-Parade*). Verbs are inflected as German roots are, with *-en* or *-ieren* as the infinitival marker (e.g., *parken, checken, managen, frustrieren*) and *ge-* and *-t* as the regular verb past participle marker (e.g., *geparkt, gecheckt, gemanagt*).

Abbreviation occurs when some part of a word or phrase is omitted, as with *Profi* from *professional* (in referring to a professional athlete), *Pulli* from *pullover*, *Twen* from *twenty*, and *last, not least* from *last, but not least*. *Twen* is particularly interesting because it originally was created as the title of a magazine for West Germans in their early twenties. As a result of the magazine's popularity, it eventually came into use to fill a lexical gap.

One last group of nativized forms are those words which result from the combination of an English word with a German word: *show business* becomes *Showgeschäft*, *test car* becomes *Testwagen,* and *playback recorder* becomes *Playback-Tonband*. This process is also used to expand the semantic range of an item. Such is the case with *Hollywood-Schaukel* which is the name for a couchlike swing with its own awning designed for patio or balcony, a feature of many middle-class West German homes.[3]

English Language Teaching

The choice of a norm to serve as the classroom model for pronunciation and usage is one obvious influence on English language teaching in West Germany. The variety that graduates of language teaching preparation programs are expected to teach is officially based on external norms, namely, that of British English. For pronunciation, this is generally understood as Received Pronunciation (RP). These norms have been followed in spite of contrary views. Atkinson (1975), one opponent of setting RP as the standard, points out that adherence to British norms produces behavior that is unidiomatic and inappro-

---

[3]See Berns (1988b) for further discussion of borrowing processes for English in German.

priate. Heinz Wittman (1981), expressing a different view in an editorial in the *Frankfurter Allgemeine*, regards the language that Atkinson labels unidiomatic and inappropriate as the result of striving toward "careful and cultivated language" among learners in both spoken and written self-expression.

However, British English pronunciation and "careful and cultivated language" do not necessarily conform to the standards represented by the teachers, many of whom can only approximate the standards themselves, or to the needs of all learners. Consequently, what began as adherence to an external British standard has been slowly developing into an internal German English standard, an inevitable development given that English instruction takes place in the institutionalized domain of the sociolinguistic and linguistic reality of the German language. Thus is it not surprising, as Hans-Eberhard Piepho, German language teaching methodologist and teacher educator, makes clear, that nonnative-speaking teachers, as a result of contact through media and their own representation of the language and the culture, bring a West German reality of English into the classroom and, with it, their own variety of English. In addition to recognition of the social and cultural realities of English, Piepho also argues for a change of attitude in the area of learner errors. He maintains that greater tolerance toward the deviations from the norm can emerge only if English is recognized as a second language and, consequently, as a variant of the standard native variety. A renunciation of norms based on a so-called Standard English is advocated, at least for those learners who will never achieve a usable, although "correct" competence when native normative standards are applied (1979).

Attitudes toward language and recognition of nonnative norms not only affect the choice of a model for learners, but they also influence approaches to language teaching. During the 1970s, two political developments, the school reform movement and revised curriculum guidelines, had a profound impact on English language teaching in West Germany. As a consequence of general school reform, a change in attitude emerged toward teaching in general and language teaching in particular. One result of general reform was the creation in some states of the integrated comphehensive school. This school type combined the traditional, separately administered forms of the lower secondary school under a joint administration. The forms brought together were the *Hauptschule* (grades 1-9), which offers a diploma qualifying graduates for training in skilled trades, the *Realschule* (grades 1-10), which offers a diploma qualifying graduates for training in business and commercial occupations, and the *Gymnasium* (grades 5-13), which prepares students for higher education.

Although one of the objectives of the new school form was to minimize the social differences the previous forms reinforced, pupils were tracked for some subjects, including English. In Hesse, for example, the "A" track was for the more proficient, with "B" and "C" for the less proficient learners. As a result of tracking, English took over the role that Latin once held of screening out the "bright" students from the masses. Christoph Edelhoff (1981), director of the teacher in-service training center for Hesse, highlights the irony of this development in observing that it is taking place at a time of greater international contact among people and a growing awareness of the practical value of being able to speak another language, English in particular.

Efforts to change tracking for English and the consequent elitist tendencies had the aim of "humanizing" the comprehensive school. Societies and groups were formed expressly for this purpose. The Society for the Promotion of English Teaching in Comprehensive Schools targeted English instruction in particular and aimed to eventually rid English of its function as an elitist and selective subject. As a means of achieving new, communication-oriented teaching goals, a communicative approach to language teaching was advocated because it would prompt simultaneous learning of the subject and processes of social interaction, goals which could be realized through materials intended for a form of teaching which sees learning in heterogenous groups (i.e., a non-tracking approach) as a process of communication (Edelhoff 1981).

The goals of the Society were not necessarily shared by the German population at large. In the same editorial in which he offered a case for striving toward careful and cultivated language, Wittmann (1981) responded to the trend toward communicative language teaching with alarm, suggesting that teaching for communicative competence alone was a reaction to the harsh demands made on the learner concerning grammar. Besides, he continued, serious study of grammar is important training for thinking. His position equates English learning with that of Latin or Classical Greek, neither of which serves as a tool of communication or learning in modern West Germany.

Such criticisms had little if any negative effect on the new direction for the teaching of English. The trend was bolstered by new curriculum guidelines, drawn up, published, and distributed by the Ministry of Education in all states, which reflected the trend toward communication as the goal of foreign language instruction. The 1980 guidelines of the State of Hesse specify the origin of the language teaching guidelines thus:

> The curriculum guidelines are not derived primarily from individual languages and their systems, but from what the learners can do with their knowledge of the language. They should be able to understand living conditions, facts, wishes, and intentions different from their own and be able to use the foreign language for their own utterances. This global learning is known as communicative competence. (*Der Hessische Kultusminister* 1980:10; my translation)

The guidelines see foreign language learning as an expansion of the learners' competence in social behavior. Therefore it must take place in forms that correspond to its character as a social activity. As concerns instruction, its purpose is to encourage cooperation among the learners purposefully and effectively, a goal which could be achieved by integrating different social forms into the classroom: individual work, partner work, small groups, and large group activities. The realization of these concepts in the classroom contributes toward the satisfaction of more global requirements that every school subject has to meet: (1) encouraging the development of the learner's personality, (2) enabling the learner to take on political responsibility, and (3) contributing to the occupational qualifications of the learners.

Japan

English serves a variety of functions which are unique to the Japanese context, yet have much in common with the functions it serves in West Germany. Perhaps the most significant difference between these two countries is the degree to which English is spoken with foreigners. In Japan, it is used less extensively among the general population with other speakers of English than in West Germany. Some reasons for its restricted use as a second language will be outlined in the following description of the nature of English language use and teaching and the processes which contribute to nativization.

Attitudes toward English

Significant contact with English which brought long-term effects for Japanese came with Commodore William Perry's arrival in Edo Bay (now Tokyo Bay) in the mid 1850s. This event ended the national policy of isolation established in 1640 to protect Japan and the Japanese against foreign influences that were considered undesirable. A new attitude of curiosity about the West developed as did widespread interest in English and in learning it well enough to speak with foreign visitors. Perry's arrival and the era of increased trade and contact with the West which followed also saw educational reforms and literacy programs for Japanese. Although learning English became highly valued as part of these reforms, Westernization of traditional Japanese thought was not a goal. Neo-Confucian ideas continued to serve as the basis for ethics and social organization.

During the period subsequent to Perry's arrival, familiarity with English in Japan was facilitated by the arrival of British and American technical advisors and the exchange of students and statesmen, along with a general fascination with Western customs and ideas. Many schools began to use English as the medium of instruction as well as to teach English, and it became fashionable for students to intersperse their conversation with English word borrowings. The new language was regarded very highly and was predicted to become "the most useful language of the future" by Mori Aronori, an influential educator and writer during the Meiji period (1868-1912) (Fukuzawa 1899:98). In part due to the recognition of English as a powerful tool of communication and as the key to the technological wealth of Western civilization and the process of modernization, serious attempts were made to designate English the official language of Japan. In the Taisho period (1912-1926), an era of relative social and intellectual freedom, English words were increasingly borrowed, for example, *rajio* 'radio', *takushii* 'taxi', and *sarariiman* 'salary man' (Stanlaw 1987).

English continued in the function of prestige language until the rise of nationalism and militarism in the 1930s and 1940s. During this phase, the Japanese government tried to purge the Japanese language of all foreign influences, including English loans. After World War II, English regained its popularity, and the presence of occupation troops increased the number of borrowings. At this time the American variety also gained acceptance in Japanese society (Tanabe 1978).

Since the second world war, Japan's unprecedented industrialization has brought about a higher standard of living and level of education. The popularity of English has been attributed to Japan's economic prosperity; industrialization has brought about need for English language skills in science, technology, and business (Morrow 1987).

The need for English and positive attitudes toward the West have led to the considerable assimilation of English loanwords into Japanese. Borrowing is so pervasive and commonplace that a number of rubrics have been coined to describe it—"Japlish," "Janglish," "Japalish," "Japangurishuu," or the more neutral "Japanized English" (Morrow 1987; Stanlaw 1987).

One indicator of the status of borrowings and their acceptance is represented by the use of loans in the poems that members of the royal family have entered in the Imperial Court poetry contest. For example, in 1965 Prince Mikasa's entry included the word *beruto-konbea* 'conveyor belt'; in 1976 the Emperor's entry contained *damu* 'dam' (Passin 1980). There is, however, no official support for the use of such loans. As a matter of policy, the Ministry of Education's Department of National Language, for example, has never published anything that contains loanwords of Western origin (Sibata 1975). "Laments" by Westerners and Japanese about the avalanche of English borrowings appear almost daily in the Japanese media (Stanlaw 1987).

Although restricted in its use as a second language, English does serve as a means of expression that is unavailable in Japanese. Stanlaw (1982) reports that the choice of English by Japanese debating societies for conducting debates enables the kind of argumentation debating activities require, a type of argumentation that is nearly impossible to conduct in Japanese, especially for women.

The Users and Uses

The Instrumental Function

Although it is not generally the medium of instruction in contemporary Japanese schools, English was the medium of instruction for some, if not all, subjects in the late 19th century. The School of Commerce, established in 1875, was a private secondary school aimed to carry on education for the promotion of commercial activities. In addition to intensive study, lessons related to foreign trade and business were conducted in English for students in the last two years of the course. When a college-level program was added in 1884, as much coursework as possible was offered in English (Omura 1978). Today, it is more important as the language of learning from such professional publications as journals, textbooks, and instruction manuals on scientific, technical, and commercial topics. Programs with dual broadcasting in Japanese and English transmitted by several television stations in Tokyo are another potential source of English as a medium of learning. In homes with newer TV sets viewers can tune in to either language. It appears, however, that the choice to take advantage of English language broadcasting among Japanese is motivated more by the desire to improve their English ability rather than to exercise bilingualism (Helgesen 1987).

The Interpersonal Function

As the language of personal communication, English is vital in the promotion of international trade and commerce for Japan. This function is one of the most important, and much of the effort at English language teaching is directed toward competence in these areas.

As noted above, English for commercial purposes has a long tradition in Japan. What began as courses in commercial correspondence developed into general business English programs. Today they are viewed as courses in English for International Business Communication (Ohtani 1978). The need for effective communication in business is perceived as great enough that some large companies in Japan have their own language programs. One example is Kobe Steel, where a study of English language use indicated that almost every employee deals with English at some time in the course of a career with the company (Baird and Heyneman 1982). Those sent overseas need it for face-to-face communication (e.g., business meetings or social functions). Those staying in Japan need English to sell and service products, make the documents used in engineering, and correspond with overseas customers.

Curriculum planners and instructors in the English language teaching program of Mobil Oil as well as Kobe Steel have been active in meeting the demands of teaching English as a tool of international business. A survey of the language needs and requirements of employees at Mobil Oil showed that promotion to section and division manager depends on advanced levels of language proficiency (Sekimori 1983). English is required for intracompany correspondence and for communication with several departments which have native English-speaking managers.

The Imaginative/Innovative Function

Like West Germany, Japan cannot claim its own body of literature written in English. However, linguistic creativity is evident in Japanese adaptation of English through a variety of phonological, lexical, and semantic processes.

Linguistic Innovation and Adaptation

English loanwords are a concrete result of contact between English and Japanese. The items in Table 2, compiled in connection with the development of materials for Japanese junior high school learners (Brown and Berns 1983), illustrate the range of words commonly used in Japanese and the topics with which they are associated.[4]

The variety of items represented is evidence of the pervasiveness of loanword use in virtually all domains and registers and by nearly all speakers. As Morrow points out, extensive use of loanwords by a range of speakers indicates something about Japanese attitude toward loans: "they are not considered second-class words appropriate only to elevated speech" (1987:51).

While use of English loans varies among Japanese depending upon the speaker's personality, speaking style, or context of use, they are common for a range of reasons and often function as communicative strategies. The loanwords allow Japanese speakers to express certain nuances which they could not express otherwise. Differences of connotation, for example, can be of formality, degree of technicality, or attitudinal neutrality. The two Japanese words for *computer* provide illustration. Speakers tend to use the native Japanese *denshikeisanki* in more formal, technical contexts, while the borrowed *kompuuta* is preferred in most other contexts. Level of formality in referring to the leader of a group is conveyed through choice of *shidoosha* (native Japanese) and *riidaa* 'leader'. *Riidaa* would most generally be preferred in casual conversation, unless the referent happens to be the prime minister, which would most likely result in the choice of *shidoosha*. Conversely, if the leader of a hiking club is being

---

[4]The list was compiled by Yukiko Abe Hatasa and Kazumi Hatasa.

Table 2. Common English Loanwords in Japanese

Sports	Music	Food	Transportation
Soccer	Harmonica	Sauce	Bus
Basketball	Violin	Barbecue	Miniature car
Jogging	Piano	Cheese	Monorail
Tennis	Rhythm	Butter	Pilot
Ping-pong	Program	Margarine	Speed
Bowling	Recital	Milk	Jet
Volleyball	Musical	Lettuce	Truck
Skate	Folk song	Cabbage	Meter
Ski	Brass band	Tomato	Seat
Racket	Flute	Hot dog	Tire
Ball	Trumpet	Celery	Headlight
Bat	Concert	Milk	Engine
Pool	Opera	Banana	Taxi
Glove	Orchestra	Grape	Helicopter
Badminton	Cello	Grapefruit	Brake
Hurdle		Pineapple	
Ballet	*Electronics and*	Fruit	
Ballerina	*Appliances*	Salad	
Pitcher		Ice cream	
Uniform	Radio	Chocolate	
Medal	Tape recorder	Cake	
Boxing	Computer	Yogurt	
Boxer	Stereo	Jam	
Whistle	Cassette tape	Hamburger	
Net	Video recorder	Curry	
Jump	Video tape	Rice	
High jump	Record	Soup	
Strike	Switch	Stew	
Game	Camera	Peanut	
Umpire	Shutter	Vanilla	
Yacht	Film	Mushroom	
Boat	Motor	Marshmallow	
Champion	Earphone	Cookie	
Tournament	Fuse	Cracker	
Surfing	Freezer	Potato chip	
Surfboard	Record player	Coffee	
Hang glider	Slide	Coke	
Coach	Lens	Juice	
Captain	Cord	Beer	
Kick	Socket	Whiskey	
Roller skate	Dial	Wine	
Camp	Channel	Sausage	

(*continued*)

Table 2. (continued)

Entertainment	Household	Miscellaneous
Recital	Sofa	Birthday
Rehearsal	Oven	Love letter
Series	Toaster	Energy
Narrator	Kitchen	Tour
Interview	Living room	Cement
Concert	Carpet	Xerox
Documentary	Curtain	Copy
Poster	Lamp	Sauna
News	Label	Service
	Tissue paper	Circus
Clothing	Toilet paper	Calendar
	Town	Capsule
T-shirt	Towel	Catalog
Skirt	Sponge	Supermarket
Jeans	Bedroom	Hiking
Blouse	Apron	Thrill
Belt	Napkin	Thriller
Vest	Bed	Honeymoon
Jacket	Cushion	Picnic
Coat	Pipe	Hitchhike
Socks	Mattress	Present
Pocket	Mop	Massage
Jumper	Bucket	Gesture
Sweater	Shampoo	Elevator
Earring		Dam
Sunglasses	Colors	Tunnel
Ribbon		Dryer
Mask	Brown	Balance
Eye shadow	Beige	Hotel
Manicure	Silver	Boiler
Boots	Red	Shopping
Bag	Orange	Bonus
Hanger	Blue	Bench
Suitcase	Green	
Fashion	White	
Dress	Black	
Wool	Pink	
Nylon	Gold	
Shirt		

referred to in a formal conversation, *shishooda* might seem inappropriate, and *riidaa* would probably be chosen (Morrow 1987).

The use of English borrowings also identifies the speakers as being modern, Western, or sophisticated. Merchants take advantage of these associations and recognize the prestige attached to the language. Stores selling clothes use the English loan *kajuaru* 'casual' in place of Japanese *hundangi* 'casual clothes' to present a modern image. It is not uncommon for more than half of the titles of hit records on the Japanese Top 100 list to be in English or to contain loanwords. Some loans may also reflect changing Japanese attitudes and priorities. A totally new social and psychological reality in Japan seeems to be highlighted by the use of *my*. This reality is described as "the notion of giving priority to one's family and to one's private realm—as against the collective entity in which one is embedded" (Passin 1980:26). Using *my* in such cases as *mai-hoomu* 'my home,' *Mai-kaa* 'my car,' *mai-pesu* 'my pace,' or *mai-puraibashi* 'my privacy' allows the speaker to avoid the somewhat selfish associations and offensive effect of Japanese terms for "my" or "self" (*watashino* or *jibun*). Use of loans also appears to permit Japanese to talk about romance, sex, and companions and girl- or boyfriends with greater ease and frequency than Japanese terms allow. It has been suggested that use of English for these subjects permits a psychological distance between the subject and the speaker, who may otherwise feel shy talking about personal and intimate relationships (K. Hatasa, personal communication, February 15, 1989).

In a study of their use, English loans were found to be used and apparently needed in men's discussions of baseball, tennis, golf, horse racing, and the Olympics. Older and younger female subjects, however, tend to use English loans in discussing fashion and cosmetics, romantic intrigues, and marriage plans (Stanlaw 1982).

Generally, loanwords are assimilated to such a degree that they are phonologically indistinguishable from native Japanese words. Thus, *leader* becomes *riidaa*. As Japanese does not allow consonant clusters, vowel epenthesis is a process necessary to break up sequences such as that in *school*, which becomes *sukuuru*, or *glass*, which becomes *gurasu*.

Phonological processes are not the only means of nativization. Semantic restriction, semantic shift, and semantic extension are also common phenomena. Limiting the meaning of *mishin* 'machine' to "sewing machine," *kuuraa* 'cooler' to "air conditioner," and *gurasu* 'glass' to refer to the industrial material, but not the drinking container, illustrates semantic restriction. Examples of semantic shift, the phenomenon of transferring the nuance from a word's original meaning, are *sain* 'sign,' which means "signature," and *sutairu* 'style,' used to refer to "figure" or "shape," not "fashion." Borrowings sometimes are given new and quite different meanings. This process of semantic extension is realized in an item such as *manshon* 'mansion,' which is not used to refer to a large, grand dwelling but to what would probably be called a condominium in American English (Miller 1967; Morrow 1987).

A further productive process for some borrowings is the coining of different forms of a word to distinguish meanings. Morrow cites Miller's (1967:252) example of the word *check*, which has at least three senses: *chekku* for "bank drafts"; *chekki* for "coat room clerk"; and *chikki* for "through check for baggage on a train." A more recent innovation is the use of *chekku* as part of a compound verb *check-suru*, literally "do check" (i.e., "to check").

Another indication of the extent of nativization is the effect of the common processes of truncation and compounding. Truncation involves deleting the first or, more commonly, the last part of a word. Examples are abundant in Japanese: *terebi* 'television,' *reji* 'cash register,' *masukomi* 'mass communication,' or *rosu* 'Los Angeles.' Compounding involves formation of new lexical items by combining two loanwords. *Salary + man (sarariiman)* means "businessman"; *ice + candy (aisukyandii)* means "popsicle"; and *paper + driver (peijraadoraibaa)* designates a person who has a driver's license but doesn't drive. Examples of this process from sports stories are *oni-koochi* 'devil coach,' with *oni* a Japanese noun for "devil" and *koochi* the nativized form of "coach" (Morrow 1987; Stanlaw 1987).

English Language Teaching

The purposes for formal English instruction in modern Japan have changed since Perry's arrival in the 19th centruy. At that time it was learned as a means of acquiring knowledge about Western civilization, particularly its industrial technology with relation to military affairs. Reading and translation were emphasized. Literature predominated as the vehicle for learning, with little if any time devoted to the development of speaking proficiency. Although it is not the only language taught, English is a popular school subject in Japan, especially among secondary school pupils. About 70% of those who begin instruction in the middle school continue instruction in high school. Ninety-nine percent of all secondary schools teach English primarily as preparation for the college entrance examinations of prestigious universities in which it is a required subject.[5] Due to the influence of the exams on the future of young Japanese and the use of English on the examination as a means of screening college applicants, one observer has gone so far as to identify the role of English on the college entrance examination as its only function in Japan (Matsuyama 1978).[6]

---

[5]English is used on these examinations because it is regarded as the most reliable indicator of students' aptitude, even more precise than mathematics or knowledge and use of Japanese itself (Matsuyama 1978).

[6]Entrance to the university does not depend upon the result of the exam in English alone; a total of 525 hours of English instruction is also required. However, the maximum possible at the end of high school is 315 hours, which leaves the learner in need of another 210 hours. English language academies and so-called cram schools provide programs to make up the difference. While these

Learning English in school is ultimately linked to one's social position. Learners know that when they enter the work force, a degree from a prestigious college, which requires high scores on the English entrance exam for admission, is a valuable commodity and can be decisive in getting a good position. As a consequence, English is simultaneously the most popular subject (in terms of numbers of students) and the most detested subject (Matsuyama 1978).

As a consequence of so much attention to the college entrance examination, school-level instruction does not emphasize the function of English as a tool for international communication. In junior high schools, the audio-lingual method has prevailed because teachers find it to be effective and less cumbersome than previous methods (Koike 1978). However, skills associated with reading and listening are increasingly found in texts in junior and senior high schools. At the university level, emphasis is again on literature and the grammar-translation method, and as such is not oriented to the purposes for which English is used in the commercial and technical communities. Thus, companies such as Mobil Oil and Kobe Steel establish their own training programs in order to develop oral communication and use of, rather than knowledge about, English.

Many specialists view the college entrance examination and the current orientation of schools toward its instruction as the major obstacle to changes in English language teaching in Japan. If the examination is not changed in content and focus or even done away with, language teaching will continue to rely on what is required on the exams—grammar-translation and reading comprehension (Matsuyama 1978). Other criticisms have been made of the exam, and suggestions have been offered for its improvement. The Council for the Improvement of English has suggested greater emphasis on listening and speaking skills and on in-service training for teachers to improve language instruction in these areas. Since these proposals were made in the 1960s and 1970s, the entrance examination has been modified and now includes a listening comprehension section.

Responding to both the communicative and symbolic functions produces a schizophrenia for those educators who recognize that English language teaching must meet the demands of international education, yet also feel responsible for preparing learners for the college entrance examinations. The short-range goal has to be met at the expense of the learners' future communicative needs. As a result, few of the learners ever learn English well enough to converse in it.

---

schools cater to the 15- to 18-year-old group, parents also send their elementary school-age children to private schools which offer English beginning at age six. In 1978, approximately 10,000 children were attending the 100 or so English language schools for this age group.

The influence of the exam also seems to contradict the goals of the *Suggested Course of Study* for languages, published by the Ministry of Education (1972), which states that pupils should be trained to acquire the four basic skills (reading, writing, speaking, and listening), always taking the cultural aspects into consideration, and should develop a desirable attitude toward the habits and customs of English-speaking countries. The latter is to be fulfilled by reading, since Japanese have few opportunities to hear and speak English in daily life (Tanabe 1978).

English language teaching is slowly but steadily changing in Japan to keep pace with the changing demands of the marketplace and of the world at large. The main industries of Japan require a large number of employees with proficiency in English, which the present system of language teaching does not supply. The establishment of English as an international language also requires that Japanese use it as a means of worldwide communication, which increases the urgency to acquire skills for oral communication (Tanabe 1978).

The communicative approach to language teaching, in particular, is currently attracting the interest of Japanese educators, and English language teaching specialists from both Great Britain and the United States are frequent visitors at professional meetings and conferences; specialists from Japan attend British and North American university programs in English language teaching to learn more about communicative language teaching firsthand. A communication-oriented approach has become attractive because it is perceived as coinciding with changes in the entrance examination and textbook contents and with the prevailing political currents of internationalism (Koike 1978).

While college entrance exams exert an influence on the teaching and learning of English among Japanese, a variety of cultural characteristics have also been identified as having an impact on second and foreign language learning. The sensitivity of the Japanese to making mistakes, or the fear of "losing face," has been given as the explanation for the inability of the Japanese to learn to speak English without hesitation. However, as a Japanese educator offers, there may be an even more profound source of learners' difficulties than fear of making mistakes:

> One of the major obstacles we encounter in the way of learning English is the difference of ideas on language between the Japanese and Europeans. For the European peoples language is the most important, and often the sole, means of communication, and through the medium of language they try to convey their thoughts and feelings as precisely as possible. . . . Yet for the Japanese, language is merely *a* means of social and cultural communication. The more complicated and delicate the matter is, the less we rely upon the language. Together with atmosphere, attitude and so on, language is no more than one of the tools to give a suggestion with. (Ohtani 1978:119)

A classic example of means other than language being involved in communication is the concept of *haragei*. It is best described as a kind of empathy which literally means "to communicate through the belly." This comes into play in the group decision-making process when the unspoken group leader intuits the position of each group member, rather than by asking them what their position is on the issue at hand (Barnlund 1975). This behavior complies with a code that marks individuals as brash if they make definite decisions regarding themselves or others. It is offensive for individuals, unless they are the group leader, to urge the acceptance of their opinion as a course of action (E. Smith and L. Luce 1979). Thus the group members reach a decision together with the leader expressing the group's consensus, which is achieved not by people expressing themselves openly but by the leader's divining the will of the group.

Major differences between Japanese and American interaction styles also influence cross-cultural communication. Where the Americans view the individual as the center of action, the Japanese value group orientation and group identity; where Americans value majority rule, the Japanese value the rights of the minority and consensus; where Americans have a competitive spirit, the Japanese see dependency upon others as desirable; Americans expect the leader to encourage participation of each group member, while the Japanese group leader divines the will of the group; and Americans encourage the expression of one's opinions, while the Japanese find it offensive to make oneself stand out from the group (Barnlund 1975). These differences in style can have consequences in the language classroom if the teacher, aware of trends in language teaching which emphasize interaction, encourages learners in situations requiring disagreement and self-expression. These activities are not likely to produce much verbal interaction. Instead of engaging in a lively debate, in which everyone participates, the group is quiet, except for the leader, who may confer quietly with the group before announcing the group's views on the topic (Berns 1982).

Significance of the Profiles

Sociolinguistic profiles shed light on the range of uses a language serves and how these uses evolve in a given context. These profiles of English in India, West Germany, and Japan offer insight into the nature of communicative competence by illustrating the differences between and among the various communicative competences in English in these countries. The differences in uses, the types of nativization, and the models of English for teaching support the notion of no single communicative competence in English. These descriptions also underscore the necessity of considering a teaching model with respect to the sociocultural context of learning and use. Recognition of these differences has profound implications for language teaching, as will be shown in Chapter 5.

The discussions of attitudes toward English in each context also show how the preferences of the speech community play a considerable role in the evolution and existence of a language and its varieties. These are forces which cannot be ignored in an attempt to understand why English has taken the form it has and serves the functions it does, not only in Japan, West Germany, or India, but in other native and nonnative contexts as well. Such adaptations at all levels make it no longer possible to think of English as the language of a particular group within a set of national boundaries. English belongs to those who use it, and English language teaching needs to be responsive to the formal and functional adaptations of its users. The next chapter explores communicative language teaching as an approach that meets this criterion of "responsiveness to context."

CHAPTER 4

Communicative Language Teaching

The term *communicative language teaching* identifies new pedagogical orientations that have grown out of the realization that knowledge of grammatical forms and structures alone does not adequately prepare learners for effective and appropriate use of the language they are learning. The inevitable outcome of increased attention to language use has been a proliferation of approaches to language teaching that claim to be communicative and of new terminology to refer to notions and concepts not addressed in previous form-oriented approaches. Understanding the nature of communicative language teaching and establishing a principled basis for its assessment depends upon familiarity with terms associated with it. Thus, the examination of communicative language teaching undertaken in this chapter begins with a review of the terms *notion* and *function*, and *functional-notional syllabus*.

Threshold Levels and Functional-Notional Syllabuses

Function and *notion* are terms closely associated with David Wilkins, a British applied linguist. His proposals for syllabuses that are organized by functions of language rather than forms are the result of his participation in the Modern Languages Project sponsored by the Council of Europe, which was interested in designing an organized program for adult foreign language teaching in Western Europe. One of the Council's first projects, which Wilkins undertook, was an analysis of existing syllabus types, which were found to be wanting for the particular needs of adult learners. In place of the existing syllabus types (structural and situational), Wilkins proposed two new designs for organizing the content for language teaching: notional and functional syllabuses. A notional syllabus would have a semantic and behavioral prediction of learner needs as its starting point. "Notional" was to be understood in this context as *meaning* based; that is, this type of syllabus was to specify what the learners were to do with language, what meanings they would need to communicate through language. According to Wilkins, a meaning-based syllabus "takes the communicative facts of language into account from the beginning without losing sight of grammatical and situational factors. It is potentially superior to the grammatical syllabus because it will produce a communicative competence . . ." (Wilkins 1976:19). In his book *Notional Syllabuses* (1976), Wilkins identifies three components of meaning: semantic-grammatical (time, quantity, space), modal (degree of certainty, degree of commitment), and communicative functions (judgment and valuation, suasion, argument, rational enquiry). While a notional syllabus would consider all three components, a functional syllabus would consider the communicative functions alone and would therefore be "the weakest application" of his proposal (1976:68). According to Wilkins, it would be used at the later stages of learning, preceded by a conventionally grammatical syllabus for the earlier stages. The notional syllabus, the stronger alternative, places more weight on semantic criteria in selecting forms to be included in the syllabus than on criteria of difficulty or order of natural acquisition. It would be most effective in, for example, English for Specific Purposes courses, whereas the functional syllabus would be suitable for the design of general courses "intended for beginners aiming to proceed towards a general and fairly high proficiency in the language" (Wilkins 1976:58).

It is the communicative functions that Wilkins considers his most original contribution to syllabus design, and it is the concepts *communicative function* and *functional syllabus* which have become associated with his name. Yet he does not claim to have created or discovered them; he acknowledges Halliday as a partial source for his interpretation of communicative functions. The influence of the British linguistic tradition and its focus on meaning and uses of language is evident in the orientation Wilkins has taken to the possible organization of syllabuses in terms of notions, or meaning categories.

Other contributors to the Council of Europe project, Jan van Ek and L. G. Alexander (1980), used Wilkins's concept of a notional syllabus as a basis for a description of the "threshold level," a specification of an elementary-level competence in English for Europeans who from time to time have professional or personal contacts in the European community. It specifies the situations for which language is used, the language functions relevant to the situations, and the notions a learner will need to express particular meanings. It also includes the language forms and vocabulary items related to each area. The "T-Level," as the threshold level has come to be known, was intended to be seen as one of a number of comparable and equivalent variants of English and to serve as a language-learning objective permitting a certain range of variation in instructional goals and methodology. Van Ek and Alexander use Wilkins's terms function and notion, but interpret them somewhat differently. In place of the *communicative function* they specify *language function*, although referring essentially to the same kind of meaning, that is, what people *do* through language.

The threshold-level specification for English has served as the model for descriptions of a number of European languages. However, these descriptions are not identical. For example, the French, who were concerned about the misapplication of their description to wrong contexts, preferred to design their version as a resource rather than a syllabus. Thus, the *Niveau-Seuil* (Coste, Courtillon, Ferenczi, Martins-Baltar, and Papo 1981) determines and specifies the needs of a variety of groups, not just those engaging in tourist travel and business, as was the aim of van Ek and Alexander's *Threshold Level*. The lists included in the *Niveau-Seuil* are comprehensive enough to reflect this. It is further distinguished in its classification of *actes de parole*, derived from the T-Level language functions, but more detailed and variously classified. The classifications include speakers' intentions underlying an utterance, utterances which are not a response to other utterances and responses to them, and functions relating to the discourse itself. Through this elaboration the French version, in effect, complements the English version (Shaw 1977).

The German *Kontaktschwelle. Deutsch als Fremdsprache* (Baldegger, Müller, and Schneider 1981) is unique as a synthesis of the French and English models and in its offering of repair strategies, for example, ways to steer, or negotiate, conversations. The Spanish *Un nivel umbral* (Slagter 1980) is the product of a deliberate experiment in which its authors attempted to see how close they could keep to the English model. This approach, however, was not appreciated by all Spaniards, some of whom regard it as a "cavalier treatment of their language" (J. L. M. Trim, personal communication, March 17, 1983).[1]

In spite of their differences in focus and aim, these documents are individually and collectively important for the development of the teaching of a variety of languages, not only English. On their own, each description is a valuable resource for teachers and curriculum designers for each language; together they are significant as an endorsement of multilingualism in Europe.

Ad Hoc Solutions and Functional Views of Language

Wilkins's development of an alternative syllabus form and the drafting of threshold levels for a number of languages have had considerable impact on

[1]Descriptions are also available for Catalan, *Atalase Maila* (King-ek *et al.* 1988); Danish *Et taerskelniveau for dansk* (Jessen 1983); Dutch, *Drempelniveau. Nederlands als vreemde taal* (Wynants 1985); Italian, *Livello soglia per l' insegnamento dell' italiano come lingua straniera* (Galli dé Paratesi 1981); Norwegian, *Et terskelniva for norsk* (Svanes, Hagen, Manne, and Svindland 1987); and Portuguese, *Nível limiar. Para o ensino/Aprendizagem do Português como lingua segunda/Lingua estrangeira* (Casteleiro, Meira, and Pascoal 1988).

language teaching around the world. Attention to language functions is included in an increasing number of materials, and learners now learn how to express various functions of language and the forms to realize them. A variety of approaches to language teaching that claim to be communicative have been developed. However, not all interpretations of communicative language teaching represent full appreciation of the implications of teaching for meaning and of the diverse competences associated with a language.

The term *communicative approach* has largely been understood to describe any approach to language teaching that claims to be based on a view of language as communication. While most interpretations have emphasized communicative needs of learners, explicit presentation of language functions, and the linguistic forms associated with functions, there is as yet no standard interpretation of the key term function. For some a function is as general as "describing a person or place" or "describing mechanical processes"; for others it is as specific as "requesting help with baggage" or "answering questions about what people have been doing," interpretations which essentially trivialize the concept and minimize its usefulness in materials design. These varied uses of the terms reflect and also contribute to confusion as to precise meanings on the part of textbook writers, publishers, and educational administrators, not all of whom are aware of these terms in their original and more restricted meanings. Although rigid prescriptivism in the use of terminology is not necessarily desirable, uncertainty and lack of uniformity can result in materials which have no basis in a view of language as communication, as often has been the case with materials designed for functional syllabuses. In one instance the selection of a particular set of materials may mean beginning with grammar and delaying any introduction to the functions of language until later in the course. In another, communicative functions may be taught from the very beginning with no systematic treatment of grammar or consideration of context.[2]

Ann Raimes (1983) offers a useful analysis of language teaching materials that were available when functional syllabuses were first becoming prominent in English language teaching in the United States. The analysis is based on the claim that available accounts of developments in ESL/EFL are often incomplete because they have only concentrated on classroom methodology. More essential to an understanding of the present state of affairs in language teaching, Raimes argues, is a look at the "underlying intellectual assumptions which generate methods" (1983:538). Using Kuhn's (1970) theory of scientific

---

[2]Berns (1984) includes a discussion with examples of English language teaching materials which claim to be communicative but have little, if any, foundation in generally acknowledged principles of communicative language teaching.

revolutions as a starting point, Raimes asserts that a look at these assumptions reveals a conflict between two paradigms, the old (audio-lingualism) and the new (communicative language teaching). This conflict is revealed in the efforts of language teachers, methodologists, and materials writers, who in attempting to adopt the new paradigm, only succeed in devising ad hoc modifications of the old paradigm.

Raimes identifies the most common modifications and organizes them into three categories. The first is the "overlay solution," found in textbooks which divide and sequence the content into grammatical structure and address the question of language use by adding a list of functions to the table of contents. The second type of modification is the "label change solution," which incorporates only the terminology, not the concepts. The material in each chapter stays the same, but chapter headings may read "Expressing need and offering help" in addition to "How many: need and want." The third and final category is the "add-a-component solution," which incorporates new theory into old practice "so that it becomes so disguised as to be unrecognizable as new" (Raimes 1983:541-542). With this solution an exercise type that ostensibly presents "communicative acts" is added to a chapter. For example, learners work in pairs and ask and answer questions (given on cards) as if they were on the telephone. As Raimes points out, such an exercise is actually little more than the audio-lingual question-and-answer drill.

What these solutions reveal, Raimes continues, is a change in design and procedure *but no alteration of the underlying philosophical approach*. Attempts to make language teaching communicative are reflected in surface features of teaching and not in the deep structure of the theoretical underpinnings. Change in the underpinnings minimally requires looking at meaning as well as form and function of language, considering the use of language in its heuristic function, and appreciating the creative power of language. In other words, the modifications need to be based on a functional view of language. Only from this perspective is it possible to design innovative syllabuses that can effect change in language teaching.

Raimes's analysis provides a starting point for a consideration of language teaching approaches that have been described as functional or communicative. The remainder of this chapter is devoted to an examination of approaches that have been influential in introducing changes into programs. However, the approaches have not been equally successful in realizing the implications of a communicative orientation. Some represent no more than the modifications in form that Raimes describes, while others illustrate substantial revisions in the theoretical underpinnings that serve as a basis for curriculum, syllabus, and materials design.

Skills and Drills

The first interpretations of communication-oriented approaches to be examined are those of Christina Bratt Paulston and Wilga Rivers, whose work
represents early responses from the United States to the need for communication-oriented language teaching. Each has attempted to integrate the concepts
of communicative competence and functions of language into her views of language and language teaching. However, since their well-established views do
not represent any change in their underlying structuralist and audio-lingual approach, their attempts are best described in terms of the ad hoc solutions Raimes
has identified in language teaching materials.

Paulston (1974, 1976), drawing on Hymes (1971), emphasizes elaboration
of the social rules of language and defines communicative competence solely
in terms of the social rules of use. She asserts that communicative competence
need not be a goal in language teaching, particularly when learners are not
interested in interaction in the culture of the second language. In her words,
"it is valid to ask how much communicative competence one needs to teach
in foreign language teaching" (1974:352). Her definition of communicative competence is basically confined to the social rules of language use "rather than
taking it to mean simply linguistic interaction in the target language" (1974:347).
This definition raises a number of theoretical and practical concerns. First, it
neglects the important interrelationship of language form to culture and society
on all linguistic levels, such as the influence of culture on lexis, syntactic structure, and realization of communicative functions, for example, apologizing, dis-
agreeing. Language use is more than simple application of correct social rules.
Further, Paulston's theoretical stance implies that a language has only one set
of social rules and that learners of a given language will always be interacting
orally and exclusively with native speakers of that language. This view fails
to take into account at least two additional aspects of language use: (1) the
sociolinguistic conventions of written language (e.g., rhetorical structure), of
which even those learners needing only reading skills must be aware, and (2)
the likelihood of nonnative to nonnative speaker interaction, which may bring
conflicting norms for appropriateness into play.

Paulston is more concerned about practical rather than theoretical implications of communication in the classroom. Along these lines she has designed
"communicative drills" which, she maintains, are a prerequisite to any interaction activities or role-plays intended to provide useful practice in the manipu-
lation of linguistic forms. Their format is that of the choral response, substitution
drill, and referred questions of the audiolingual era.

TEACHER: Describe the weather in your country.
STUDENT: It's (beautiful/wonderful.)

TEACHER: What is your responsibility?

STUDENT: My responsibility is (to learn English/learning English.)

These "communicative" drills, which bear little resemblance to any real form of communication, are distinguished from pattern drills only in that they require learners "to answer truthfully" rather than with prescribed responses (1976:9). This attempt at innovation is essentially Raimes's overlay solution, which identifies incorporation of new terminology (i.e., the term communicative), but not new concepts.

An example of the label-change solution is Rivers's (1971, 1973) division of language teaching into two stages—the skill-getting and the skill-using. These stages organize classroom activities in a sequence which moves from controlled structure practice to creative use of language, that stage at which learners eventually progress to the use of language for communication. Although the latter stages are referred to as skill-using, the theory upon which the skill-using stage is based is essentially audio-lingual. Learner responses in the creative and communicative phases are to be of the same quality as teacher-directed exercises, that is, error-free and complete. Control of language is a necessary prerequisite to moving on to the skill-using level where learners interact in the second or foreign language. Practice in autonomous interaction is to be incorporated into the language program. As such, Rivers's model represents an add-a-component solution. Although perfection at the pattern-drill level is no longer an end in itself, it is still the aim in "autonomous expression" (1971:77).

In further development of her model of teaching, Rivers (1976, 1983) does attempt to provide theoretical support from Halliday's (1975) work on child language development. She finds his identification of seven microfunctions and three macrofunctions particularly applicable to second language teaching. The implication she appears to draw from Halliday's proposal for these two sets of functions is that language teaching should begin with the learning of the microfunctions, which she calls microlanguage learning, and then proceed to macrolanguage use. She argues that learners' acquisition of the simple microfunctions is the means to performance on the macrolevel and stresses that this acquisition "is essential if efforts at macro-language use are to be rich and expressive" (1983:108). In using the terms microlanguage learning and macrolanguage use, Rivers appears to be relabelling her previous model of skill-getting and skill-using, but not changing that part of the theoretical framework that concerns the nature of language.[3]

---

[3]While Halliday found that a child learning a first language progressed from microfunctions to the development of a more complex system of macro- (or meta-) functions, Rivers application of this developmental model of second language teaching is problematic. Classroom instruction is an activity quite different from the process Halliday describes. Classroom language learners, who are Rivers's concern, come to the formal learning situation well beyond the transitional phase which

Thus, Rivers's models of language teaching and learning illustrate both the add-a-component and the label-change solutions. Interaction is added and stages of functional development label parts of the model, but the behaviorist and structuralist theories that shaped audio-lingualism remain intact.

New Names for Old Concepts

A more comprehensive interpretation of the role of function in language teaching syllabus and materials design is offered in Mary Finocchiaro and Christopher Brumfit's (1983) account of the sources and characteristics of an approach to language teaching they label "functional-notional." This approach is based upon the theory of syllabus design outlined in Wilkins (1976). Because their discussion is extensive, their treatment provides an opportunity for close consideration of the concept "communicative approach" as well as "function" and their implications for language teaching.

Finocchiaro and Brumfit identify the functional-notional syllabus as an "innovative approach" (1983:xi) to language learning and teaching which has as its primary focus the learners and the function or functions of language, that is, the communicative purpose learners wish to express and to understand. They describe sensitivity to individual learner needs, interpreted in terms of functions of language, as the core of the functional-notional syllabus and as the major characteristic of the functional-notional approach to language teaching.

Features of language identified as characteristic of learner-focused teaching include the necessity in materials design of taking into account the meanings and ideas that learners want to express, the uselessness of skilled organization of course content if there are no effective classroom activities, and the learners' choice of the use of the language, which in many cases may not be essential to their objectively perceived needs. In addition to these general ideas, techniques and procedures are offered which are designed to involve learners in purposeful classroom communication, for example, problem-solving tasks requiring small group work, and subsequent large group evaluation of the solutions offered by the groups.

Although Finocchiaro and Brumfit's discussion of the approach to language teaching they call functional-notional is comprehensive, there are several weaknesses in their discussion that seriously compromise the adequacy of this approach as an interpretation of communicative language teaching. One impor-

marks the first language learner's shift from the developmental functions to the adult language system of three metafunctions. Organizing second language instruction on the same pattern as first language development will not necessarily lead to free and independent interaction.

tant omission is a lack of a review of theoretical and pedagogical issues that clarify the relationship of their functional-notional approach to a communicative approach. Such a review, when related to current applications of the terms function and notion would provide insight into the concepts themselves and into their usefulness for language teaching practice. Similarly, they fail to consider the implications of a functional-notional approach for materials development and methodology. Thus, it is difficult to relate their conceptions of function, notion, and communicative competence to considerations of cultural and social parameters which determine meaning and the formal realizations of these meanings, as has been outlined in the discussion of British linguistics and Halliday's semiotic perspective in Chapter 1.

In its discussion of practical applications for the classroom, Finocchiaro and Brumfit's description of a functional-notional approach reveals an adherence to the philosophy of audio-lingualism. It is more concerned with *practicing* communication than with engaging learners in communication itself. A further example of lack of change in theoretical underpinnings is the use of the terms *mastery* and *control* to describe the outcomes of teaching. In a communicative approach, learners' competence is not viewed in terms of mastery or control; rather, development of competence in communication is recognized as variable and dependent upon the learners' abilities, attitudes, and rate of learning, as well as upon their needs for learning the language and the degree of competence required for those purposes.

The lack of a change in the theoretical underpinnings for the language teaching they describe is also evident in their view of errors. The claim that "most teachers are understandably unwilling to encourage their students to make errors without good reason" (1983:94) betrays a lack of consistency with the communicative principles these authors appear to espouse. In communicative language teaching the concern is not whether learners make errors or not, but whether and how the errors they inevitably make interfere with their ability to express, interpret, and negotiate meaning.

The limitations of their treatment of the relationship between form, function, and culture in particular contributes to the failure of their account of a functional-notional approach to be anything more than an overlay of new terms on old concepts. While Finocchiaro and Brumfit point out that the language forms a speaker uses are influenced by the function of the message, the situation, and the topic, they do not call attention to the role that the speaker's cultural background plays in determining the appropriateness of linguistic structures and lexical items selected to realize a function. Failure to do so ignores the effects of sociocultural constraints on language form and function as a crucial consideration in materials development and curriculum design. As shown by the example of the Zambian's and American's experience in cross-cultural greeting in English illustrated in Chapter 2, recognition that forms associated with a function in one culture may differ from those associated with it in another culture is essential. As the anecdote illustrated, association of functions with particular forms depends on more than speaker's purpose, situation, and the topic; the formal realization of a form is closely linked to the cultural context of the speaker.

As a consequence of these shortcomings, Finocchiaro and Brumfit's interpretation, like those of Paulston and of Rivers, fails to demonstrate that the functional-notional approach is anything new; it simply offers new names for old concepts.

Although the interpretations of communicative language teaching discussed up to this point have been inadequate primarily because of their basis in structural linguistic philosophy and audio-lingual methodology, interpretations of communicative language teaching have been made that are based upon a functional view of language and offer innovative approaches and methodologies. Prominent examples of these interpretations are presented in the remainder of this chapter.

Savignon's Interactional Approach

The concept "communicative competence" has gained prominence in pedagogical circles in North America primarily through the research of Sandra Savignon (1972, 1983). Her work, representing an extension and reinterpretation of Hymes's concept, has had considerable impact on language teaching, initially on the teaching of French and other modern languages in the United States and Canada, and more recently on the teaching of English as a second and foreign language.

Her initial contact with the term can be traced to her interest in language testing and Jakobovits's (1968) views of the importance of teaching for communicative competence and the testing of school-made bilingual competence. In a 1972 study of the effects of teaching for communicative competence on the achievement of learners in a foreign language course, she first demonstrated the viability of communicative competence as a pedagogical concept. A more recent publication (Savignon 1983) documents her commitment to communicative language teaching and the development of her views.

Savignon's approach is based on a view of language as "meaning making." Language is a mode of human behavior, and to "know" this form of communication means knowing how to use it for creating meaning as well as knowing about the forms of the language. The goal of any language teaching program, in her view, is the development of learners' communicative competence, which she defines as "the *expression, interpretation,* and *negotiation* of meaning involving *interaction* between two or more persons or between one person and a written or oral text" (1983:249).

As a preliminary step toward understanding communicative competence for the classroom, Savignon explores the individual concepts of communication and competence. The central characteristics of competence in communication are associated with (1) the dynamic, interpersonal nature of communicative competence and its dependence on the negotiation of meaning between two or more persons who share to some degree the same symbolic system; (2) its application to both spoken and written language as well as to many other symbolic systems; (3) the role of context in determining a specific communicative competence, the infinite variety of situations in which communication takes place, and the dependence of success in a particular role on one's understanding of the context and on prior experience of a similar kind; and (4) communicative competence as a relative, not absolute, concept, one dependent on the cooperation of all participants, a situation which makes it reasonable to speak of degrees of communicative competence (1983:8-9). These four characteristics evidence the vital role Savignon acknowledges for sociolinguistic parameters. Her recognition of the role of social and cultural experience in the act of communicating and the variable nature of meaning and its dependence upon linguistic and nonlinguistic factors is a reflection of Halliday's influence on her approach to language teaching.

The Components of Communicative Competence

The theoretical framework upon which Savignon bases her model of communicative competence is that developed by Canale and Swain (1980) and refined by Canale (1983), which suggests four components of communicative competence:

1. *Grammatical competence.* Knowledge of the sentence structure of a language.
2. *Sociolinguistic competence.* Ability to use language appropriate to a given context, taking into account the roles of the participants, the setting, and the purpose of the interaction.
3. *Discourse competence.* Ability to recognize different patterns of discourse, to connect sentences or utterances to an overall theme or topic; the ability to infer the meaning of large units of spoken or written texts.
4. *Strategic competence.* Ability to compensate for imperfect knowledge of linguistic, sociolinguistic, and discourse rules or limiting factors in their application such as fatigue, distraction, or inattention.

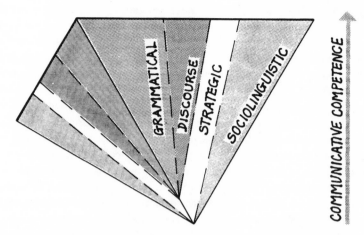

Figure 5. Components of communicative competence. Source: Sandra J. Savignon, 1983, *Communicative Competence: Theory and Classroom Practice*, Addison-Wesley, p. 46.

Savignon (1983:46) visualizes these components interacting in the manner shown in Figure 5. As the figure illustrates, no hierarchical relationship exists among these components. They are interdependent: communicative competence is greater than any one single component, Savignon explains, and a learner does not proceed from one to another "as one strings pearls on a necklace" (1983:45).

A Communicative Curriculum

Savignon's work, primarily focused on the classroom, includes a model for a language teaching curriculum based upon her interpretation of communicative competence. This curriculum differs considerably from the traditional approach to language teaching curriculum design which divides language programs into reading, speaking, listening, and writing components. In place of this four-skills approach she puts forward a framework which is consonant with the four characteristics of competence in communication and the four components of communicative competence outlined above.

The curriculum she proposes has five areas, with no sequence or hierarchy prescribed. The first of the components is *Language Arts*, which focuses on rules of usage and provides explanation of how language works, but is not restricted in content to analysis alone. Systematic practice in the application of rules is also recommended. Spelling tests, vocabulary expansion exercises, and pronunciation exercises would be typical activities. This component could be interpreted as focus on the textual function of language. It is here that grammar, in the traditional sense of focus on formal relationships, finds its place in language teaching. Savignon stresses that it is important to keep the formal aspects of language in perspective. The Language Arts component is regarded as *interrelated* with the others and is not to be considered any more or less important than the other four components.

Language for a Purpose is the second component. This relates to authentic use of language in the classroom as in bilingual immersion programs. This could be achieved by establishing the L2 (second language) as the lingua franca of the classroom. The purposes could range from comprehension of basic classroom commands (e.g., "Open your books to page 10") to the learning of a new game or craft activity through the L2. Here the focus can be interpreted as the ideational function since attention is on concepts and relationships rather than formal structures of language or strictly on the skills and strategies required for the expression of meaning between or among individuals.

The third component is related to *Personal L2 Use*. It involves the affective aspects of language acquisition, the expression of one's own attitudes, values, and beliefs, ranging from acceptance of cross-cultural differences or a learner's rejection of native-like competence in the L2. This component highlights the fact that *"it is one thing to analyze and appreciate native language behavior, quite another to adopt that behavior for one's own"* (1983:201). This component can be interpreted as focus on the interpersonal function. Activities for learners which incorporate this use of language in the curriculum include the keeping of a personal journal or the construction of family trees with important information about family members. A key feature of these activities is the learners' use of the language to express their own view of the world and their own culture.

The fourth and fifth components provide opportunities for the natural blending of the three functions represented in the other three components.

Theater Arts includes such activities as the "class play," but more importantly calls attention to other facets of the theater such as roles, simulations, and rehearsal. This component provides opportunities to analyze the total set of behaviors involved in communication and also provides opportunities to try them out.

The final component, *Beyond the Classroom*, involves the exploration of the L2 community, either by stepping outside the classroom, if learners are in the L2 setting, or through the media and local representatives of the L2 culture(s).

Savignon's approach does not draw a specific relationship between communicative competence and its formal exponents. Her earlier work (1972) has been criticized for providing no description or specification of the grammatical and other skills required in, for example, information getting (Canale and Swain 1980). Such criticism is unwarranted since it is neither possible nor necessary to definitively describe or specify these skills. A speaker's communicative competence cannot be described in terms of discrete elements and skills; it is not possible to determine how much competence is required to communicate in a particular situation. Attempting to do so is like answering the question, "How much light is sufficient to find your way out of the forest," which John Oller has posed in the context of critiquing so-called integrative language tests. As he explains, finding one's way out of the forest depends "hardly at all on any particular discrete rays of light" (1978: 55). The same can be said about discrete skills and elements of communicative competence.

Savignon's later work specifically addresses the inappropriateness of a monolithic view of communicative competence and stresses the need to take learners' individual goals for learning a language and the contexts in which the language will be used into account: "In the first place there may exist not *one* but *several* L2 cultures, each with a different set of rules. More important, the L2 may be widely used as a means of communication among nonnative speakers *outside a community to which it is native*" (1983:26).

Savignon's curriculum proposal is a cogent summary of her interactional approach to communicative language teaching. By extending the definition of communicative competence beyond that offered by Hymes, she provides a framework for curriculum design and a basis for principled realization of a curriculum in materials and classroom practice. This proposal is a significant contribution to primary and secondary language education and university undergraduate foreign language programs which are designed to help learners develop general language competence rather than specific areas of language use. It is especially suited to integrated language programs since such programs do not focus on particular aspects or modes of communication such as oral communication skills or writing skills, which are often the concern of more narrowly focused language programs such as advanced-level ESL courses at the college level in the United States.

Widdowson's Discourse-Based Approach

Significant contributions to the development of communicative competence as a pedagogical concept and extensive insight into the nature of discourse is illustrated through the work of the British applied linguist Henry Widdowson (1978, 1979). His views have gained global recognition in part due to the popular concerns he has addressed, most notably the development of programs and materials for English for Specific Purposes, and the activities of the British Council, through which British applied linguists make recent developments in language teaching known outside of Great Britain.

Widdowson's approach to communicative language teaching with respect to specific-purpose programs can be characterized as "discoursal." He maintains that the real problem in a communication-oriented approach is not to teach the linguistic realization of specific illocutionary acts as suggested by the functional syllabus but to teach the realization of the connected structure of these acts, or discourse. For Widdowson, this is achieved by the development of the learners' use of pragmatic skills in the second language, skills such as interpretive strategies relating to knowledge of the use of discourse conventions or nonverbal elements and to skills which they already have developed in their first language.

The goal in Widdowson's approach is to have learners achieve competence in the use of the rule system of the language. They begin with discourse analysis, which involves them in discerning the meaning of text and organizing their means of analysis. As a result, learners develop language skills through the use of existing interpretive skills which they routinely bring to bear on text interpretation in their first language. Focusing on the interpretation of meaning as the starting point for language study provides learners with an incentive to communicate and the experience of communication, both of which, in Widdowson's view, are basic for the development of linguistic competence.

Language Use and Usage

Widdowson's discoursal approach stems from two concerns. The first is his argument for sociolinguistic analysis of language as opposed to a strictly linguistic analysis of language. The latter, he maintains, is inadequate to deal with the inexact nature of communication: "If meaning could be conveyed by exact specification, if it were signalled entirely by linguistic signs, then there would be no need of the kind of negotiation that lies at the very heart of communicative behavior, whereby what is meant is worked out by interactive endeavor" (1979:243). This feature of negotiation is central to all communication but is of particular concern in second and foreign language teaching because the variables that can confound communication (i.e., mutual understanding), are compounded and intensified through cultural and social differences. It is not that these differences do not already exist among speakers of the same language with a common social and cultural background; opportunities for miscommunication are greater, however, between those who do not share the conventions and expectations shaped by culture and society.

The second concern to which Widdowson is responding is the distinction between language *usage* and *use*. Language usage is the language system and language use is the manifestation of that system. Linguistic behavior is the production of utterances in a context for a purpose. Or, to put it another way, sentences are used for the creation of discourse. The language learner's task is to develop the ability to create and interpret discourse. This ability refers to the knowledge of how the language system is realized as use in social contexts, or communicative competence. While he acknowledges that it is possible to separate use from usage for research and study, he insists that both are necessary for a complete description of language. He supports this claim by pointing out "we are generally required to use our knowledge of the language system in order to achieve some kind of communicative purpose. That is to say, we are generally called upon to produce instances of language *use*" (1978:3).

With the discoursal approach, teaching for the development of learners' communicative competence requires attention to linguistic skills (usage) and communicative abilities (use). It cannot be supposed, however, that once the skills "are acquired in reasonable measure the communicative abilities will follow as a more or less automatic consequence. . . . The question is: how can the skills be taught, not as a self-sufficient achievement but as an aspect of communicative competence? How can skills be related to abilities, usage to use?"(1978:67-68).

To answer this question, Widdowson, in making reference to general-purpose (as opposed to specific-purpose) language courses, proposes that learners use the second/foreign language the same way they use their native language—as a communicative ability. For example, in a general English course for children, teachers should relate the second/foreign language to situations which are part of the children's real world, including the classroom, where experiences familiar to the learners are formalized and extended into new concepts. The language class, then, can relate to the world outside the classroom through history or geography. The content of the classroom should, therefore, be drawn from other school subjects, providing learners with opportunities for meaningful communicative behavior about relevant topics for realistic purposes, for example, to classify, predict, or describe.

Thus, discourse will be created in the classroom, and learners through use will work out, or negotiate, meaning through these interactions. Through creating discourse, or through communicating in the second language, and negotiating points of misunderstanding, they will develop their ability to cope with the interactive structuring of discourse, that is, their communicative competence. This approach is summed up in Widdowson's views on the purpose and specifications for learning: "It does not seem to me to follow that what is learnt needs to be explicitly taught. It is perfectly possible to teach one thing in order to facilitate the learning of something else" (1979:245).

This approach to language teaching bears some resemblance to two methods, the Direct Method and the Natural Method, that have evoked controversy since their introduction in the 19th century. Widdowson's approach differs from these significantly in that the focus of the teaching in his view is on the *content* of texts and the learners' ability to interpret texts, not on language learning.

The language is not the object of study, as in the Natural and Direct Methods. However, these approaches do share with Widdowson's approach the view that learners learn best by doing, by using the language, and not simply by learning about it.

Language for Specific Purposes

Widdowson's approach has been used in classroom application through the development of English for Specific Purposes (ESP) materials and for secondary school language teaching curriculum design. The series *English in Focus* (Allen and Widdowson 1974), written for various areas of ESP (e.g., physical sciences, metallurgy), attempts to apply a theory of discourse to ESP reading materials. The aim is to directly teach communicative acts and to teach students the realizations of major illocutions such as assertion, generalization, and inference as they appear in written texts.

Reviewers have found this application of Widdowson's theory to practice to be unsuccessful. The major difficulty stems from the lack of exercises which simulate the kind of communication that goes on in the real world (Huckin 1980; Ross 1981). The result is texts which do not challenge learners (unless they are beginning students of the subject) because they are too simple and exercises which are overcontrolled to the point of requiring little more than mechanical responses or the production of odd-sounding discourse that may be grammatically feasible, but strikes the native speaker as odd (Coulthard 1977; Huckin 1980).

Although Widdowson's approach has generally been used in the teaching of English to restricted groups, his insights into language use have implications for general language programs primarily because of his view that language should be taught through language use. In this respect, his views are similar to Savignon's. If learners are given the opportunity to create discourse as well as discover the features of cohesion and coherence that given texts display, the notion of "teaching language as communication" (Widdowson 1978) is fully realized and can be the basis of both general- and specific-purpose programs. This means taking issue with Widdowson's claim that the teaching of "general" language cannot be defined in terms of communicative requirements, a counterview which finds support in the Firthian and Prague interest in language as primarily a tool of communication in the most general sense: it is used by individuals to interact with one another for a wide variety of purposes, among which the purposes of the members of the discourse communities of science and technology is only one set.

Widdowson has provided valuable insights into the nature of language and communicative competence and, as Huckin (1980) has expressed it, has played a "pioneering" role in the movement from emphasis on grammatical correctness to emphasis on appropriate use. The shortcomings of his work, which lie prin- . cipally in the application of his approach and in his view that discourse is a combination of logical statements, do not diminish its potential in the area of curriculum design and materials development. Focus on use of language in the classroom has resulted in greater attention to cognitive skills and the incorporation of problem-solving activities in a variety of teaching contexts. One of these contexts, South India, in which Widdowson's approach has been applied to curriculum and syllabus design, is described in Chapter 5.

Piepho's Communication-Based Approach

An approach to communicative language teaching rather different from those of Savignon and of Widdowson is that developed by Hans-Eberhard Piepho (1974, 1979), a West German methodologist who is known throughout Europe as an innovator and leader in language pedagogy. He has had considerable impact on curriculum design, materials development, and teacher training and is largely responsible for new orientations in the teaching of German as a first and second language as well as English as a foreign language. His communicative approach to English language teaching is distinguished by the two major educational concerns it addresses. The first is minimalizing, if not possibly doing away with, the discrepancy in West Germany between school and the reality of socialization. The second is establishing English language teaching and learning as a means of developing a careful and systematically sequenced approach toward expression, interpretation, and negotiation within learners in their experiences with the sociocultural reality of English.

When it was introduced in the 1970s, Piepho's approach to language teaching was not generally accepted and proved controversial, in large part due to his use of Jürgen Habermas's (1970, 1971) social theory and interpretation of communicative competence as a basis for his communicative approach.[4] The most important critique in this regard was that the concept of communicative competence would conceive "a class internal didactic revolution," the effects of which would be expressed in changed teaching strategies (Piepho 1979:9). While this did eventually come about in the course of the development of communicative language teaching materials, such changes were not Piepho's original aim. His objective was to democratize language teaching and to break down elitist barriers to the development of communicative competence for all learners.

---

[4]One especially outspoken critic, H. Gustschow (1976), ridiculed the notion of *Kommunikative Kompetenz* by labeling it "Koko" and declaring it a "passing fad."

Piepho's interpretation of communicative competence is oriented toward ability and is similar to Savignon's interpretation in this respect. For Piepho, communicative competence is:

> the ability to make oneself understood, without hesitation and inhibitions, by linguistic means which the individual comprehends and has learned to assess in terms of their effects, and the ability to comprehend communicative intentions even when they are expressed in a code which the speaker him or herself does not yet know well enough to use and is only partially available in his or her own idiolect. (1974:9-10, my translation)

This definition is significant for its inclusion of "hesitation and inhibitions," a reference which can be traced to Habermas. Piepho has drawn on the work of this West German philosopher because he finds Habermas's concern with the dynamics of interaction useful in meeting the changing needs of language teaching. This concern contributed to Piepho's exploration of Habermas's concept of communicative competence from a pedagogical perspective.

Habermas and Communicative Competence

In defining communicative competence, Habermas is concerned with the notion in terms of the ideal; however, he rejects Chomsky's narrowly conceived notion of competence, perceiving it as inadequate to account for culturally determined interpretation and expression of meaning. In his view, the general competence of the (ideal) speaker extends beyond the mastery of the abstract system of linguistic rules to include the ability to produce a situation of potential ordinary communication.

For Habermas, communicative competence is the mastery of the ideal speech situation, which he describes in terms of two qualifications: (1) the potential to produce an ideal speech situation and (2) knowledge and competence in role behavior (which he calls "symbolic interaction") (1971). These qualifications are also part of Piepho's interpretation of communication for pedagogical purposes ("to make oneself understood . . . by linguistic means which the individual has learned to assess in terms of their effects").

While Habermas's theory is founded on the nature of language and communication, it is primarily a basis for a critique of society and is emancipatory in aim. *Communication*, or *communicative activity*, is associated with communicative competence. When understood in terms of an ideal, communication is realized when the actual motivations of the hearer are identical with the linguistically apprehensible intentions of the speaker. Its prerequisite is an unhindered agreement between the participants about the thematic and situational parameters, the inherent meaning relationships, and the social conventions appropriate to the context. During communication, as Wells (1986) interprets Habermas in a discussion of problems associated with technical writing, all statements in the dialogue are assumed to be true, appropriate, sincere, and comprehensible. This ability to enter into such a dialogue is communicative competence. However, communication ends when a participant questions the claim and implication of validity made by the other participant. This may happen in communication involving nonidentical norms of appropriate interpersonal behavior. In such cases, the rules are not identical for each participant in the speech act; and, as a result, participants will not conduct themselves reciprocally toward one another's expectations.

At this point, discourse begins, which is the discussion (negotiation) between the participants oriented toward reestablishment of agreement on basic principles, reaching a consensus, or resumption of communication. This distinction between pure communication and discourse is central to Habermas's theory. His critique of the condition of communication in society is contingent upon the communication/discourse dichotomy, since it is through discourse, through negotiation, that change in society is effected and the ideal of communication can be attained between and among all members and groups of a society. This distinction proved to be important to Piepho for the design of techniques and strategies for English language teaching which aims to develop in learners the ability to work toward communication through discourse and to expect the same from others.[5]

Habermas's social critique focuses on communicative inequality and the conflict between an ideal speech situation and communication distorted and inhibited by actual patterns of socialization and interaction. Realization of an ideal speech situation is dependent upon freedom from two types of hindrance: (1) external, contingent influences, such as uneven distribution of power inherent in a given social structure, and (2) tensions which result from the structure of communication itself which might conceivably require repetitions, redundancies, or use of formulaic expressions at particular points in the speech situation. The desire to remove external and contingent influences gave impetus to the school reform movement in the late 1960s and throughout the 1970s in West Germany, a movement with which Piepho's "Kommunikative Didaktik" (communicative approach) was initially related.

[5]It is important to note here that the value on negotiation and equality in problem-solving acts in Habermas's theory and Piepho's Kommunikative Didaktik is not generic to communication in all cultures. While these values do exist in the West German context and may also be features of social behavior in other European countries, it may not be possible to generalize to other cultures. As illustrated in an example provided by Hymes (1980), what may appear as restriction from one point of view may be the existence of structure from another perspective, as in the Japanese convention of constraint, or of giving way to the opinions of the leader and not expressing opposing views openly. Such cultural contrasts can be observed within one culture, where there is a continuum of norms for negotiation.

The Development of a Kommunikative Didaktik

Development and recognition of Piepho's views were made possible partly through the efforts of Piepho's fellow progressive educators who "have been particularly concerned with the communicative approach since it promotes simultaneous learning of the subject and the processes of social interaction" (Edelhoff 1983:14). Their aim is the creation of a more democratic base in the schools and the breakdown of elitist barriers to a quality education which would recognize, among other things, the legitimacy of language variety and deviation from the norm as well as the necessity of developing critical thinking in the learners. This critical thought would be expressed through language, whether it be in the first or second language classroom. The relationship between these aims is realized when learners are encouraged to engage in discourse in Habermas's sense, that is, challenge, criticize, and suggest improvements in the status quo, be it of class texts, activities, or the society at large, with the language being learned as the medium for the discourse.

Freedom from tensions resulting from the structure of communication is more directly related to Piepho's Kommunikative Didaktik, which is concerned with the structure of communication as much as it is with the formal realizations of communicative acts.

The distribution of political and economic power, the distinction between communication and discourse, and the potential of language to change society is the basis for Piepho's definition of communicative competence and his approach to communicative language teaching. The ultimate aim of his approach is to empower language users through language and thus enable them to participate in the sharing of social and political responsibility. Communicative activity takes on particular importance for Piepho as a means for learners to act upon their surroundings. As he expresses it,

> Every society displays a range of socially varied rituals realized by particular conventional modes of communicating. Through these modes of communicating human beings adjust to their surroundings, and mould them, making use of a set of well-defined ways of expression. What this means in concrete terms for language learning is the provision for learners of ways of making changes in his immediate environment, among his fellow-learners and his teachers. (1981:17)

When applied to the classroom setting, Kommunikative Didaktik implies that early on the classroom learner is to make use of utterances such as "I don't understand," "Repeat it please," "Could you speak a little slower?" and "What's the meaning of X in English?" At a later point, other communicative acts in other situational domains (e.g., obtaining goods or services) would be added to prepare learners for contacts they are likely to make with other English speakers outside of school. These communicative activities are one function of a speaker's communicative competence.

HARPER COLLEGE LIBRARY
PALATINE, ILLINOIS 60067

The next function of competence is the ability to use discourse, or "a co-herent pattern of speech acts in context" (1981:18; a phrase Piepho considers preferable to discourse because of possible confusion with the nontechnical sense of discourse as "talk, conversation"). Like communicative acts, these pat-terns are also restricted by sociocultural realities and conventions, although they may be less ritualized. Language learners' capacities to handle a pattern of speech acts is related to their ability to select those particular linguistic real-izations required to communicate their own particular point of view. Concretely, this means learners are given opportunity to express their views (e.g., "I don't like that story") and are provided with the means to justify their position. This self-expression, considered vital to unrestricted communication, makes demands on the linguistic resources available to the learners.

By relating Habermas's social analysis to culture and communication, two basic concerns in language teaching, Piepho relates the facts of West German culture to the organization and content of activities and teaching materials. How-ever, Piepho deviates from Habermas in the priority given to communication. Attainment of the ideal speech situation is not to be the learning and teaching objective. Rather, it is development of learners' ability to cope with the real situation, which is usually far from ideal. In emphasizing discourse, Piepho does not intend to imply that communication is not ever possible, a condition which would render any attempts at language teaching useless. Learners also have to be prepared to deal with the manifestations of diversity which can hinder communication. Miscommunication and faulty communication also have to be regarded as situations in the real world with which learners are familiar in their own language and culture.

Language Teaching and Social Change

The progressive education movement, Habermas's theory of communica-tive competence, and alternative directions in language teaching are brought together in a Kommunikative Didaktik to reveal the inauthenticity of the lan-guage and of the situations presented in most language classrooms. In doing so, Piepho is reacting to the situation in which "we are constantly demanding that learners relocate themselves in some fantasy world when we ask them to hear, see and imitate English dialogues" (1981:19). As a consequence, a variety of stock figures and social and national stereotypes continue to be represented in materials:

> Women appear as "'Mummies," men as "Daddies" who drive cars, hand out pocket money, make the family holiday plans and so on. In the school, teachers rule as friendly, gently reproving, unassailed kings of the classroom, boys play football, fight and bash each other about, girls turn out like sissies, or as older sisters with very self-conscious ideas of "right" and "wrong." (1981:19)

To correct this situation, Piepho suggests changing the orientation of language teaching textbooks in two ways. The first is to make room for a hard look at the roles and relationships behind human behavior and to examine more closely relationships between men and women, children and parents. As a result, these stylized, idealized representations of society might be replaced with a more honest attempt to involve learners in freer and more open communication with those who have authority over them and with their speech partners. The second means of changing the textbooks would be to seek out and present texts as opinion and point of view, rather than fact, an approach known in German as the *Problematisierung* of texts. Such presentation of texts would encourage learners to assess and evaluate the texts critically, and ultimately lead to refinement of learners' communicative abilities and the achievement of the "overall scholastic goals of being able to get their ideas across, of evaluating ideas carefully and of committing themselves to interpretation and communication" (1981:19).

Essentially, Piepho's Kommunikative Didaktik is based on the belief that learners can become completely competent when they know what they have to communicate and when they are sure of their roles and function. The objective of language teaching is to help learners become confident of the diverse roles and various functions associated with the language they are learning and the contexts in which it is used.

Similarities and Differences

Although distinctive in a variety of ways, the approaches to communicative language teaching of Savignon, of Widdowson, and of Piepho share in the high value they assign language use in relation to its social context. In this aspect, their interpretations draw upon the implications of Hymes's view of communicative competence as including social dimensions.[6] All three share in a view of communication as the expression, interpretation, and negotiation of meaning. However, they vary considerably in the specific characteristics of their approach, which differ according to the perspective each takes on the purposes of teaching. Savignon is primarily concerned with general-purpose foreign and second language programs. Although Widdowson addresses the situation of general En-

---

[6]See David Taylor (1988) for an extensive discussion of the notion of communicative competence and a critique of its use by a number of scholars, including Savignon and Widdowson. For discussions of Taylor's article and additional views on the theoretical and practical value of communicative competence, see Volume 10, Number 2, of *Applied Linguistics*, which contains selected papers from the 1988 conference "Communicative Competence Revisited" held at Coventry, England, and jointly sponsored by the British Association for Applied Linguistics and the American Association for Applied Linguistics.

glish, his efforts in the area of communicative language teaching have concentrated on teaching English for specific purposes. Piepho has addressed language teaching at political and pedagogical levels, but is, like Savignon, primarily interested in general language programs such as those typically found in primary and secondary schools.

Savignon's and Piepho's approaches are more broadly based than Widdowson's in their concern with face-to-face interaction as well as reader-to-text interaction. This emphasis makes their models more appropriate for general language programs. Although Widdowson's attention to the particular concerns of reading in the area of science and technology, which can be identified with Savignon's curriculum component "Language for a Purpose," characterizes his approach as less broadly based, this attention can be recognized as appropriate given the narrowly focused concerns of text interpretation in specific subject areas, concerns limited to the linguistic realizations of a discourse and the nonlinguistic features determining cohesion and coherence. It must also be recognized that the appropriateness of Widdowson's interpretation of the nature of discourse is somewhat limited and thus weakens to some degree the potential usefulness of his approach, particularly to the interpretation of verbal and nonverbal behavior in cross-cultural interaction. Chishimba (1985) has pointed out that while a view of discourse as primarily a matter of cohesion and coherence and the stringing together of logical statements might contribute to understanding the meaning of a text, its interpretability also depends upon knowledge of the role of silence, implication, or inference.

A strong feature of Widdowson's discoursal approach is his emphasis on learning the language through using the language. His notion of "teaching language as communication" is also at the center of Savignon's and Piepho's communicative teaching. They differ, however, in drawing attention to the importance of engaging learners in use of the language in the classroom and of making it possible for them to express their own views, that is, to express themselves with appropriate cultural and social markers which may not be shared with native-speaker or other nonnative-speaker groups. This allowance for diversity contrasts with Widdowson's ESP materials, which are concerned with the expression of one kind of international English that is associated with the world community of scientists and technologists.

Much of the significance of Savignon's and Piepho's work is their development of communicative language teaching beyond Language for Specific Purposes, which has been equated with communicative language teaching in some circles (Ross 1981). This conception of communicative teaching can be traced perhaps to Widdowson's claim, with respect to English language teaching, that

> so long as our concern is with the teaching of "general" English without any immediate purpose, without knowing in any very definite way what kind of communicative requirements are to be made of it, then the need to teach language as

communication is not particularly evident. Once we are confronted with the problem
of teaching English for a specific purpose then we are immediately up against the
problem of communication. (1979:12)

The viability of these three distinct communicative approaches and their
potential for the classroom will be illustrated in Chapter 5 through an examination of three language teaching curricula and materials based on either
Savignon's, Widdowson's, or Piepho's model of communicative language teaching. Through these illustrations, the communication-oriented language teaching
principles the approaches have in common and the uniqueness of their interpretations will be outlined. From the examination of these illustrations, it will
become clear that communicative language teaching cannot be conceived of in
monolithic terms or be understood as an exclusively British, North American,
or continental European phenomenon. It will also be shown that the strength
and value of a communicative approach to language teaching lie in its responsiveness to the diversity of contexts in which languages are taught and used
around the world.

What Is a Communicative Approach to Language Teaching?

The communicative approach is different from previous approaches to language teaching in a number of significant areas. Although it has frequently
been associated with functional syllabuses, it has evolved into a basis for culturally and socially responsive language teaching that does not dictate or pre-
scribe a syllabus type or teaching methodology. This development is due to its
concern with communication as a meaning-based activity and with the role of
functions, or uses, of language in the expression, interpretation, and negotiation
of meaning. Communicative language teaching is founded on an understanding
of the nature of communication and the variability of norms for communication
from context to context. Since it draws on the functional approach to linguistics,
exemplified in the theory of Halliday, for its theoretical perspective on language,
language use, and language development, the concepts of function and use refer
not only to function in the sense of apologizing or describing but also, and
more importantly, to the ideational, interpersonal, and textual functions of language, that is, the metafunctions of Halliday's theory. This abstract interpretation
of function becomes especially important in the choice of appropriate language
teaching models and materials.

At issue in appreciating the need for rejection of a monolithic view of
communicative language teaching is the identification of appropriate approaches
to language teaching for a variety of contexts. Communicative language teaching
has the potential to meet the needs of situations as diverse as those found in
India, West Germany, and Japan and to provide for the development of materials

suitable for each context, either through guidelines for the modification of existing materials or the local production of materials. This potential can be realized most effectively when communicative language teaching is understood in terms of the following characteristics:

1. Language teaching is based on a view of language as communication, that is, language is seen as a social tool which speakers use to make meaning; speakers communicate about something to someone for some purpose, either orally or in writing.
2. Diversity is recognized and accepted as part of language development and use in second language learners and users as it is with first language users.
3. A learner's competence is considered in relative, not in absolute, terms of correctness.
4. More than one variety of a language is recognized as a viable model for learning and teaching.
5. Culture is recognized as playing an instrumental role in shaping speakers' communicative competence, both in their first and subsequent languages.
6. No single methodology or fixed set of techniques is prescribed.[7]
7. Language use is recognized as serving the ideational, the interpersonal, and the textual functions and is related to the development of learners' competence in each.
8. It is essential that learners be engaged in doing things with language, that is, that they use language for a variety of purposes in all phases of learning.

As these characteristics indicate, qualification as a communicative approach requires more than addition of the word "communicative" or "function" to the language teacher's lexicon. It also requires an orientation toward language based on a set of assumptions which are radically different from the formalistic views of the structuralist period of influence or the dominant generative model. As the language teaching curricula and materials described in the next chapter illustrate, it is this broader interpretation which makes it possible for approaches to language teaching to be fully responsive to a learner's needs as a social being who interacts in a variety of roles and contexts in particular social and cultural settings.

---

[7]While particular techniques and procedures (e.g., group and pair work) are generally associated with communicative language teaching, these are not a feature of all communicative materials and by no means are they organized into a prescribed sequence to be identified as a "method" (as this has been understood with "audio-lingual method" or the "Natural Approach").

CHAPTER 5

Functionally Based Communicative Approaches to Language Teaching

Functional linguistics serves as a perspective from which to gain insight into the key sociolinguistic concepts of communicative competence, intelligibility, and model, the nature of English language use in nonnative contexts, and the underlying framework of communicative approaches to language teaching. It further provides a theoretical basis for relating the practical concerns of materials and methodology design to learner needs and the sociocultural context in which the learning occurs. This link between theory and practice is achieved when materials identified as communicative are examined with respect to their functional basis.

One means of determining the functional basis of curricula, syllabuses, materials, and methodologies is to evaluate them using criteria drawn from the distinguishing characteristics of functional approaches to linguistics. In light of the discussion of functional approaches in Chapter 1, the following set of criteria can be identified:

1. The communicative function of language
2. The symbolic function of language
3. The individual language user as a social being
4. The analysis of language in context
5. Meaning
6. Actual texts
7. Context
8. Situation
9. Culture
10. Learning how to mean

The Criteria

To be useful as a framework for the examination of the functional basis of materials, the criteria need to be elaborated upon in pedagogical terms and examples provided of the aspects of materials to which they apply.

Communicative Function of Language. Language is viewed as a means by which members of social groups communicate thoughts, ideas, beliefs, wishes, needs, and desires. It is regarded as the primary means for social interaction. In language teaching materials, this criterion is evident in a primary focus on learners doing things in the language they are learning rather than in reciting contrived dialogues, manipulating grammar in mastery exercises, following repetitive drills, or analyzing decontextualized language. For example, learners are asked to use language to interact with others (their teacher or peers in the classroom or others outside of the classroom) for a variety of purposes through written as well as spoken texts.

Symbolic Function of Language. This criterion refers to the function language serves as a result of speakers' attitudes about language, which in turn influence norms, standards, and models. This function has a bearing on the model of language selected for learners to approximate, the varieties of language to which they are exposed, and the particular communicative competence they are to develop. For example, learners may be expected to conform to a model which may be a nonnative instead of a native model. The symbolic function also is reflected in educational policies that determine which students are eligible for foreign/second language instruction and the standards set for learner achievement in learning. This criterion can be applied in looking for acknowledgment of the instrumental, interpersonal, or regulative functions a language serves learners.

Individual Language User as a Social Being. This criterion is reflected in materials writers' concern for the learner as an individual with unique interests and needs. This is acknowledged in the individualization of content and objectives which permit learners to establish their own agenda for learning and use of the language and their own preferences in the use of the language, for example, in the choices of vocabulary, registers, and levels of formality/informality. While the focus is on the individual, it is recognized that each individual is a member of at least one social group and that each individual ultimately uses language to establish, maintain, and develop membership in a group. This is reflected in opportunities for learners to take on a number of social roles and points of view and to develop the corresponding communicative competence.

Analysis of Language in Context. This criterion is applied to the tasks and activities that focus on the lexicogrammatical system. Are the forms of language related to the functional meanings they express? Are learners presented with texts which exemplify formal and functional features of language at all levels, phonological through discoursal? Do the explicit descriptions of formal and functional relationships include an account of the role of context in determining their relationship?

Meaning. Meaning is viewed as the result of choices available to users in the meaning systems of a language. This criterion is evident in the materials' focus on what learners want to say, or the meanings they want to make, as well as on how they say what they are saying, that is, the form in which they express these meanings. It is also evident in activities and tasks which offer learners opportunity to make selections from the available choices in meaning offered by the language being learned.

Actual Texts. Actual texts are those spoken and written by users of a language for the purposes of communicating with other users of that language. They are contrasted with texts created solely for the purpose of display or illustration of grammatical features. In language pedagogy, actual texts are frequently described as "authentic" and are contrasted with contrived dialogues and reading passages designed to highlight particular structural and formal features. Actual texts are represented by excerpts or reprints from a variety of sources—magazines, newspapers, or school textbooks, and transcripts of conversations, meetings, or other face-to-face encounters—or, in cases where no suitable actual text is available, by "genuine" texts, which, although not written or spoken by users for communication with other users, are considered to be acceptable representations of such texts. This criterion is evident in texts (either authentic or genuine) which illustrate a variety of uses and represent a range of text types.

Context. This criterion concerns the relationship between form and situation. It focuses on the relationship of the elements of a situation to the formal and structural features of an utterance and the way these formal features of language are dependent on and structured by the context. In language teaching materials this criterion is applied to the manner in which texts are presented and to the types of activities and tasks surrounding the texts. Is enough background provided about the speakers and hearers for the motivation of their choice of forms and interpretations of these forms to be clear? Are participants specified? Is enough text provided for learners to identify possible participants? Is the setting (location) of an instance of language seen as being only potentially significant to the meanings being expressed and interpreted by the participants?

Situation. Situation refers to the environment of the utterance (text), for example, what is being talked about, the participants and their purpose in interacting, and the particular characteristics of the participants which lead them to choose the particular utterances and to formulate them in the way they do or to interpret the utterances as they do. This criterion can be applied to the texts included in the materials and the range of situations they represent. It can also be applied to tasks and activities for learners. Are learners provided with the variety of situation types performed by a variety of speakers appropriate to their purposes? Do the speakers represent various backgrounds, take on a variety of roles, and use language at a variety of levels of formality? Are learners also provided the opportunity to use language in a variety of roles, at different levels of formality, and for various purposes?

Culture. As a criterion for evaluating functionally based communicative approaches, culture is related to the appropriate use of language. It is regarded as determining the situation types in which users of a language engage and the forms appropriate to these situations. Attention to culture is evident in explicit and implicit references to cultural features. For example, explicit attention to culture includes examination of what it means for native speakers to make an apology, the form the apology is to take, and how this compares and contrasts with what it means for nonnative speakers to make an apology and the form it would take. Culture is also acknowledged as a determinant of the success of a teaching approach or methodology. Evidence of culture in this sense is reflected in the types of activities and tasks selected or rejected as suitable for learners. For example, role-playing may not be considered appropriate in a particular setting due to the value placed on a traditional teacher-centered classroom.

Learning How to Mean. When used to evaluate the functional bases of communicative language teaching materials, this criterion is related to the underlying view of the goal of language learning. When viewed as learning how to mean, language learning is a process of developing a meaning potential and its concomitant behavior potential. The meaning potential represents the repertoire of meanings that a given language, or variety of language, expresses. In language teaching materials, the nature of learning and language-use tasks and activities and the objectives with which they are associated are evidence of this view of language development. Are the purposes for the completion of tasks restricted to formal analysis and learning about the forms to realize meanings? Or, are they aimed at the learners' mastery or control of structural features and linguistic forms? Are the purposes related to doing things with language, to interacting with other users of the language for the purpose of achieving some aim, realizing some intent? Is the goal for learners to learn how to make meaning, to express, interpret, and negotiate meaning in a variety of situations, that is, to develop a communicative competence that is appropriate to their needs?

In the following sections, the criteria will serve as the framework to guide an examination of the functional basis of three examples of communicative language teaching. Each example will be examined with reference to each criterion.

The first example is *Contacts* (Piepho and Bredella 1976), an English language teaching series designed for the West German context based on Piepho's Kommunikative Didaktik. The second is Savignon and Berns's (1983) proposal for a set of materials for Japanese learners of English based on Savignon's interactional approach to communicative language teaching. The final example is Prabhu's (1987) communicational language teaching project, set in the context of South India and based on Widdowson's discourse-based approach.

Contacts: Communicative Language Teaching for the West German Context

Contacts is an English language series prepared for West German primary and secondary schools.[1] It represents a curriculum for grade 5, the first year of instruction in most West German schools, through grade 10 and is a comprehensive example of materials designed with the sociocultural context of both the learners and the language being learned in mind. As described in Chapter 4, social concerns are at the center of Piepho's approach. As a functionally based communicative language teaching program, *Contacts* illustrates how the impulses of social change and socioculturally determined needs of learners, the essence of Piepho's Kommunikative Didaktik, have been realized in language teaching materials. The application of the criteria to these materials highlights this focus on social concerns.

Communicative Function of Language. In *Contacts*, an understanding of English in its communicative function is evident in many forms. Emphasis is on involving learners in using and working with the new language. Attention to analysis of the uses of English as well as experiences in using it is highlighted in activities which address a range of language uses, for example, buying in a department store, returning an item, writing a letter of complaint, participating in a formal meeting, giving and asking for directions, following instructions, or writing a letter of inquiry. These activities are specifically designed to involve learners in using English for a variety of communicative purposes. Typically the tasks presented call on skills in expression as well as interpretation, which learners are to apply to complete the tasks. "Making an Itinerary" (Figure 6),

---

[1] Publication of the first edition of *Contacts* began in 1976. The team of authors for individual first edition volumes, which are the source of illustrations in this chapter, include Margie Berns, Vera Breuer, Werner Genzlinger, Lore Gerster, Louanna Heuhsen, Rainer Iwen, Delia Krause, Jutta Kruger, Dieter Mulch, Colin Oakley, Harald Ponader, Heike Rautenhaus, and Franz Wenisch. The entire series is in revision for a second edition, under the general editorship of Hans-Eberhard Piepho, Lothar Bredella, and Franz Wenisch.

⓲ Contacts Tips for Tourists

Part One: Making Contacts with America by Bus

Enjoy unlimited travel in the U.S. and Canada year 'round!

The new Greyhound AMERIPASS lets you travel about anywhere in the U.S. and Canada. You decide when, where and how often. You also set your own schedule. Your own itinerary — because there are four great AMERIPASS plans!

Adult Fare (U.S. dollars):

15 Days	$ 165 ⁰⁰
21 Days	$ 199 ⁰⁰
One Month	$ 225 ⁰⁰
Two Months	$ 325 ⁰⁰

Part Two: Making an Itinerary

In small groups solve the following itinerary problems.

Problem description:

1. You and your friends have bought 15-day Ameripasses.

2. You have decided to start and end your trip in New York City.

3. After reading several travel guides, you have decided to visit the following cities:
New York City
Toronto, Ontario
St. Louis, Missouri
Boston, Massachusetts
Nashville, Tennessee
Chicago, Illinois
Washington, D.C.
Cincinnati, Ohio
Philadelphia, Pennsylvania

4. You have agreed to spend at least one day (24 hours) in each city and to spend no more than 3 nights altogether sleeping on the bus. Pay close attention to the time·it takes to travel from one city to another (on the map).

5. You assume that you can get a bus to the next city at any time between 6:00 a.m. and midnight.

Now make an itinerary. **Solution:**

Day One:	Arrival in New York	Sightseeing in New York
Day Two:	Departure for . . . at . . .	Arrival in . . . at . . .
Day Three:	Departure for . . .	

Figure 6. *Contacts* Tips for Tourists. Source: H. E. Piepho and L. Bredella, 1980, *Contacts 8: Topics 2, Enriched Course*, Kamp, pp. 4-5.

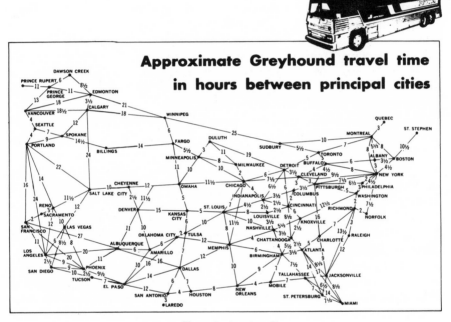

Figure 6. *(continued)*

for example, engages learners in a set of problem-solving tasks that require reading and interpretation of map information and sharing of knowledge and ideas for the successful completion of the activity.

Symbolic Function of Language. The instrumental and interpersonal functions are taken into account through choice of content for texts and the nature of activities and tasks learners are to complete.

The interpersonal function is illustrated in situations in which West Germans interact with both native and nonnative speakers and in which English functions as a lingua franca. English as a language of intra-European communication is acknowledged in dialogues between West Germans and other Europeans in likely places for these contacts. For example, a children's summer camp is the setting for the fifth-grade textbook. Since it is an international camp, the children, who come from all over Europe, use English to communicate with one another. Through this setting, learners are introduced to English as a language they can use with their peers outside as well as inside the classroom. As Piepho (1974) has emphasized, English is the medium for making other people's reality, values, wishes, plans, and history (past, present, and future) accessible to the learner. Therefore, texts are not restricted in content to topics about American or British culture; while familiarity with these (and other native English-speaking cultures) is one objective of this curriculum, English as a medium for finding out about others and oneself is also important. Figure 7 offers an example of an activity designed to involve learners in using English for self-understanding.

Attention to self suggests a further category of the symbolic function, one which can be considered a subcategory of the interpersonal function. This subcategory could be called the "personal function" because it is concerned with individual users' development of unique identities, a process directly related to the ideational component of the semantic system. In the materials for grades 7 and 8, learners are given opportunities to broaden their own field of experience through activities designed to encourage creative skills and talents and to articulate their own experience in other than oral expression. Poetry (Figure 8), diaries, and short pieces of fiction are means of achieving this.

Although it is difficult to predict the role the instrumental function of English will play in the careers and employment of the learners or to know how many will need and use English in higher education, ample opportunities for the development of study skills and subject matter texts are provided. Study skills (Figure 9) include note taking, summarizing, outlining, skimming and scanning, categorization and classification, determination of fact and opinion, and defending a point of view. Text types include recipes, assembly instructions, "brain teasers," charts, graphs and tables, time lines of historical events, encyclopedia excerpts, and newspaper and magazine articles.

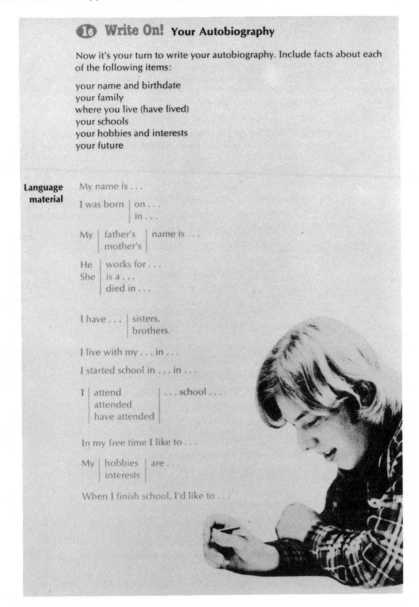

Figure 7. Write On! Your Autobiography. Source: H. E. Piepho and L. Bredella, 1980, *Contacts 8: Topics 2, Enriched Course*, Kamp, p. 119.

Relating with Poetry

In the last approach you wrote your autobiography as a way of relating to
yourself. In this approach you have the chance to write a poem expressing
your feelings or ideas. This is another way of relating to yourself or your
friends. You don't have to be a great poet to write a poem that says something interesting or important.

Poems have many different forms. In this exercise we want to introduce
you to a form called the cinquain, which is about 600 years old. The
classical cinquain has five lines and 22 syllables arranged like this:

line 1   2 syllables
line 2   4 syllables
line 3   6 syllables
line 4   8 syllables
line 5   2 syllables

Here are two examples of a cinquain. Count the syllables in each line.

My friend – Fun, laughter, tears. Please be there when I call. Waiting, hoping, dreaming with me. Partner.	CONTACTS – Lively learning. Look across the ocean! Time to make friends with each other. People.

Relating with Poetry: Have a Try

Each line of a cinquain has a different function.

Line 1 names the subject of the poem;
line 2 describes it;
line 3 describes an action of the subject;
line 4 expresses your feelings about the subject;
and line 5 names the subject again with a different word, or words.

Follow this guide and write your own cinquain. It doesn't matter at all if
your poem isn't exactly like the guide – after all, it is your poem.

Figure 8. Relating with Poetry. Source: H. E. Piepho and L. Bredella, 1980, *Contacts 8: Topics
2, Enriched Course*, Kamp, p. 123.

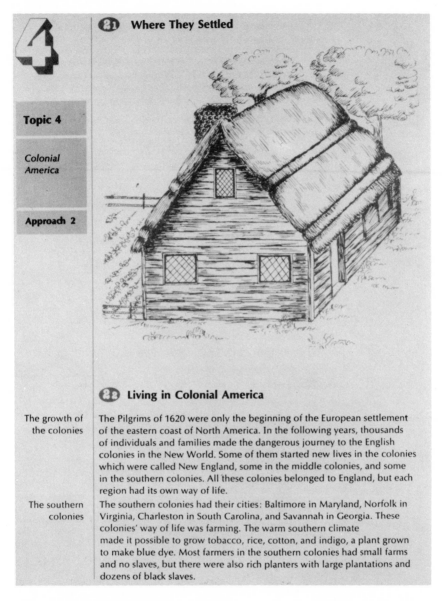

4

21 Where They Settled

Topic 4

Colonial America

Approach 2

22 Living in Colonial America

The growth of the colonies

The Pilgrims of 1620 were only the beginning of the European settlement of the eastern coast of North America. In the following years, thousands of individuals and families made the dangerous journey to the English colonies in the New World. Some of them started new lives in the colonies which were called New England, some in the middle colonies, and some in the southern colonies. All these colonies belonged to England, but each region had its own way of life.

The southern colonies

The southern colonies had their cities: Baltimore in Maryland, Norfolk in Virginia, Charleston in South Carolina, and Savannah in Georgia. These colonies' way of life was farming. The warm southern climate made it possible to grow tobacco, rice, cotton, and indigo, a plant grown to make blue dye. Most farmers in the southern colonies had small farms and no slaves, but there were also rich planters with large plantations and dozens of black slaves.

Figure 9. Study Skills Text. Source: H. E. Piepho and L. Bredella, 1980, *Contacts 8: Topics 2, Enriched Course*, Kamp, pp. 78-79.

The middle
colonies

The middle colonies were known as the "bread colonies". Most of the colonists there had small but successful farms without slaves. The farmers lived in stone and brick houses far apart from one another. In the growing cities of Philadelphia, Pennsylvania, and New York, many people worked as shopkeepers and craftsmen. Many non-English colonists came to the middle colonies: German, Scotch, Irish, Swedish, and French colonists. The middle colonists were most tolerant of different religious and ethnic groups.

New England

Like the other colonists, most New Englanders were farmers. However, their farms were small and the soil was poor and rocky. Many colonists lived in seaports catching fish, making rum, building ships, or trading slaves for southern plantations. Boston, Massachusetts, was the center of trade, whereas Newport, Rhode Island, was the center of the slave trade.

23 Taking Notes about Living in Colonial America

Copy the following headings onto another sheet of paper and organize the information in 2.1. and 2.2.

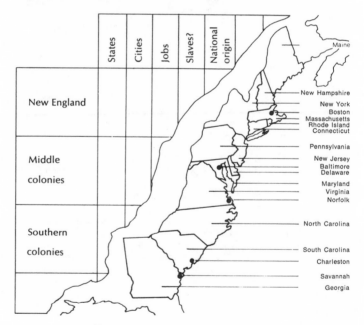

Figure 9. *(continued)*

Since *Contacts* was designed with the aims of the school reform movement in mind, diminishing the effect of the prestige function of English is a feature of the contents and approach to these materials. This feature is represented in three ways: (1) through the content of the texts, which are not solely literary, (2) in the nature of activities, which are not translation exercises and comprehension questions, but which represent efforts to create social awareness among the learners and to develop their ability to engage in discourse, and (3) in the presentation of both British and American variants of expression as acceptable models.

Responsiveness to the variation in models to which learners are likely to be exposed is also evident in *Contacts*. Teachers' unique competences and models of pronunciation, usage, and use are recognized as influencing the English that learners eventually use in speaking and writing. While norms and standards may be derived from native models, and, more likely, British models, the *Contacts* authors acknowledge that teachers themselves can only approximate these norms and that their English reflects German linguistic and sociocultural influences in general and the individual teacher's own experience with English in particular.

Individual Language User as a Social Being. The individual learner as a member or potential member of particular social groups is accounted for in the variety of roles the learners are called upon to play, the range of groups in which they have membership or with which they come into contact. In the eighth-grade text, for example, the social context of texts and activities includes the members of the school community at large, the English class, a school club, the family, the neighborhood, a circle of friends, a hobby club, a school activity committee, and a sports team. The language appropriate for participation in these groups is presented in articles, brief reports, and dialogues. "A School Meeting" (Figure 10), for example, provides the context for the introduction of one situation type, a formal meeting, and corresponding language items. Learners are subsequently provided with an opportunity to use these particular lexical and structural items in a setting similar to that presented in the textbook.

Analysis of Language in Context. Analysis of language form and function is explicit and implicit. Explicit analysis highlights the nature of the formal realizations of English. The textbooks for grades 7 and 8 focus on form in the recurring section, "Using Language" (Figure 11).

It is appropriate at this point to address the issue of systematic presentation of lexical and grammatical items, in which *Contacts* departs from a traditional view. As explained in the teacher's manual:

Examples   Chairman: I call this meeting to order. The secretary will now read the
                      minutes of our last meeting.
           Secretary: The chairman called the meeting to order on Monday,
                      September 10, 1977 at 4.00 p. m. . . .

           Chairman: At our last meeting we decided to have a school fair. When?
           John: I think . . .
           Michael: Well . . .
           Karen: November . . .
           Gwen: What about . . .
           Chairman: Everybody can't talk at the same time.
                      John, you raised your hand first. Michael is next.

           Michael: The fair should be in June. It's warm then.
           Chairman: Karen.
           Karen: I think November would be better.
           Chairman: Gwen.
           Gwen: I agree. People can buy Christmas presents then.

           Chairman: Any more discussion? John.
           John: I move that we have the fair in June.
           Chairman: Mary.
           Mary: I second the motion.
           Chairman: Let's vote on the motion. Raise your hand if you're for a fair
                      in June. Now raise your hand if you're against a fair in June.

🕹 Getting things done: a school meeting (II)

Language   I call the meeting to order.   I second the motion.
material   We should have our . . . in . . .   Let's vote on the motion.
            I think . . . would be better.   Raise your hand if you are for . . .
            I move that . . .   Raise your hand if you are against . . .

Practice   Form groups of 5 pupils. Practise using the rules for a meeting.
            Take turns being the chairman.

            Decide when to have
            a school fair,
            a class trip, or
            a handball tournament.

Figure 10. A School Meeting. Source: H. E. Piepho and L. Bredella, 1979, *Contacts 7: Topics 1,
Enriched Course*, **Kamp**, pp. 54-55.

2.6 Taking minutes

At a meeting the secretary takes notes.
Then he writes a report about the meeting.
This report is called the minutes of the meeting.
Complete these minutes.

Minutes of School Meeting – October 22, 1977

The pupils decided to form six committees for the school fair.

1. The . . . Committee will organize the work of all committees and classes during the fair.
2. The . . . Committee will tell the newspapers about the fair. It will also make advertising posters for the school and the shops in town.
3. The . . . Committee will collect and count all money at the fair.
4. The . . . Committee will sell drinks and food at the fair.
5. The . . . Committee will plan and make decorations for the fair.
6. The . . . Committee will empty wastebaskets and sweep the floors during and after the fair.

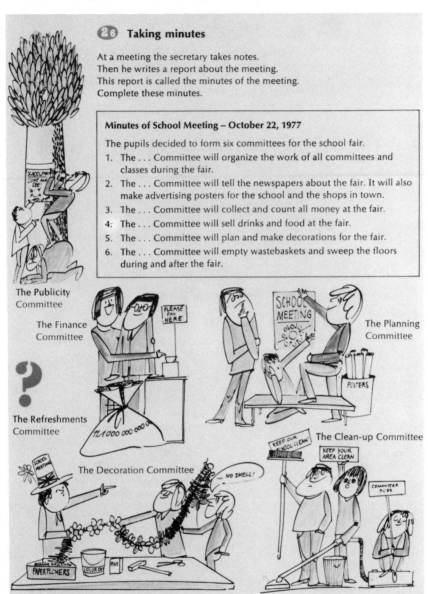

Figure 10. *(continued)*

④s Classroom Contacts

Janie, Martha, and Carol are sitting in study period, but they're not doing their homework because they've got so much to chat about.
The only problem is they have to whisper, and Janie and Carol can't hear each other. Martha has to report what each of them says.
What does Martha say?

Janie: I've finished my homework. I'm bored.
Martha: Hey, Carol. Janie says . . .
Carol: I'm bored, too. And I'm hungry.
Martha: Carol says . . .
Janie: I'll give her my candy bar.
Martha: . . .
Carol: Great. I have to buy something to wear on my date.
Martha: . . .
Janie: I'm going to wear my new sweater.
Martha: . . .
Carol: She looks really nice in that sweater.
Martha: . . .
Janie: Thanks. We can all go shopping after school. My mom will take us.
Martha: . . .
Carol: O.K. I'll call you when I get home.

Figure 11. Classroom Contacts/Using Language. Source: H. E. Piepho and L. Bredella, 1980, *Contacts 8: Topics 2, Enriched Course*, Kamp, pp. 46-47.

(4A) Using Language to Retell What Someone Said

Do you remember what Georgia said?

A	Georgia:	"I **am** in ninth grade."

B	Georgia said to the interviewer	that she **was** in ninth grade.

A	Georgia:	"I **do** my homework in the study period."

B	Georgia told the interviewer	that she **did** her homework in the study period.

A	Georgia:	"In the evening we **have** dinner with our parents."

B	Georgia remarked	that in the evening they **had** dinner with their parents.

reporting clause	reported clause

When you retell something, the reporting clause is usually in the PAST TENSE. In this case, present tense verbs in direct speech (A) are changed into past tense in the reported speech (B).

(4B) More about Tenses in Reported Speech

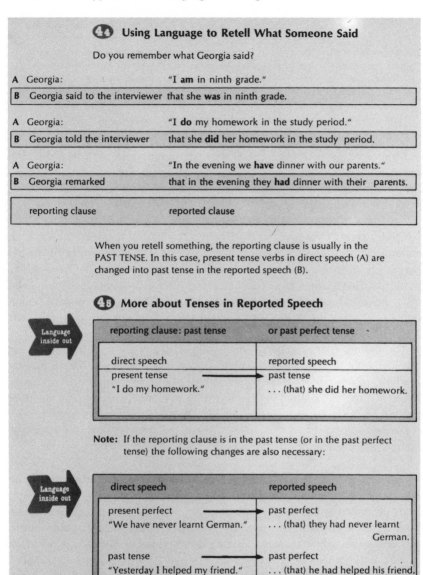

reporting clause: past tense	or past perfect tense
direct speech	reported speech
present tense	past tense
"I do my homework."	. . . (that) she did her homework.

Note: If the reporting clause is in the past tense (or in the past perfect tense) the following changes are also necessary:

direct speech	reported speech
present perfect	past perfect
"We have never learnt German."	. . . (that) they had never learnt German.
past tense	past perfect
"Yesterday I helped my friend."	. . . (that) he had helped his friend.

Figure 11. *(continued)*

Learning of rules is not to take place ad hoc and chapter by chapter, but rather in
a long-term process of recognition, practice, and application. When information, rules,
and explanations of the language are to be formalized, it is the concern of the teacher
and not any prescriptive teaching plan. Therefore, all grammar explanations are given
very carefully in the textbook. Under no circumstances should the user of *Contacts*
assume that the grammar as it is presented in the textbook is completely or formally
presented as a pedagogical grammar. . . . The system of the grammar is inherent
and implicit, and only seldom, if ever, explicit. (Piepho and Gerster 1979:5, my
translation)

Implicit analysis of language is required in nearly every task and activity
in these materials to the extent that correct interpretation of any text depends
on an understanding at all levels, from the phonological to the discoursal.

Meaning. Contacts offers two illustrations of meaning as choice. One is
the activity type "Chatter Chain" (Figure 12) which represents choice as determining meaning and the effect of these choices on the responses of the next
speaker. The interactive nature of language is conveyed by the form of this
activity: the first learner makes a choice from the two options given; a second
learner makes an appropriate choice from "2"; the first, or yet a third, learner
chooses a response from "3." Variations and combinations are allowed if they
are meaningful and contribute to the creation of a coherent text.

The second type of activity which is specifically concerned with meaning
as choice is the "Everyday Encounter" (Figure 13). The choice in the meaning
potential ("can mean") is from three options: (1) placing blame, (2) opting out
of dealing with the situation, or (3) suggesting an alternative plan. The utterances
presented in the activity represent preselections in "can say." Learners are to
make meaning choices, discuss their effects, and provide possible alternative
meanings and realizations of meanings.

Actual Texts. Contacts uses a variety of actual texts, both authentic and
genuine, which includes texts presented to and created by learners. Examples
of texts presented to learners include newspaper stories, magazine features (e.g.,
quizzes and questionnaires), interviews, encyclopedia and biographical entries,
letters and notes, advertisements, catalog descriptions, poetry, songs, short stories, and diary entries.

Actual texts, either written or spoken, are contextualized and intended for
a communicative purpose; in other words, they are not for the pedagogical purpose of determining whether or not learners can manipulate particular formal
features, for example, formation of the present perfect tense. Texts of this kind
contrast with drills or responses to display questions (e.g., "What is this?" intended to elicit "a pencil" or "a book" from learners while the teacher holds
a book or pencil up before them). Texts created by learners include letters,
autobiographical statements, reports, summaries, messages, or poems.

⓲ **Chatter Chain:** What Do You Like to Read?

1	**2**
What do you like to read? Do you like to read | magazines? 　　　　　　　　　| novels? 　　　　　　　　　| comics? 　　　　　　　　　| love stories? 　　　　　　　　　| mysteries? 　　　　　　　　　| science fiction? I like to read . . .	I like to read . . . 　No, they're | boring. 　　　　　　| all alike. 　　　　　　| a waste of time. 　　　　　　| too expensive. I prefer . . . . . . are more exciting. Yes, | especially | hobby | magazines. 　　　　　　　　　| sports 　　　　　　　　　| fashion 　　　　　　　　　| teen 　　　　　　　　　| music 　　　　　　　　　| news 　　I buy one almost every week.
3 I do, too. | What's your favorite? 　　　　　| What have you read? I don't. They're | boring. 　　　　　　　　| . . . Want to look at my newest one? Could I | see it 　　| sometime? 　　　| borrow one | Reading is | a great way to make contacts. 　　　　　| better than . . . You can't play football | all the time. 　　　　　　　　　　| all night. 　　　　　　　　　　| . . . That's too bad. Reading is fun. I think they're . . . Last | week 　| I read . . . 　　| month | My favorite is . . .	I don't have time for that. 　　　　I have too much reading for school. I don't like to read at all. I'd rather | play football. 　　　　　　　　　　　　　　| watch TV. 　　　　　　　　　　　　　　| ride my bike. 　　　　　　　　　　　　　　| listen to records. 　　　　　　　　　　　　　　| . . . Why? 　　| What's your favorite? I do, too. | What have you read?

Figure 12. Chatter Chain: What Do You Like to Read? Source: H. E. Piepho and L. Bredella, 1980, *Contacts 8: Topics 2, Enriched Course*, Kamp, p. 136.

Context. Context is taken into account with features of the context of situation often explicitly referred to in tasks and activities. In "Everyday Encounter" (Figure 13), participants' roles and relationships are under analysis. Learners are encouraged to speculate on the effects of the utterances chosen. Attention is drawn to the social and cultural background of the participants, for example, their nationality, how well they know each other, or their age.

When learners are to create texts in role-plays and situations, for example, background information is given. In a simulation, learners are presented with

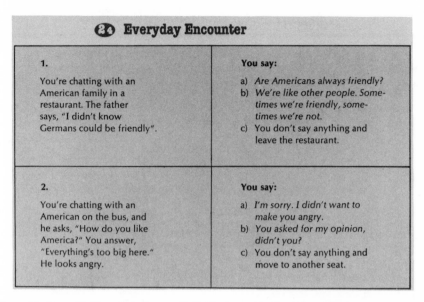

Figure 13. Everyday Encounter. Source: H. E. Piepho and L. Bredella, 1980, *Contacts 8: Topics 2, Enriched Course*, Kamp, p. 13.

a complex problem, as in the "Parking Garage Controversy" (Figure 14). Background information, roles and relationships, and relevant objects are outlined in the tasks and activities. The texts learners produce in the "town meeting" section of the simulation are the result of their interpretation of these features of the context and of appropriate behavior and meanings.

In addition to considering the context of simulated and role-played interactions which may be removed from the learners' present, the classroom also provides an immediate context relevant to the learners as school pupils. As they are already familiar with the particular features of the classroom context, these do not require explicit description; the participants in the roles of learner and teacher, for example, and relevant objects as they interact are a given, and therefore they are not in need of analysis.

Situation. "Situation" in these materials is best understood by considering van Ek and Alexander's interpretation of this concept. Rather than refer to "at the post office," situation specifies "the complex of extra-linguistic conditions which determines the nature of a language act" (1980:17). These conditions are the psychological and social roles the learner will be able to play (e.g., neutrality, private person). In the role-plays and simulations of *Contacts*, for example, roles are situated in the settings in which the learner will be able to

③① The Parking Garage Controversy

In this approach you'll encounter a new language learning activity: the simulation. In a simulation you and your classmates take the roles of people who are trying to solve a difficult problem. First you gather information about the problem. Then you try to find a solution.

Topic 5

An Environment Simulation

Problem:

A controversial plan to build a parking garage on the site of a park in the center of town.

Background information from a local newspaper:

Approach 3

Angry citizens meet with mayor

Yesterday afternoon 25 members of the "Save the Elm Street Park" campaign met at Mayor Young's office to give him a petition. The spokesperson for the group, Mrs Barbara Bennett, told reporters, "This is only the beginning of our fight. We're against the city's plan to build a garage on Elm Street. We owe it to ourselves and our children to save the Elm Street Park." In his statement Mayor Young said that he understood the group's wish to save the park, but he continued, "The parking garage on Elm Street is absolutely necessary for the shoppers." The next meeting of the Elm Street Park campaign will be held on Friday evening at 7:30 in the basement of the Catholic Church.

③② The Roles

Divide the class into four groups. Each group takes one of the following roles:

A: The shopkeepers in Monroe. They are in favor of the plan to build the parking garage on Elm Street.

B: Citizens who have to drive into the city to work and to shop. They are also in favor of the plan.

C: "Save the Elm Street Park" campaign. This citizens' group is against the plan.

D: Teachers and students at Monroe High School next to the Elm Street Park. They are also against the plan.

Figure 14. Parking Garage Controversy. Source: H. E. Piepho and L. Bredella, 1980, *Contacts 8: Topics 2, Enriched Course*, Kamp, pp. 102-105.

🔢 The Tasks (I)

Task 1   Organization:

Look at this list. Which of these reasons can your group use to support its opinion?

more money for the town	a place for adults to relax
more shoppers	fewer cars parked on the street
more traffic on Elm Street	new stores in town – more jobs
more pollution on Elm Street	safer streets
more noise on Elm Street	a place for teachers to park
more accidents	too loud for the school
no park	too expensive
a place for children to play	

Put your reasons in rank order, with the most important reason first, the next most important second, etc.

Task 2   Advertising:

Write slogans for advertisements in the newspaper and design posters to hang in store windows.
Exercise 5.2.5. may help you.

Figure 14. *(continued)*

84 The Tasks (II)

A letter to the editor of a newspaper is a good way to speak out on a problem that interests you. It is a kind of business letter.

Example

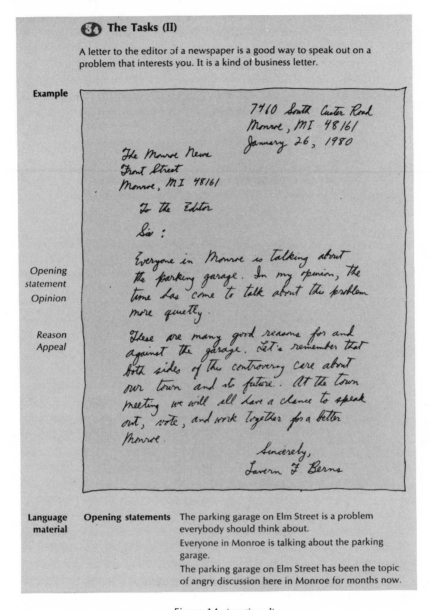

7460 South Custer Road
Monroe, MI 48161
January 26, 1980

The Monroe News
Front Street
Monroe, MI 48161

To the Editor

Sir :

Opening statement
Opinion

Everyone in Monroe is talking about the parking garage. In my opinion, the time has come to talk about this problem more quietly.

Reason
Appeal

These are many good reasons for and against the garage. Let's remember that both sides of this controversy care about our town and its future. At the town meeting we will all have a chance to speak out, vote, and work together for a better Monroe.

Sincerely,
Lavern F Berns

Language material   **Opening statements**   The parking garage on Elm Street is a problem everybody should think about.
Everyone in Monroe is talking about the parking garage.
The parking garage on Elm Street has been the topic of angry discussion here in Monroe for months now.

Figure 14. *(continued)*

Opinions   In | our | opinion, | the parking garage would be a mistake.
            | my |

            I | think | we (don't) need a parking garage here in Monroe.
            We |

Reasons   A parking garage | would bring more . . . into Monroe.
                     | would be too . . .

                     | would cause | more . . .
                                | too much . . .
                                | too many . . .
                     | would help . . .

If we (don't) build a parking garage, people won't want to . . . in Monroe.
. . . are more important than . . .
The Elm Street Park . . .

Appeal   Let's come to the Town Meeting and vote | for | the parking garage.
                                       | against |

Let's work for a better Monroe. Vote | for | the parking garage.
                                 | against |

Task   Write a letter to the editor from your group. Either the group or the spokesperson may sign it.

3.5 Getting Ready for the Town Meeting

Prepare a short statement on your group's opinion for your spokesperson to read at the Town Meeting. Be sure you have found out about the arguments of the other groups from their letters to the editor.
The language material in 3.3. and 3.4. will help you.

3.6 The Town Meeting

At the Town Meeting the mayor of Monroe (your teacher) calls on each of the groups to read their statements. After all statements have been read, everyone may give his opinion. Remember to follow the rules of parliamentary procedure (Exercise 2.2.2.).

At the end of the meeting, vote: Do you, the citizens of Monroe, want a parking garage on Elm Street?

Figure 14. *(continued)*

use the language, for example, in terms of a country such as West Germany, Great Britain, or the United States, or a more specific location such as a beach or cafe, and are related to topics familiar to the learner. Representative topics in the table of contents for the eighth-grade volume range from major cities in the United States and the geography of surrounding regions to the hobbies and pastimes of reading, biking, and cooking, and sports events and activities.

The sociocultural reality of language use in West Germany and in Europe in general plays a role in the situation types represented. Because learners' use of English may be specific to interaction with other continental Europeans as well as American, British or other native speakers, the social contexts for making meaning are diverse. Simulations and role-plays in addition to immediate classroom situations provide opportunities for developing a competence in English.

Culture as a determinant of situation types is closely linked to consideration of context. While Americans and West Germans may share many situation types, the selections they make in meaning options in a particular situation may differ. In an "Everyday Encounter" (Figures 13 and 15), for example, learners may not find any of the options presented viable unless they are familiar with the meaning these options realize in this particular setting. It is possible, for example, that a particular option presents a problem of interpretation, as in Figure 15, in which the option of inviting the complaining neighbor to the party may not match West German notions of privacy and appropriate behavior toward relative strangers.

Culture. Culture is not restricted in interpretation to descriptions of American or British monuments or social institutions. While outstanding representatives of each are the topic of texts, the information included is not an end in itself (e.g., description of an important architectural achievement). Rather, these texts also provide data for subsequent exercises aimed at developing study skills, as shown in Figure 16, in which learners are to draw comparisons between the features of two architecturally and historically significant places of worship in England.

Learning How to Mean. The tasks and activities are designed to develop learners' potential to mean. A range of the opportunities in which learners can express meaning in a variety of situations for various purposes have been illustrated under the first nine criteria. Learners are involved in the interpretation and negotiation of meaning when interacting with spoken and written texts. Negotiation of meaning is seen as relevant when communication breaks down and the learners no longer understand a particular text, that is, it is no longer intelligible, comprehensible, or interpretable. The interpretation, expression, and negotiation of meaning come together in such activities as simulations in which learners make use of their meaning potential. Integration of interpretation, ex-

⏰ Everyday Encounter

1. Your American neighbors have their radio on so loud that you can't hear your own radio. You say to them:	a) *Are you deaf? Turn that radio down!* b) *Your radio is bothering me. Would you please turn it down?* c) You don't say anything to them, but think to yourself "Typical Americans!".
2. You are having a party and are playing loud music. Your American neighbors come and ask you to turn it down. You say:	a) *What are you complaining about? You play loud music, too.* b) *Sorry, we'll turn it down.* c) *Wouldn't you like to join our party?*

Figure 15. Everyday Encounter. Source: H. E. Piepho and L. Bredella, 1980, *Contacts 8: Topics 2, Enriched Course*, Kamp, p. 145.

Places of worship: Stonehenge

Stonehenge in Wiltshire is one of the oldest and most mysterious ruins in Great Britain. An old legend says that Merlin, the magician of King Arthur's court, transported the stones magically from Ireland to Stonehenge in the eighth century A. D. The legend still lives today, although archaeologists have concluded that these circles of huge stones were built between 1800 B. C. and 1400 B. C. In that period the stones were carried to their present site, eight miles north of Salisbury, from all over Wales and England. No one has been able to explain the function of the circles. The most popular theory has been proved wrong. It says that Stonehenge was a place of worship for Druids, who were sun worshippers. Archaeologists think that Stonehenge was a place of sky worship for men who lived many hundreds of years before the Druids. The arrangement of stones seems to point to the risings and settings of the sun and moon.

Figure 16. Places of Worship. Source: H. E. Piepho and L. Bredella, 1980, *Contacts 7: Topics 1, Enriched Course*, Kamp, pp. 132-133.

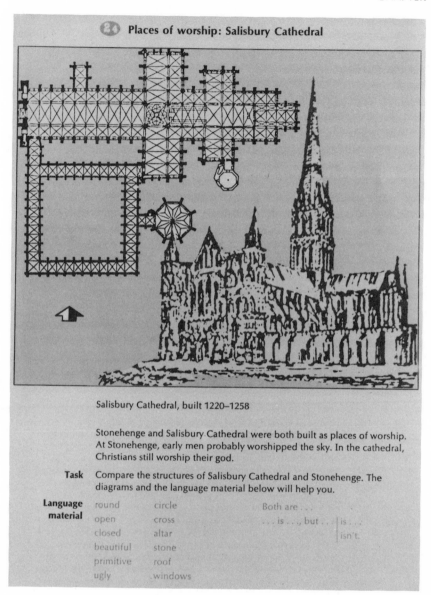

Places of worship: Salisbury Cathedral

Salisbury Cathedral, built 1220–1258

Stonehenge and Salisbury Cathedral were both built as places of worship. At Stonehenge, early men probably worshipped the sky. In the cathedral, Christians still worship their god.

Task Compare the structures of Salisbury Cathedral and Stonehenge. The diagrams and the language material below will help you.

Language material

round	circle	Both are . . .
open	cross	. . . is . . ., but . . . is . . .
closed	altar	isn't.
beautiful	stone	
primitive	roof	
ugly	windows	

Figure 16. *(continued)*

pression, and negotiation of meaning are designed to provide the learners with an opportunity to apply and develop their competence in each of these aspects of language use.

English Around the World: EFL for Japan

English Around the World is a proposal for a beginning-level English as a foreign language (EFL) series for Japanese junior high school pupils. It is an application of Savignon's (1983) interactional approach to the design of a full-scale EFL curriculum. These materials aim to develop a communicative competence consistent with the reality of English in Japan, where learners have limited contact with native speakers and few opportunities to use English. The materials take the ideational function into account by giving learners opportunities to use it as a means for exploring English language settings outside of Japan. At the same time the materials introduce the interpersonal function by giving attention to situations in which English is used for communication between and among nonnative as well as native speakers. Savignon's (1983) five component curriculum (Language Arts, Personal L2 Use, Language for a Purpose, Theater Arts, and Beyond the Classroom) is the framework for the focus of the materials.

Communicative Function of Language. Language as a tool for social interaction is the view of language upon which these materials are based. Not only is this stated as one of the goals in the introduction to the lessons ("to engage learners in the purposeful use of English"), but it is also evident in tasks and activities for the learners. Tasks and activities include several types of "doing": getting information from spoken and written texts; selecting and classifying relevant information; performing such particular uses as asking for repetition or clarification, or giving and following directions. Some of these uses are presented to learners in dialogues (Figure 17) which illustrate a range of situations for use of language, for example, greeting, requesting information, or describing.

Learners also "do" things with language in the establishment of contacts with others outside their immediate context. In "My letter to Rob" (Figure 18), learners also become familiar with letter-writing conventions in English as preparation for writing letters on their own in later lessons.

Activities of the nature of "Finish the Picture" (Figure 19) engage learners in problem-solving tasks. In this particular activity, interpreting a set of clues is essential to successful completion of a picture.

Other activities which require problem-solving skills are describing one's home; finding out more about the relationship between different types of homes,

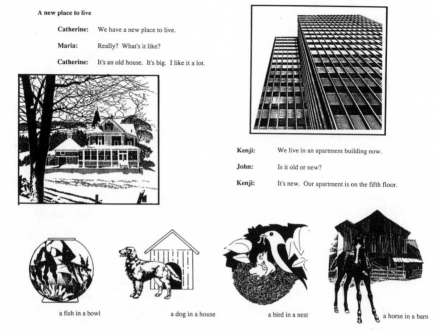

Figure 17. A New Place to Live. Source: S. Savignon and M. Berns, 1983, *English Around the World*, Unpublished manuscript.

their occupants, and their cultural setting; or finding out about the cultural settings of a city in the United States. Each of the activities illustrating this criterion are more representative of the Language for a Purpose component than of the other four curriculum components.

Symbolic Function of Language. Due to the influence of the United States in Japan, American English is a viable model in English language instruction. This series provides American English as the model for pronunciation, intonation, spelling, syntax, and lexical items. The goal for pronunciation is intelligibility, not native-like pronunciation. This orientation is explicit in the "teachers' notes": "Without insisting on native-like pronunciation, help learners to distinguish in both listening and speaking between the sounds *sh* and *ch*" (Savignon and Berns 1983:13). This teachers' note refers specifically to the Language Arts activity of Figure 20.

As outlined in Chapter 4, English serves the instrumental and interpersonal functions in Japan. While the interpersonal function is the focus of a number of the illustrations selected from *English Around the World*, the instrumental

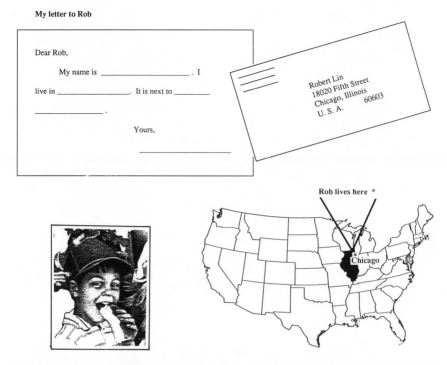

Figure 18. My Letter to Rob. Source: S. Savignon and M. Berns, 1983, *English Around the World*, Unpublished manuscript.

function is also taken into account. This is done through short texts containing factual information such as one might find in a tourist information brochure (Figure 21). Such texts are not included solely for the information they contain about the United States; they also provide information the learners need to complete subsequent tasks and activities.

The interpersonal function of English is illustrated in "A Letter from a Pen Friend" (Figure 22). Since learners of this age are not likely to have much opportunity to interact with Americans, letters provide a context in which English can be used to illustrate this function.

Individual Language User as a Social Being. One of the goals stated for this unit is to aid learners in using English to situate themselves with respect to their family, neighborhood, city, country, and the world. The tasks and activities designed to help learners in meeting this goal are part of the Personal L2 Use component. Within this unit, the learner is considered as a member of

Finish the picture.

1. The church is on the corner of Church Street and School Street. It's across from the school.

2. The toy store is on School Street. It's across from Green Park.

3. The hospital is on Church Street next to the river.

4. Tim's house is across from the school. It's on the corner of Second Avenue and School Street.

5. Kenji's apartment is next to the toy store. It's next to the river.

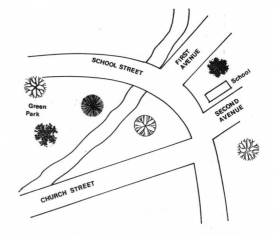

Figure 19. Finish the Picture. Source: S. Savignon and M. Berns, 1983, *English Around the World*, Unpublished manuscript.

the school community, an English class, a family, and a neighborhood. "A Letter from a Pen Friend" (Figure 22) shows how the learners' membership in an English-speaking peer group and the world community is addressed. This text also presents the form a letter in English takes when used to establish and develop membership in this group.

Learners as *individuals* are also considered in terms of the development of their competence in English. They learn not only about Americans their own age but also how to use English to express themselves on familiar topics. "My Neighborhood" (Figure 23) represents an American neighborhood and ways of describing its features. The dialogue and drawing are a basis for learners' drawings and descriptions of their neighborhoods and situating themselves there.

A further example of development of the learner as an individual is represented in the feature "My Page" (Figure 24). Here learners are to note words, phrases, and images that have become important to them as they have learned to use English throughout each unit.

Attention to the ideational function of language is also considered in the Personal L2 Use component. Development and application of learners' cognitive skills is one of the curricular aims of this series. Puzzles and problem-solving activities popular with junior high age learners are useful in addressing this aim. Simple crossword puzzles, finding the word that does not belong in a set

Figure 20. Say It in English. Source: S. Savignon and M. Berns, 1983, *English Around the World*, Unpublished manuscript.

of words, categorization, and matching activities are represented in these materials.

Inclusion of these skills is in response to the recognition that language is used not only in interpersonal communication, as Savignon and Berns point out in their introduction to the materials, but it is also necessary for the conceptualization of thoughts and ideas that individuals communicate to one another (the ideational function). The skills of classifying, categorizing, and summarizing are considered among those which underlie the traditional four skills of reading, writing, speaking, and listening. They also serve as a reference point for transfer to the learning situation of the new language. "My Page" (Figure 24) for example, requires that learners apply their skill of categorization to make entries on these pages.

Analysis of Language in Context. Analysis of formal features of language (e.g., morphology or syntax) is presented in these materials as an aid in interpreting and creating texts. Lexis and grammar are considered the means through which the learners realize the ideational and interpersonal functions of language.

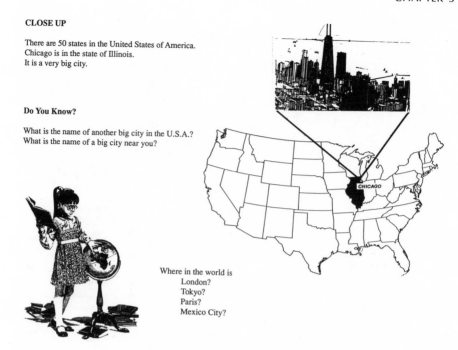

CLOSE UP

There are 50 states in the United States of America.
Chicago is in the state of Illinois.
It is a very big city.

Do You Know?

What is the name of another big city in the U.S.A.?
What is the name of a big city near you?

Where in the world is
    London?
    Tokyo?
    Paris?
    Mexico City?

Figure 21. Close Up. Source: S. Savignon and M. Berns, 1983, *English Around the World*, Unpublished manuscript.

These materials provide "Grammar Notes" (Figures 25 and 26), a feature intended for learner reference, not for memorization or drilling. As stated in the teachers' guide, "They provide learners with an opportunity to observe and make inferences about the patterns of English" (Savignon and Berns 1983:12).

Meaning. The Language Arts component is also realized in the attention given to meaning as choice. While attention is implicit rather than explicit, learners' exposure to the meaning system of English inevitably creates an awareness of the formal features realizing it and their distinctiveness from Japanese forms used for similar meanings. Texts (Figures 21 and 22) and "Grammar Notes" (Figures 25 and 26) focus on the formal choices. In the case of semantic choices, for example, the Japanese learner comes into contact with the English system of address which is comparable to, although less complex than, the Japanese system of honorifics. In "At Home" (Figure 27), learners are introduced to two common forms of address, one appropriate for an adult speaking to a child and the other which is appropriate for the child speaking to the adult in

A Letter from a Pen Friend

October 2 7, 198···

Dear ···,
My name is Rob. I am 12
years old. I live in an old
apartment building next to a big
river. Here's a picture of it.
Our apartment is big. It's on
the fourth floor. I like my home
a lot. Do you live in an
apartment?

Yours,

Rob

Rob lives in _____ .

His apartment is next to _____ .

It's on the _____.

Rob likes _____ apartment a lot.

Robert Lin
18020 Fifth Street
Chicago, Illinois 60603
U.S.A.

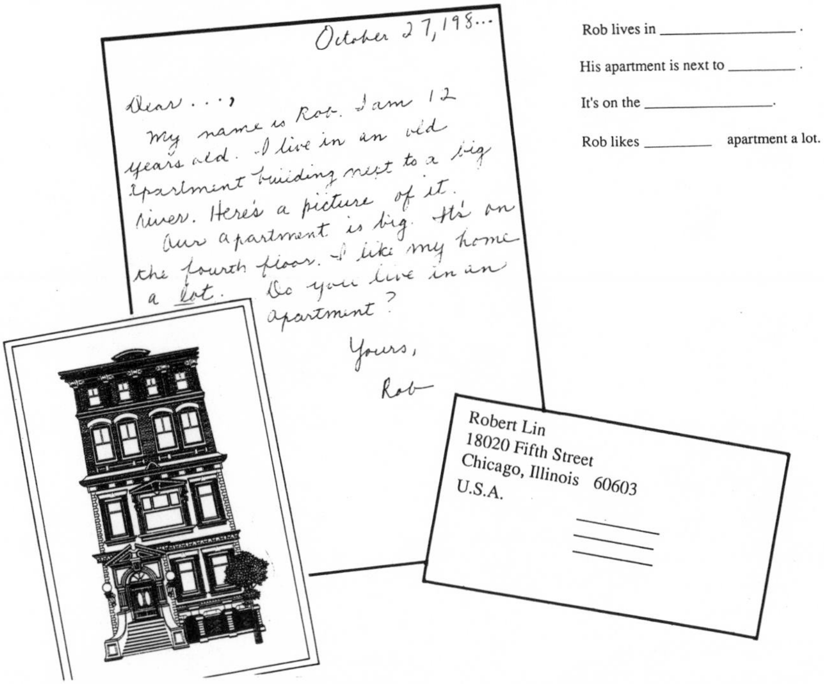

Figure 22. A Letter from a Pen Friend. Source: S. Savignon and M. Berns, 1983, *English Around the World*, Unpublished manuscript.

this context. Presentation of these forms in similar texts and a variety of settings represent the meaning they can convey in "showing respect and deference."

Actual Texts. The criterion of actual texts has two interpretations in these materials: (1) presentation of language in authentic linguistic, semantic, and pragmatic contexts and (2) provision of an assortment of texts and situations for interpreting and using informal and formal language in both spoken and written form.

Here, as in *Contacts*, authentic and genuine texts created by and for speakers of the language are included. Figure 21, "Close Up," is an approximation of travel brochure information. Actual contexts of language use are represented in "Finish the Picture" (Figure 19) and "My Neighborhood" (Figure 23), which directly refer to the contexts of map reading and puzzle solving, tasks which require conceptualization of special relationships.

Actual text is also considered in terms of the texts learners create. Learners are not required to respond artificially to questions in complete sentences but

MY NEIGHBORHOOD

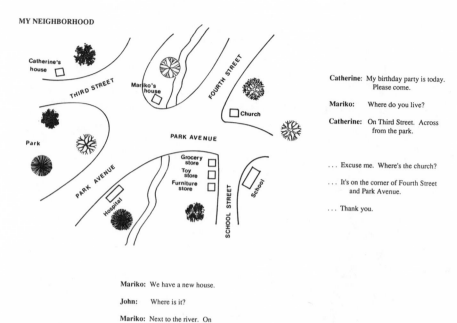

Catherine: My birthday party is today. Please come.

Mariko: Where do you live?

Catherine: On Third Street. Across from the park.

... Excuse me. Where's the church?

... It's on the corner of Fourth Street and Park Avenue.

... Thank you.

Mariko: We have a new house.

John: Where is it?

Mariko: Next to the river. On Park Avenue.

Figure 23. My Neighborhood. Source: S. Savignon and M. Berns, 1983, *English Around the World*, Unpublished manuscript.

My Page.

Important new words

T _____
H _____
I _____
N _____
G _____
S _____

P _____
L _____
A _____
C _____
E _____
S _____

Important New Phrases

_____
_____
_____
_____
_____

An Important Picture

Figure 24. My Page. Source: S. Savignon and M. Berns, 1983, *English Around the World*, Unpublished manuscript.

Where is Pedro?   What's Tim Doing?

Grammar Notes

<u>Pedro</u> is in <u>his</u> bedroom.
   <u>He</u> is in <u>his</u> bedroom.

<u>Catherine</u> is in <u>her</u> bedroom.
   <u>She</u> is in <u>her</u> bedroom.

<u>Maria</u> is brushing <u>her</u> hair.

<u>Kenji</u> is brushing <u>his</u> hair.

Is	Mr. Carson	watching TV?							
		brushing	his	hair?				she	
			her		Where's	Mrs. Garcia?	What's	he	doing?
	Mr. Carson	at home?				Tim?		Tim	
	Maria	in the kitchen?				......		Kenji	

Figure 25. Where is Pedro? What's Tim Doing? Source: S. Savignon and M. Berns, 1983, *English Around the World*, Unpublished manuscript.

are permitted to respond with short answers ("yes," "no," "nine"), as native speakers frequently do. Similarly, the English names for objects and actions are negotiated in the context of "What's this called in English?" or "What's this in English" rather than "What's this?", a question that implies that the learner does not know the identity of the object rather than its English name. Expanding the question to include "in English" more accurately describes the purpose of the activity, which is not the identity, but the names for objects.

Situation. Attention to situation is illustrated in the exchange presented in "At Home" (Figure 27), a brief interaction which represents a complex of features that define its context of situation. The participants live in the United States; one is a child and one an adult. The child's name, Pedro, suggests that English may not be his first or native language and that the culture of the United States may be his "second" culture. The name of the adult (Mrs. Carson) suggests that English is her first language and the culture of the United States is her first culture. These two individuals are speaking about one person not present who is a friend or classmate of the child. The adult (Mrs. Carson) and the child referred to (Tim) are members of the same family living in a mid-

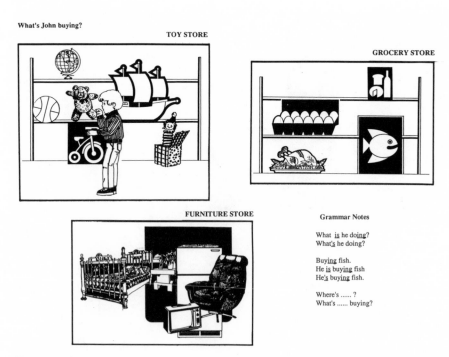

Figure 26. What's John Buying? Source: S. Savignon and M. Berns, 1983, *English Around the World*, Unpublished manuscript.

dle-class neighborhood, as indicated by the size of their home, the car in front of the garage, and the sharing of household chores referred to in the exchange. The situation is one of asking about a person's whereabouts ("Is Tim at home?"). The content of the response to the child's inquiry ("He's in the kitchen") is not expected, which is indicated by the echoing of the response with rising intonation ("In the kitchen?"). This question can be interpreted as the child's attempt to negotiate meaning through a request for clarification or repetition of the response and the circumstances it describes. His need to negotiate meaning at this point is understood when the possiblity is explored that Pedro holds a cultural view that differs from Mrs. Carson's about the places in a home where younger and/or male family members are likely to be found and the activities they are likely to engage in there. When attitudes among the speech participants differ, such negotiation is appropriate and often necessary if communication is to continue.

Context. Since text is presented as the means through which learners are to express, interpret, and negotiate meaning, these materials keep the relationship

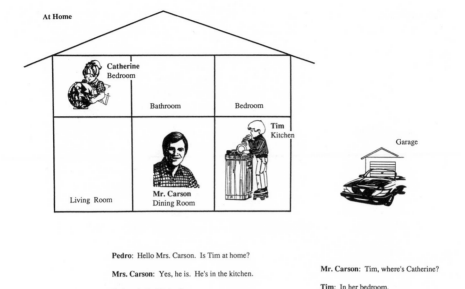

Pedro: Hello Mrs. Carson. Is Tim at home?

Mrs. Carson: Yes, he is. He's in the kitchen.

Pedro: In the kitchen?

Mrs. Carson: Yes, he's washing dishes.

Mr. Carson: Tim, where's Catherine?

Tim: In her bedroom.
She's feeding her fish.

Figure 27. At Home. Source: S. Savignon and M. Berns, 1983, *English Around the World*, Unpublished manuscript.

of the situation to the text in view. Variability in meaning with respect to situation is accommodated in these materials by focus on appropriate behavior choices and ways of realizing meaning through language, rather than focus on the settings themselves. In "At Home" (Figure 27), for example, the fact that this exchange takes place in a private home is not as essential (if it is essential at all) to the meanings made by the participants as are the particular meanings expressed and interpreted and the options in meaning available to the participants. It is more important to attend to Pedro's need for clarification at learning that his friend is in the kitchen, that is, in a location he does not anticipate finding his friend, than that his friend is actually in the kitchen.

Culture. Culture is used in two senses: (1) to refer to learners' unique, personal culture as determined by their own experiences (the ideational function) and (2) to refer to values, beliefs, institutions, and customs associated with groups (e.g., Americans or Japanese). "Questions to Ask My Classmates" (Figure 28), "My Neighborhood" (Figure 23), and "My Page" (Figure 24) illustrate culture in the first sense.

Questions to ask my classmates.

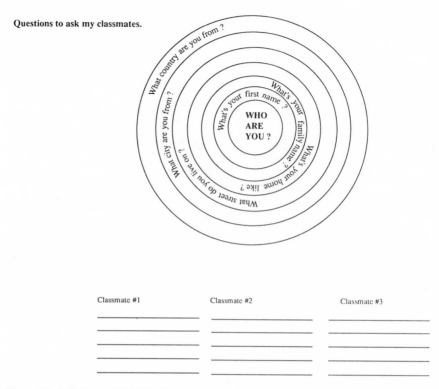

Classmate #1	Classmate #2	Classmate #3

Figure 28. Questions to Ask My Classmates. Source: S. Savignon and M. Berns, 1983, *English Around the World*, Unpublished manuscript.

"At Home" (Figure 27) illustrates the reference to a traditional view of appropriate behavior for men held by some cultures. It is this second example which highlights the relationship of culture and text. The utterance "My father is in the kitchen" means something very different to Japanese children if their experience and tradition do not include men performing household duties in the kitchen. It may mean "my father is not a 'real' man" or "my mother is not a good homemaker," whereas for a growing number of American children it could mean "my parents share the work in the kitchen" or "my mother does not like or have time to cook."

Similarly, the phrase "my own room" may present difficulties in interpretation for learners who live in a culture where the notion of a bedroom as a room specifically for sleeping or the association of a room with one person differs from American notions. This difference may make the concept "one's own room" difficult to interpret. The learners' interaction with these realizations of cultural differences necessarily involves negotiation of meaning if they are to understand the text and find it interpretable. These materials seek to use awareness of these differences to engage learners in the negotiation of meaning.

Learning How to Mean. The criterion of *meaning potential* is directly related to an appreciation of the interrelationship of factors discussed under the other nine criteria. The development of this potential, therefore, is the underlying purpose of the tasks and texts presented. This is explicitly referred to in goals set by the authors: (1) to build upon existing communication skills and develop learners' ability to exploit these in using and learning English, (2) to exploit the potential of learning through communicating about content as well as about language, and (3) to develop the learners' ability to express, interpret, and negotiate meaning with one or more individuals or a spoken or written text, that is, develop their communicative competence.

Attention to tasks which encourage learners to conceptualize, generalize, and summarize, that is, to apply their cognitive skills, also contributes toward the development of learners' meaning potential. The new names for objects, places, and actions learners encounter, for example, may introduce new concepts or new interpretations of concepts (privacy, showing respect). Understanding the use of the new names is a means for understanding Americans and their culture and for discovering the meaning of English when it is used to talk about these topics. Thus, facts about Americans can be learned through learners' negotiation with the meaning and interpretation of these new names. Meaning potential is developed through the interpersonal function of language through use of language in interaction with classmates, teachers, or other English speakers through spoken or written texts.

The Communicational Teaching Project: ESL in South India

The Communicational Teaching Project is the name of a research program undertaken from 1979 to 1984 in South Indian schools under the direction of N. S. Prabhu, former English officer of the British Council in Madras. It involved a new type of syllabus and methodology for the teaching of English in government schools in Madras and Bangalore.[2] The innovations introduced were

---

[2]Significant innovations associated with the Communicational Teaching Project are not limited to syllabus and methodology. As Prabhu has pointed out, it is also unique as a form of inquiry in that "it constitutes essentially a classroom *exploration* of pedagogic principles and procedures (and its lesson-reports, consequently, represent a public presentation of that exploration rather than teaching 'materials' for large-scale use)" and in its relationship "to current theories of second language acquisition (and to language acquisition generally, in a Chomskyan sense) as much as (perhaps even more than) to specifically 'communicative' perspectives on the nature of language" (N. S. Prabhu, personal communication, March 4, 1986).

an outgrowth of general dissatisfaction among language teachers with the then-current approach to language pedagogy which included a structurally and lexically graded syllabus and a primarily oral/structural approach to the presentation and practice of language items. Discontent with this approach and its failure to develop learners' grammatical competence (the primary objective of English teaching) coincided with awareness of so-called communicative syllabus design and teaching methodology which eventually led to the design of the syllabus and methodology that has come to be known as "procedural." This term refers to the basis of the classroom procedure, which is teacher-class negotiation in a sequence of exchanges related to tasks completed through collaborative efforts between teacher and class or independent work by individual students.

The term "procedural" is apt because it reflects the project's concern for developing teaching procedures that are realistic and replicable in the Indian classroom. Meeting these criteria means responding to the norms, expectations, and opportunities associated with English language teaching in this context. Various reports on the project (see RIE 1980a, 1980b, 1980c, and 1980d) make reference to a number of these features. Available teaching aids, for example, are generally limited to chalk, blackboard, paper, and pencil. Class size ranges from 30 to 45 for primary school and 40 to 60 in secondary classes. Learners expect classroom material to be of a serious and substantive nature. Teachers are expected to act as teachers and learners as pupils, in the traditional sense, as they do in the rest of the school's work. For the Indian context, this implies that all activities are teacher centered. Finally, learning is regarded as directly linked to the requirement of the written examinations in English given at the end of each school year and at the point of leaving school.

In contrast to the syllabus (organized as a list) that preceded it, the procedural syllabus is considered a specification of what might be done, as a source for teaching, not a course in itself (Prabhu 1987). The possible activities, however, are sequenced in a manner essential to their usefulness and potential for success. The sequence has three parts: pre-task, task, and feedback. The *pre-task* is a whole class activity which is oral and teacher directed. Its purpose is to make the nature of the task known, to bring relevant language into consideration, and to provide the teacher an opportunity to gauge the difficulty of the task that is to follow and make any necessary adjustments. The *task* is an activity which requires learners to arrive at a solution from given information through some processes of thought while also allowing teachers to control and regulate that process. The sequence concludes with *feedback*, which is the teacher's response to the content of the learners' solutions or answers. Due to its reliance on this three-stage task sequence, the methodology accompanying the syllabus has been referred to as "task-based teaching." Figure 29 provides samples of pre-tasks and tasks from a Madras school.

<u>Pre-task</u>: Teacher draws a square on the blackboard and asks the class:
What have I drawn? How many corners has it got? How many at the
top/bottom? Which is the left-hand corner at the top? What name shall we give
it? Which is the right-hand corner at the bottom? What name shall we give it?
Where shall we now write D?
Individual pupils are asked to perform (on the blackboard) the
following:
     (i) Draw a square.
    (ii) Name the corners at the top: C on the left and D on the
         right.
   (iii) Name the corners at the bottom: A on the right and B on
         the left.
    (iv) Join B, D.
     (v) Continue B, A; name the end of the line E.
    (vi) Join D, E.
   (vii) Continue A, B; name the end of the line F.
  (viii) Join C, F.

<u>Task</u> 1: All pupils carry out, on sheets of paper, the following
drawing tasks. (The sequence of instructions is indicated by numbers).
Instructions given orally.

  1. (i) Draw a square.
    (ii) Name the corners at the top: A on the left and C on the right.
   (iii) Name the corners at the bottom: B on the left and D on the right.
    (iv) Join AD
     (v) Continue AC. Name the end of the line E.
    (vi) Join DE.
   (vii) Continue BD. Name the end of the line F.
  (viii) Join CF.

  2. (i) Draw a square.
    (ii) Name corners at the top. A on the left and B on the right.
   (iii) Name the corners at the bottom. C on the left and D on the right.
    (iv) Continue DB. Name the end of the line E.
     (v) Continue AB. Name the end of the line F.
    (vi) Join EF.
   (vii) Join AE.

  3. (i) Draw a square.
    (ii) Name the corners at the top. E on the left and A on the right.
   (iii) Name the corners at the bottom. F on the left and D on the
         right.
    (iv) Continue EA. Name the end of the line B.
     (v) Continue FD. Name the end of the line C.
    (vi) Continue DA. Name the end of the line G.
   (vii) Join EG.
  (viii) Join BC.
   (ix) Join BG.

Figure 29. Examples of Tasks and Pre-tasks. Source: Regional Institute of English. 1980. Bangalore.

The principal feature of the theoretical framework supporting the project is Widdowson's (1979) distinction between *use* and *usage*. Although the teaching objective is the development of learners' grammatical competence, features of the language system are not the content of teaching or the basis for organization of the content. Use is the means by which usage knowledge is expanded. Meaning-focused activity occupies learners with understanding or conveying meaning and coping with language forms demanded by those processes. As a consequence of attention to meaning, it is expected that learners will be able to make use of, or "deploy," their linguistic resources, an ability which learners in project schools typically did not have. Prabhu describes the orientation of these syllabus and methodological orientations as "teaching language through communication," which he contrasts with "teaching language for communication," the formulation generally associated with British proponents of communicative language teaching, which addresses itself primarily to the development of situational appropriacy in language use outside the classroom (Prabhu 1980:23).

The classroom communication achieved through tasks and negotiation between teacher and pupils is described as "a matter of understanding, arriving at, or conveying meaning" (Prabhu 1987:1). Because of its attention to meaning rather than social appropriacy the project was designated as *communicational*, not *communicative*, in orientation. Although Prabhu has explicitly distanced his model from communicative language teaching by using the label "communicational" rather than "communicative," the Communicational Teaching Project is an example of communicative language teaching. The variation in methodology, scope and range of the language situations it represents underscore that communicative language teaching is not a neatly packaged method, that is, it is not possible to identify a well-defined set of techniques and procedures as the "communicative method." In addition, because the procedural syllabus and its communicative methodology are responsive to the realities of English language learning and use for the South Indian setting, they are significant in discussions of communicative methodology precisely because they illustrate that all of the procedures commonly associated with the communicative approach (e.g., group and pair work, role-plays) are not essential for language teaching to be communicative.

Communicative Function of Language. Explicit focus on grammatical competence and exclusion of concern with social appropriateness is an essential characteristic of the Communicational Teaching Project. However, this does not imply that the communicative function of language is not represented in learner tasks and activities. Rather than address issues of sociolinguistic appropriateness or represent the diversity of social roles and relationships that are part of the sociolinguistic profile of India, the materials focus on the interaction

Teacher:	Good morning, children.
Students:	Good morning, sir.

(Preliminary pre-task)

Teacher:	Sit down. Look at that. (The teacher writes '0600 hours = 6 a.m.' on the blackboard. That means.....
Students:	Six a.m.
Teacher:	Now, what does this mean? Zero six three zero hours. (The teacher writes '0630'.)
Students:	Six thirty p.m.
Teacher:	Six thirty...?(pause)
Students:	p.m.
Teacher:	Six thirty...?(pause)
Students:	a.m.
Teacher:	a.m.....yes. (pause) Zero eight zero zero hours. (The teacher writes '0800'.)
Students:	Eight a.m.
Teacher:	Eight a.m. (pause) Now, next question. Don't give the answer. Just put up your hands. Zero nine one five... (the teacher writes '0915'.) Whom shall we ask? Uh... (indicates student 1)
Student 1:	Nine--nine--nine fifteen a.m.
Teacher:	Nine fifteen a.m. Yes, good... One one four five. (The teacher writes '1145'.) Eleven four five hours.
Students:	(indistinct)
Teacher:	Say it again.
Student:	Eleven forty-five.

Figure 30. Language of Student and Teacher Roles. Source: N. S. Prabhu, 1987, *Second Language Pedagogy*, Oxford University Press, p. 123.

that the materials generate between teacher and learner. Because the roles for the learning of English are explicitly determined by the methodology, the communication that takes place is between one individual in the role of "teacher" and a group of individuals, each with the role of "pupil." Consequently, the language used in the classroom is that associated with these roles as they are realized in an Indian school. As there are social relationships already familiar to teacher and pupils, explicit attention to analysis or practice of the language relevant to them is not required. Figure 30 provides an excerpt from the transcript of a lesson which illustrates the language of the teacher and pupil roles.

This brief exchange illustrates teacher-centered instruction. The teacher determines the topic and the questions to be asked and also knows all the answers to the questions. Pupils listen, respond to questions, and repeat responses when asked to do so. This representation of the teacher-learner relationship, although it is not one that is usually associated with communicative language teaching, is typical in the Indian context and is one with which teachers and pupils are comfortable and familiar.

Symbolic Function of Language. In India, as outlined in Chapter 3, English is considered to be the language of opportunity and a means of opening the door to higher education, better jobs, and upward social mobility. As such it serves an instrumental function. However, for the learners, the potential usefulness of English in their future is somewhat removed from the reality of their present concerns as school children. In a discussion of the project, one teacher reports that "most of the time our students really don't know what they are going to do with English" (Bhasker 1980:iii). Another teacher observed with respect to this reality, "There is little attraction for them in a vague future unless they have specific ambitions, and you will not have a class full of such pupils, especially in a government school" (Bose 1980:86). Recognition of this reality led to the development of the types of tasks that shaped the syllabus. Through the tasks, learners develop the skills needed to write a letter or complete a job application in the event they would need to perform these tasks sometime in the future.

Another aspect of the symbolic function is related to the model of English that learners are to approximate. Prabhu points out that English is taught in India—as it is in other parts of the world—by nonnative speakers, which may seem to be a disadvantage since the competence of these teachers is in general limited or deficient when compared to native speaker competence. However, he does not see this perceived disadvantage as a problem at all, and he challenges the appropriateness of the concept of deficiency in speaking of Indian teachers' competence. The status of English as a world language requires recognition that standards of adequacy pertaining to it are those that arise from its role as such, not from its role in native-speaking contexts. Consequently, native-speaker standards cannot constitute the measure of adequacy for learners in India (1987:99-100).

Individual Language User as a Social Being. Learners as individuals are associated with two distinct groups. One is the immediate community of the classroom; the other is the community of English users of which learners may become a member if they find themselves in or aspire to positions in higher-level administration, higher education, one of the professions such as law or medicine, or participation in large-scale industry and commerce. The relationship of the learners to these two groups is a function of English as a second, rather than foreign, language in India. Although English may be used outside of the classroom by only a very small percentage of the learners, it does have an institutionalized role in Indian culture and society which supports its learning and use in the classroom. One feature of this role, which Prabhu identifies as a small advantage to the project, is the existence of a number of English words which are borrowings into Indian languages and the school "dialect." *Blackboard, chalk, notebook, first, last, map, drawing,* and *timetable* are pertinent examples.

Learners' membership in the classroom community is established and maintained through the familiar role of "pupil." The important difference is the use of English rather than the local vernacular to realize this role. Using English, however, does not mean learning how native speakers (e.g., American or British English speakers) behave as pupils, since the learner, as an Indian and as a speaker of Indian English, must rely on Indian ways of behaving in this role.

Since the school is viewed as the context for the development of cognitive, rather than social skills, the role of pupil is oriented toward interactions which focus on the exchange of ideational, not interpersonal, meanings. As one teacher expressed it, attention to interpersonal meaning would be regarded by learners as having "superficial relevance to their present or future life" and as not relevant to the development or expansion of the general repertory of skills and knowledge required by the school setting (Bose 1980:84).

As a result, individual solutions to problems and tasks is stressed. Teachers' evaluations are based on individual performance on tasks, not on group interaction. It is through interaction with texts and involvement in problem solving that learners develop an awareness of the nature of the ideational and textual functions of language. Cognitive skills emphasize reasoning activities that directly focus on categorization, numerical relationships, and space and time relationships. Figures 31 and 32 are tasks relating to the notions of time and quantity.

Analysis of Language in Context. Identification of grammatical competence as the focus of the Communicational Teaching Project is based on the project developer's concern with learners' inability to be correct at all in their use of English (Prabhu 1980:17). It seems that whatever they had previously learned *about* English simply was not brought to bear in their *use of* English. Relevant evidence given by Prabhu of this lack of transferability of knowledge into use is learners' inability to write a letter or an application in correct English when attention is on the application or the letter and not on the structure of language. But Prabhu's decision to concentrate on grammatical competence is not to imply that language structure is to be the content and focus of the language teaching. He interprets the role of grammar quite differently and deliberately chooses to avoid planned progression and preselection in terms of language structure as well as form-focused activity (or planned language practice) in the classroom.

Instead, through preoccupation with thinking or understanding prompted by the problem-solving activities, learners are involved in an incidental struggle with language use; the learners try to cope on their own with the language required for the task, an endeavor considered essential to the process of grammar construction. The teacher provides recurrent models for the formal realization of functions that are relevant to the completion of the tasks.

Pre-task : Teacher writes up the following four problems — one at a time — on the blackboard, and invites individual pupils to state (sometimes to write on the blackboard) their answers. The class agrees or disagrees with each answer.

1. Sekar's school has holidays from 27th September to 5th October.

    How long is the holiday?

2. The railway strike went on for ten days. It started on 26th August.

    When did it end?

3. I reached Bangalore on 8th September, and stayed there for some days. Then I left Bangalore and reached Mysore on 12 September.

    How long did I stay in Bangalore?

4. Sudha went to Coimbatore and stayed there for five days. The next day, she went to Calicut, and stayed in Calicut for 2 days. She returned from Calicut on 2nd April.

    When did she go to Coimbatore?

    Several pupils volunteer to state answers, and do so successfully, on the first three problems. The last problem proves too difficult for all but two pupils.

Task : A sheet of paper containing six problems is given to all pupils.

1. Kamala's school has holidays from 28th October to 2nd November.

    How long is the holiday?
    _____

2. The bus strike stated on 29th March.

Figure 31. Numerical Tasks. Source: Regional Institute of English, 1980, Bangalore.

An excerpt from a lesson transcript (Figure 33) illustrates incidental focus on form. It is contrasted with deliberate focus on form illustrated in Figure 34. Each type of focus is concerned with form in terms of spelling and capitalization.

Prabhu summarizes the project's approach to structure and the avoidance of language under five points:

(1) No lesson is to be consciously geared to introducing, practising or revising particular items of structure or vocabulary.

(2) At no stage are the learners to be asked to do things (e.g., say, repeat, make sentences) to language items as such; that is to say, no response from the learner is to be judged merely by its correctness in form.

(3) No activity should be used merely or primarily as a guise for exemplifying or "feeding" language items; that is to say, saying and doing—by the teacher or the learner—should be treated as serious objectives, never as an excuse for mere "speaking."

It went on for five days.

When did the strike end? _____

3. My ~~brother~~ had Examinations for six days.
They ended on 3rd January.

When did the examinations begin? _____

4. I reached Delhi on 10th September.
I stayed there for seven days. The next day, I left Delhi.

When did I leave Delhi? _____

5. Sekar reached Bombay on 28th June, and stayed
there for some days. Then he left Bombay and
reached Poona on 4th July.

How long did Sekar stay in Bombay? _____

6. My uncle went to Tiruchi and stayed there for
three days. The next day, he went to Thanjavoor
and stayed there for four days. He left Thanjavoor
on 7th June.

When did he go to Tiruchi? _____

They take about 15 minutes aswering them, and are seen to be
generally struggling.

Homework : A copy writing task—the fourth since teaching began — is given to
pupils to be done over the work—end.

Figure 31. *(continued)*

(4) Occasional and explicit attention to language itself (e.g., Do you know what X
means?) is legitimate, provided that (i) it is incidental to—and seen by learners as
necessary for—performing the tasks on hand and (ii) it is done frankly and openly
. . . not as a hidden "moral" of some pretended activity or communication. Similarly,
errors in learners' expression are to be treated by the teacher in the way a child's
errors are treated by an adult, for example, rephrased more acceptably or corrected
explicitly (not, however, elaborately, through a drill) or simply accepted provisionally
as being adequate for the occasion—all as a form of temporary digression from (or
clearing the way to) more important business, viz. the activity, task on hand.

(5) It is also, of course, legitimate to base certain tasks themselves on language (e.g.,
picking the odd man out from sets of words or sentences) or to set (in activities
that justify it, e.g., role-play) correctness of language itself as one of the targets to
be achieved—provided that such correctness is not treated/perceived as the sole (or
primary) criterion of success, thus undermining the importance of substantive correctness and thereby reducing the genuineness of the task itself. (RIE 1980b:15)

Pre-task : Questions of the following kind asked, answered (by individual pupils), sometimes written up on the blackboard — one at a time.

1. Raju was born in 1965.

   How old is he now?

2. Girija is 20 years old now.

   When was she born?

3. Sankar was born in 1960.

   How old was he in 1970?

4. Suresh was 10 years old in 1976.
   When was he born?
   How old is he now?

Two questions of each of these four types are dealt with. Forms of answer established (from occasional writing-up on the blackboard, both by the teacher and by pupils) are : "15 years" and "in 1960".

Pupils are occasionally puzzled — especially on types 3 and 4 — but can work out and state answers after the first example of each kind.

Task :   All pupils write down their answers to the following questions, each stated twice.

1. Ravi was born in 1974.

   How old is he now?

2. Ramesh is 8 years old

   When was he born?

3. Revathi was born in 1962.

   How old was she in 1974?

4. Rekha was 12 years old in 1972.

   When was she born?

5. Radha was 5 years old in 1960.

   How old is she now?

Figure 32. Numerical and Classification Tasks. Source: Regional Institute of English, 1980, Bangalore.

Pre-task: Sets of four words are prescribed (most of them on the blackboard) to the class, from which they pick out the one that doesn't belong.

Examples are :

(1)	teacher	(2)	curry	(3)	big
	pupil		coffee		small
	blackboard		tea		sick
	headmistress		milk		large

(4)	beans	(5)	tall	(6)	kerosene
	egg		short		candle
	cabbage		fat		dark
	tomato		rich		oil

Task : Fifteen sets of words are given, on paper, to each pupil. The class takes about 15 minutes to complete the exercise, and is seen to be finding it less easy than the pre-task work.

1	hand	2	story	3	uncle
	bag		pencil		grandmother
	head		paper		sister
	foot		pen		doctor

4	chair	5	apple	6	green
	table		orange		red
	teacher		rose		small
	desk		mango		white

7	speak	8	late	9	teacher
	read		run		brother
	write		stand		tailor
	absent		walk		doctor

10	bus	11	cow	12	hot
	train		horse		food
	bullock		car		cold
	bicycle		pig		warm

13	long	14	slowly	15	look
	short		fast		love
	black		quickly		listen
	small		clever		smell

Figure 32. *(continued)*

Pre-Task

Teacher   Now, the first period on Wednesday for this class, VI-B, the first period on Wednesday is English. Who will come and write that? (Some students raise their hands. The teacher calls on one.) Yes, come. (The student writes 'english' in the first period for Monday.)

Student   Teacher - Teacher! (making a bid to correct)

Teachre   Is that right?

Student   No--wrong...Teacher - Teacher!

Teacher   The first period on Wednesday is English. (The student re-writes 'english' in the right slot.). Is this correct?

Student   Correct.

Teacher   This is correct....You have to make a capital, big E. (The student corrects the mistake.)

Teacher   The second period on Tuesday is for Kannada. Who will write that? The second period on Tuesday is for Kannada. Yes? (A student writes the correct answer on the board.) Good.

Teacher   The last period on Thursday is for Games....The last period on Thursday is for Games. Who will do that? Who will write that? (A student comes up.) The last period on Thursday is for Games. Yes? (Peer consultation is followed by the student writing 'G-o-m-e-s' in the last period for Thursday morning.)

Teacher   Yes?

Students   Wrong - Wrong!

Teacher   What is wrong?

Student   G-a-

Teacher   G-a. The spelling is wrong. OK. Change the spelling. G-a-m-e-s. (The student corrects the spelling, but the entry is still in the wrong slot.) Is this correct? Listen to my question. The last period on Thursday is for Games.

Student   Teacher - teacher!

Teacher   Yes, Shyambai. Yes, come along. (Shyambai writes 'Games' in the right slot.) Is that correct?

Students   Yes. Correct.

Figure 33. Focus on Form I. Source: N. S. Prabhu, 1987, *Second Language Pedagogy*, Oxford University Press, pp. 132-133.

Teacher	The Science lessson, the Science lesson on Friday is just before History. The Science lesson on Friday is just before History. Who will do that? Yes? (A student comes up and writes 's-c-i-n-s'.)
Teacher	Is that all right? Yes?
Student	Wrong.
Teacher	What is wrong?
Student	Spelling.
Teacher	The spelling is wrong. OK. Who can give me the right spelling? Who can give him the right spelling? Stand up and say the right spelling.
Student	S-c-i-n...
Teacher	S-c-i....
Student	S-c-i-n-...
Teacher	No. -e-n-c-e, S-c-i-e-n-c-e. Yes, Science. (The student corrects the spelling, but begins the word with small 's'.)
Student	Big 'S'.
Teacher	Yes....Yes. Good. The next question--listen--The first period after lunch on Tuesday is Geography. The first period after lunch on Tuesday is Geography. (peer talk; No hands go up.)

Figure 33. (continued)

Meaning. Meaning as choice is realized in the texts that learners draw upon as the source of information for problem-solving tasks and in the text learners produce to express their solutions. However, it is through interaction with the task and with the teacher that learners are given the opportunity to explore the potentialities of the language for formal and semantic choices. Since neither linguistic nor semantic preselection is the basis for the organization of the syllabus, there is a greater possibility of "learning to mean, of purposeful exploitation of the language" (RIE 1980b:38). Through making choices on one's own (choices which may be incorrect as well as correct) learners have additional opportunities to understand the nature of language on their own terms, at their own rates, and in their own sequences. Attention to the solution to the problem, rather than to the form of the solution, emphasizes the relationship of form to meaning—incorrect choices in meaning can result in wrong solutions to the problems.

Emphasis on problem-solving tasks is emphasis on ideational meaning. For the learners, this implies engaging in "reasoning-gap activities," which are de-

Pre-task: Teacher calls out a word, asks all pupils to write it down,
then invites individual pupils (from among volunteers) to write it on
the blackboard. The rest of the class agrees/disagrees and suggests
corrections. The words thus dealt with are a selection from those that
have occurred--in the context of various tasks, in earlier teaching.
They are:
  left, first, morning, evening, join, office, pencil, last, bread,
  coffee, sister, give, draw, year, glass, old, take, day, name,
  school, class, beginning, square, continue.
Pupils make various mistakes (e.g. 'jain', 'bred', 'coffice', 'neim',
'cals', 'squier', 'continew') and are corrected either by other pupils
or by the teacher.

Task: A dictation test of the following words:
  name, class, school, left, square, morning, coffee, first, pencil,
  glass, year, sister, give, old, join, continue, beginning, farmer,
  road, grandmother.

Pre-Task: Work on spelling continued.
  Teacher calls out short phrases for pupils to write in their
note-books and for particular pupils to then write on the blackboard.
Examples of the phrases called out are: to the left, in the class,
from the school, under the table, at the beginning, to my sister, with
a pencil, make coffee, leave home.
  Pupils make occasional mistakes (in writing words on the
blackboard) which other pupils (or the teacher) point out. The teacher
insists, repeatedly, on adequate space being left between words.
  Then, the teacher calls out some short sentences, and insists on
capitalisation at the beginning and appropriate punctuation (period or
question mark) at the end. Examples of sentences are:
      Who is Rani?
      Make some coffee.
      Go to my sister.
      What is this?

Task: A dictation test of the following phrases:
  a school,   the man,   to the right,   in the school,   on the
  chair,   at last,   break the glass,   come late,   next year,
  two apples.   What is this? Where is the table? Go to the
  school. Eat some rice. Give me the paper.

Pupils mark their own work and then hand it to the teacher.

Figure 34. Focus on Form II. Source: Regional Institute of English, 1980, Bangalore.

scribed as involving the learner in "deriving some new information from given
information through processes of inference, deduction, practical reasoning, or
a perception of relationships or patterns" (Prabhu 1987:46). Deciding upon the
best course of action for a given purpose and within given restraints is one
means of engaging learners in the expression of ideational meaning. Asking
learners to solve problems with information from a timetable (Figure 35) illustrates focus on such meaning.

SOUTHERN   RAILWAY

List of Fares :   Ramnagar / Alandur / Mandia

	Rupees
Alandur to Hosalpur	8
Alandur to Bapnahalli	7
Hosalpur to Alandur	8
Hosalpur to Ramnagar	10
Hosalpur to Devanahalli	5
Ramnagar to Hosalpur	10
Devanahalli Hosalpur	5
Devanahalli to Bapnahalli	7
Bapnahalli to Devanahalli	7
Bapnahalli to Alandur	7
Bapnahalli to Mandia	5
Mandia to Bapnahalli	5

Figure 35. Southern Railway. Source: Regional Institute of English, 1980, Bangalore. Bangalore Group Lesson Report, pp. 16-17.

Actual Texts. The texts which serve as the source of information about the language are of two types: (1) the discourse (spoken and written) that learners and teachers create in the process of solving the tasks and commenting upon the solutions offered and (2) the texts learners work from in solving the tasks.

In the first type, the emphasis is on the nature of the interaction with the task. For Prabhu, it is important to recognize that such interaction shares certain features with real-life communication, such as (1) attention on saying or doing something rather than on mere "speaking" (i.e., making sentences), (2) saying and doing with a perceived purpose (i.e., other than the acquisition/practice of language), and (3) making an effort in the selection, reapplication, or extension of strategies (i.e., thinking) while performing the task. Communication in the classroom is ensured if tasks are based on the preconditions that the learners' minds are engaged and there is a resultant need for them to communicate. Preoccupation with understanding, thinking out, doing or saying something while

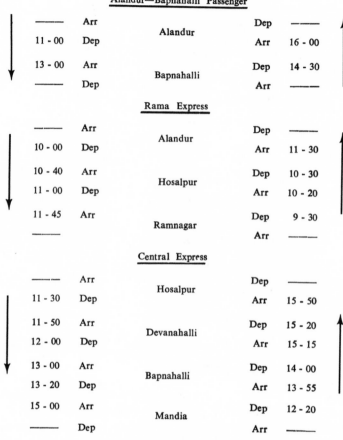

Figure 35. *(continued)*

learners cope in the process, as well as they can with the language involved, is a prerequisite to communication.

"Natural" language is to be modeled in the teacher's use of language; the teacher is to control language as an adult does in conversing with a child—"by glossing/rephrasing/explaining or ascertaining the understanding of such expressions and modifying his assumptions (about what is within or beyond his audience's competence) continually in the light of ongoing (interactional) evidence" (RIE 1980b:16).

Pre-task: oral stimulus and response; answers written on the blackboard:

   How do you get from Mandia to Alandur by train?

   What time do you leave Mandia?

   Where do you change trains?

   At what time do you get down there?

   How long do you wait there?

   What time does the train leave for Alandur?

   How long does it take to travel from Mandia to Alandur?

Task: How do you get from Ramnagar to Mandia by train?

   What time do you leave Ramnagar?

   Where do you change trains?

   What time do you reach that place?

   How long do you wait there?

   Which train takes you from that place to Mandia?

   What time does it leave?

   What time does it reach Mandia?

   How long will it take to get from Ramnagar to Mandia?

Figure 35. *(continued)*

   The authenticity of the discourse in the interaction between learners and teacher is ensured by the spontaneous use of language that is involved in the solution of problems and tasks. There are no set formulas, responses, or forms that can be imposed on the teacher and the learners that could replace or approximate the meaning-making process necessary to solve the problem.

   In addition to discourse created by teacher and learner in the process of solving the tasks, actual texts are presented to learners in the range of written and spoken texts that contain the information they are to act upon in applying their cognitive skills. The excerpts from lesson transcripts presented in previous sections illustrate one form of learner and teacher created discourse. Illustrations of prepared texts are timetables (Figure 35), reading passages (Figure 36), and maps (Figure 37).

Rajan is ten years old. He is now in the fifth standard at his school. He has a younger sister called Revathi. She is two years younger than Rajan and is studying in the third standard. Revathi is a clever girl. She gets good marks in her class. Rajan is not so good in his class. He spends most of his time playing with other boys.

Figure 36. Reading Passage. Source: Regional Institute of English, 1980, Bangalore.

Scale : $\dfrac{1\ \text{inch}}{1\ \text{km}}$

Autorickshaw Charge :   Rs. 0 . 75 per kilometre

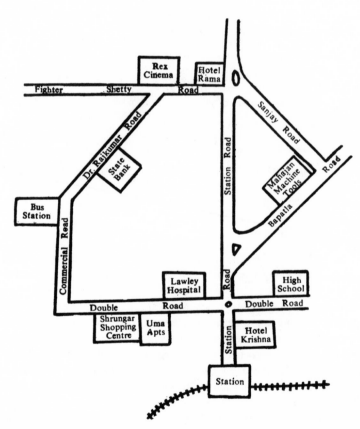

Figure 37. Map of Tenali. Source: Regional Institute of English, 1980, Bangalore. Bangalore Group Lesson Reports, p. 60.

Context. The context of the texts created by and presented to the learners can be considered in terms of the classroom and of the context beyond the classroom. In each, the relationship between the text and situation is a given, familiar to teachers and learners alike. English is not being learned for use with speakers of British or American English, but with other Indians. This reality precludes the need to analyze the Indian classroom context or attend to appropriate nonverbal actions or relevant objects, that is, socialize the learners into appropriate classroom behavior, verbal or nonverbal.

The context within which the classroom is situated is related to the environment of the text and its formal features. The use of the names of local towns (Madras, Katpandi) and of familiar objects (*bullock cart, puris, sarees*) establish the context as Indian. The behavior of learners and teachers in the classroom and the texts which correspond to this behavior also reflect the Indianness of the setting. Examples of such behavior are the teacher-centered instruction and the expectation that learning has to do with "serious, substantive content," not "having fun" (Prabhu 1987:4).

Situation. Perhaps the most striking feature of the materials and setting of the Communicational Teaching Project is the lack of reference to uses of language, participants, roles, objects, or situations that are abstract or removed from the "here and now" of the learners. The context for learning and use of English is not deferred for future uses; it is immediate and one within which the learners are immersed. It is woven into the reality of the school and their participation in the activities of the school as an Indian institution.

The general situation types represented in the procedural syllabus are germane to the Indian school setting, for example, asking for and providing specific information, making inferences, or giving and following directions. The relevance of these situations is to be seen in terms of the learners' present needs as school pupils and of their potential need for English outside the school setting in the future.

Culture. The sociocultural reality of English language use in India plays a role in determining the general situation type that defines English instruction in the government schools which participated in the project. As already mentioned, the dominant teacher-pupil relationship in this setting is also determined by the culture. The power of this norm is demonstrated by the project's failed attempts to introduce role-plays and group activities to learners in its early phases. These activities were unsuccessful because they did not meet learners' preconceived notions of learning and teaching, which did not include playing games, acting out nonclassroom roles, or managing without a teacher (Prabhu 1987:4).

Indian culture is also represented in the contexts of the problems them-selves. Indian names for places and persons as well as local objects (e.g., *bullock cart)*, are used in the texts. Their use underscores that English is being learned with reference to the Indian reality inside and outside the classroom, not to British or American contexts.

Learning How to Mean. Learning and teaching in the Communicational Teaching Project is achieved through making ideational meaning. Communica-tion in the classroom is embedded in and emerges from meaning-focused activity which occupies learners with understanding, conveying, or extending this mean-ing as they cope with the language forms demanded by the meaning-making process.[3] The difference between focus on meaning and focus on form is il-lustrated in one teacher's reflections of learners' tendency to focus on the dis-crete lexical items of a teacher's question rather than on the meaning of the question as signalled by question words. In a series of questions based on in-formation given in a train schedule, learners would not distinguish between "When does the train reach Katpandi?" "When does the train leave Katpandi?" and "How long does the train stay at Katpandi?" Instead, they would treat each question as being the same except for lexical changes, which were not recog-nized as cues for semantic changes (Bose 1980:85).

Learning to mean for the learners is described as learning to solve problems and as creating texts that realize the conceptual solution; these texts are to gradually approximate the language of an adult speaker of the language. By creating and interpreting discourse, learners are to develop and expand their knowledge of the structure of English. The progression is from the expression of meaning to a refinement of the understanding and use of the structures which realize this meaning.[4]

Similarities and Differences

Application of a functionally-based framework to determine the functional bases of these materials reveals a number of significant similarities and differ-

[3]In comments made during observations of the project's early development, Keith Johnson (1982) recognized the influence of Halliday's concept "learning how to mean" on the nature of the communicational approach. Of particular importance, he notes, is Halliday's observation that language is learned by a child in relation to use, which has been applied literally in project materials through use of English by learners to expand their repertoire and acquire language not previously known.

[4]A number of scholars have described, discussed and critiqued aspects of the Communicational Teaching Project. See, for example, Beretta (1987), Brumfit (1984), Greenwood (1985), and Johnson (1982).

ences between and among them. Their shared and unique features can be summarized by examining the communicative competence, learner model of language, and expectations for intelligibility each identifies as appropriate for the learners in each particular setting. The similarities and differences also reflect the capacity of a functionally-based interpretation of communicative language teaching to respond to a variety of social and cultural contexts of language learning and use.

Communicative Competence

With respect to the selection of communicative competence as a goal, *Contacts* and *English Around the World* have more in common with each other than either does with the Communicational Teaching Project. Having specified communicative competence as the teaching objective, Piepho as well as Savignon and Berns make use of learner-learner interaction; offer a wide variety of task and activity types; have a multicomponent curriculum; and place value on the development of social as well as cognitive skills. However, their materials are distinguished by the particular communicative competence each aims to develop. The Japanese learners' communicative competence differs significantly from that of the West German learners, for example, with respect to the range and type of situations in which the learners are expected to be able to communicate. *Contacts* is designed to engage learners in critique and questioning of the status quo, in keeping with the goals of the school reform movement of the 1970s. These activities require competence in critical-thinking skills and the means of expressing this process and its outcome in English. In contrast, the Communicational Teaching Project emphasizes ideational meaning, the cognitive aspects of language development, and language as a discourse-creating tool rather than a means of interpersonal communication. This focus explains the lack of learner-learner interaction, the limited range of task and activity types, the one-dimensional nature of the curriculum, and the premium placed on cognitive skills.

The context for developing competence in Japan requires an ability to interpret, express, and negotiate meaning with respect to a rather short-term goal, the college entrance exam, which does not reflect the broader uses that English serves for a growing number of Japanese. The communicative competence required of the school-age learners is not related to immediate communicative uses, but almost exclusively to grammatical competence and comprehension skills. Yet, there is growing awareness that the internationalization of Japan requires the ability to use English—to speak and write and to interpret the meaning of a variety of texts for a variety of purposes and the ability to interpret being Japanese in a world context. Thus, communicative competence in English also increasingly means being able to talk about one's self, native country, ideas, and history—goals similar to those outlined in *Contacts*. *English Around the World* is designed to be responsive to both types of competence.

The rationale for the identification of unique competences for each of these contexts rests in the social and cultural realities of English language use in West Germany and Japan. Traditionally, in each of these settings English has been described as a foreign language. Yet, as shown in Chapter 3, this "foreignness" differs depending upon the uses and users. West German school-age learners are frequently interacting with and through the language by means of the media, contacts with tourists, or school exchange programs and excursions abroad. Japanese school children, on the other hand, are less likely to have contact with native or nonnative speakers other than their teacher. While some words and phrases have become part of the vocabulary of many Japanese, the influence of English is not as extensive in Japan as it is in West Germany.

For these reasons, the adequacy of the term "foreign" to describe the status of English in the West German pedagogical setting is called into question. English in Europe in general and in West Germany in particular is increasingly regarded as a tool for inter- and intracontinental communication and less as an academic subject. Given the scope and breadth of its use in these performance contexts and the purposes for learning it, the term "English as an international and intranational language" (read "intracontinental" for Europe) seems more appropriate. This notion also reflects the changes in what is being taught and how it is being taught.

While English is not the language of wider communication in either West Germany or Japan, its role in a variety of functions does have implications for language teaching. The notion of English as a language of interpersonal communication has been integrated into Piepho's approach to communicative language teaching.

Prabhu claims that the Communicational Teaching Project is not concerned with communicative competence defined as social appropriateness (1987:1). However, when "learning how to mean" is seen as compatible with Hymes's view and with interpretations of communicative approaches such as those of Savignon and of Piepho, the purpose of English learning in the Communicational Teaching Project is, in fact, the development of communicative competence. The Indian school-age learners are developing the ability to express, interpret, and negotiate meaning in the classroom setting in which they use English, a particular competence unique and specific to their needs and the sociocultural features of their situation.

Intelligibility

The question of intelligibility, which is related to the notions of model and communicative competence, has also been answered differently by each approach. In the Communicational Teaching Project, Prabhu has selected an Indian English model of language use for the learners, the features of which are represented in the spoken and written texts presented to the learners. Since these texts are produced locally, rather than taken from materials produced in the United States or Great Britain, the cultural and social contexts represented are South Indian. Thus it can be expected that the English competence the learners develop will enable them to be intelligible (and comprehensible and interpretable) with other South Indians. That is, the choice of a local model implies that the learners will be intelligible locally, although not necessarily internationally.

Intelligibility has been considered somewhat differently for Japanese learners. The classroom model of English for these learners is American or British because the purpose for learning English is its use as an international lingua franca. Yet, as discussed in Chapter 3, learners' English will display local features of pronunciation or lexical items.

The choice of a native-speaker model suggests that the learners are to be intelligible to those who find American and British English intelligible. Yet, as shown in Chapter 2, being intelligible involves more than decoding the noises made by speakers or the marks they put on paper. It also involves comprehending and interpreting spoken and written texts. Recognition of the complexity of intelligibility is important with respect to West German learners who are going to use English not only with native speakers but also with other Europeans. Thus, while the noises and marks they make may be American, the meanings will be West German or, more broadly, European.

Model

Given the influence of the teacher's individual use and perception of the English language in addition to the diversity of models, West German learners are exposed to in the media, Piepho has emphasized the prudence of realistic aims for classroom models of English. Savignon and Berns similarly emphasize realistic goals, although they understand that the range of native-speaker models for Japanese learners is likely to be less broad than those for West German learners. As a consequence, the Japanese teacher's own experience with English is likely to be less diverse than that of the West German teachers. The materials for the West German and Japanese learners are also similar in their attention to ideational and interpersonal meanings.

Focus on English for rational rather than emotional uses of language in the Prabhu curriculum implies that the model of English presented to the Indian learners will differ from the model presented in the West German and Japanese materials. Differences on this point are most pronounced when comparing *Contacts* and the tasks of the Communicational Teaching Project. At an early stage, *Contacts* presents learners with the means for expressing displeasure, dislike, or preference, for example, whereas Prabhu's communicational tasks ask learners neither to express their own opinions and feelings nor to interpret or evaluate the views of others. *Contacts*, reflecting the philosophy of Habermas, also stresses questioning the status quo of social relationships in the classroom as well as in the society at large. In contrast, Prabhu is concerned not with analyzing or changing social relationships but in using language in an established set of roles, that of teacher-pupil.

Conclusion

The discussion of the three examples of communicative language teaching materials undertaken in this final chapter brings together the various aspects of language use, learning, and teaching discussed in previous chapters and demonstrates their interconnections as well as their relevance for program and materials assessment and design. As such, these aspects are shown to be integral parts of a comprehensive sociolinguistic approach to the establishment of language teaching programs that are communicative in theory as well as practice.

The functional linguistics of the Prague School and the British tradition outlined in Chapter 1 served as the point of departure for the discussions of concepts, contexts, and pedagogy taken up in the subsequent chapters. The exploration of communicative competence, intelligibility, and model in Chapter 2 showed how a functional perspective on these terms illuminates their relationship to one another and their centrality in informing pedagogy. The sociolinguistic profiles of India, West Germany, and Japan described in Chapter 3 presented the formal, functional, and attitudinal features of English for each context and illustrated particular communicative competences, available models of English for the classroom, and the parameters of intelligibility associated with them. In Chapter 4 functional linguistics provided the framework for assessing the theoretical bases of a variety of interpretations of communicative language teaching. The implications of more than one communicative competence for a language, of nonnative standards for intelligibility, of differences in the forms and functions of one language across contexts, and of the comparative soundness of the theoretical underpinnings of various approaches to communicative language teaching became salient in Chapter 5 when the 10 criteria were applied to language teaching materials. The salience was evident in the considerable variation across the tasks and activities included in the materials and their representation of objectives for learners.

This lack of uniformity, rather than revealing a weakness in the materials or the approaches upon which they are based, offers insight into one of the most significant features of communicative language teaching: its potential to be sensitive and responsive to the relationship between communicative competence and the social and cultural context in which a language is learned and used.

It is this context-specific response which is the strength of these materials. They demonstrate that identification of the broad goal of communicative competence does not imply adopting a particular syllabus or methodology. In fact, they show that teaching for communicative competence cannot mean rigid adherence to one way of teaching or the use of one kind of syllabus, one set of materials, or a fixed selection of learner activities if the goal of communicative competence is to be achieved effectively across a variety of contexts.

Like meaning, a teaching approach has to be negotiated anew for each context. As no two contexts for the development of communicative competence are alike, no two responses to the social and cultural realities of those contexts can be identical. A functional basis to communicative language teaching provides a framework that is sufficiently flexible to adapt to diverse contexts of language learning and use. This flexibility and adaptability in approach is essential if the communicative needs of learners of any language, second or foreign, and in any setting, native or nonnative, are to be met.

References

Abercrombie, D. (1951). R.P. and local accent. In D. Abercrombie (1965), *Studies in phonetics and linguistics* (pp. 10-15). London: Oxford University Press. (Reprinted from *The Listener, 6*)

Adeyanju, T. (1987). *Rule-bending creativity in Nigerian English.* Unpublished manuscript.

Allen, J. P. B., & Widdowson, H. G. (Eds.). (1974). *English in focus.* London: Oxford University Press.

Atkinson, R. (1975). RP and English as a world language. *International Review of Applied Linguistics, 13*, 69-72.

Baird, D., & Heyneman, J. (1982). A look at a company in-house English program. *JALT Newsletter, 16*, 10, 12-13.

Baldegger, M., Müller, M., & Schneider, G. (1981). *Kontaktschwelle. Deutsch als Fremdsprache* [The threshold level in German]. Munich, West Germany: Langenscheidt.

Bamgbose, A. (1971). The English language in Nigeria. In J. Spencer (Ed.), *The English language in West Africa* (pp. 35-48). London: Longman.

Bamgbose, A. (1982). Standard Nigerian English: Issues of identification. In B. Kachru (Ed.), *The other tongue: English across cultures* (pp. 99-111). Urbana, IL: University of Illinois Press.

Bansal, R. (1969). *The intelligibility of Indian English.* Hyderabad: Central Institute of English and Foreign Languages.

Barnet, V. (1972). Learning the spoken language. In V. Fried (Ed.), *The Prague school of linguistics and language teaching* (pp. 29-42). London: Oxford University Press.

Barnlund, D. (1975). *Public and private self in Japan and in the United States.* Tokyo: Simul Press.

de Beaugrande, R. (1980). *Text, discourse, and process.* Norwood, NJ: Ablex.

Beneš, E. (1972). The syntax of scientific German in foreign language teaching. In V. Fried (Ed.), *The Prague school of linguistics and teaching* (pp. 142-159). London: Oxford University Press.

Benson, J., & Greaves, W. (1973). *The language people really use.* Agincourt, Canada: Book Society of Canada.

Beretta, A. (1987). The Bangalore Project: Description and evaluation. In S. Savignon & M. Berns (Eds.), *Initiatives in communicative language teaching II.* (pp. 83-106). Reading, MA: Addison-Wesley.

Berns, M. (1982, May). *Culture and communication: English for Japanese.* Paper presented at the International Meeting of TESOL, Honolulu, HI.

Berns, M. (1984). Functional approaches to language and language teaching: Another look. In S. Savignon & M. Berns (Eds.), *Initiatives in communicative language teaching II.* (pp. 3-22). Reading, MA: Addison-Wesley.

Berns, M. (1988a, June). *English in West Germany: Contact and conflict of attitudes.* Paper presented at the International Conflict-Symposium Contact + Confli(c)t 88, Brussels, Belgium.

Berns, M. (1988b). The cultural and linguistic context of English in West Germany. *World Englishes, 7,* 37-49.

Bernstein, B. (1964). Elaborated and restricted codes: Their social origins and some consequences. *American Anthropologist, 66,* 55-69.

Bernstein, B. (1971). *Class, code and control I: Theoretical studies toward a sociology of language.* London: Routledge and Kegan Paul.

Berry, M. (1975). *Introduction to systemic linguistics: 1. Structures and systems.* New York: St. Martin's Press.

Bhasker, W. (1980). Foreword. In RIE (1980a), pp. i-iii.

Bokamba, E. G. (1982). The Africanization of English. In B. Kachru (Ed.), *The other tongue: English across cultures* (pp. 77-98). Urbana, IL: University of Illinois Press.

Bose, M. (1980). A teacher's experience. In RIE (1980a), pp. 81-90.

Brown, H. D., & Berns, M. (1983). *Junior action English.* Tokyo: World Times of Japan.

Brumfit, C. (1984). The Bangalore procedural syllabus. *ELT Journal, 38,* 233-241.

Bühler, K. (1934). *Sprachtheorie.* Jena, East Germany: Fisher.

Butler, C. (1982). Recent developments in systemic linguistics. In V. Kinsella (Ed.), *Surveys I* (pp. 38-57). Cambridge: Cambridge University Press.

Campbell, R., & Wales, R. (1970). The study of language acquisition. In J. Lyons (Ed.), *New horizons in linguistics* (pp. 242-260). London: Penguin.

Camutaliová, I. (1972). Some principles of stylizing a dialogue for foreign language teaching. In V. Fried (Ed.), *The Prague school of linguistics and language teaching* (pp. 160-181). London: Oxford University Press.

Canale, M. (1983). From communicative competence to communicative language pedagogy. In J. Richards & R. Schmidt (Eds.), *Language and communication* (pp. 2-27). London: Longman.

Canale, M., & Swain, M. (1980). Theoretical bases of communicative approaches to second language teaching and testing. *Journal of Applied Linguistics, 1,* 1-47.

Candlin, C. (1976). Treating language functions in language teaching. In C. Edelhoff (Ed.), *Kommunikative kompetenz durch Englischunterricht* (pp. 36-49). Fuldatal, West Germany: Hessisches Institut für Lehrerfortbildung.

Candlin, C. (Ed. and Trans.). (1981). *Communicative teaching of English: Principles and an exercise typology.* London: Langenscheidt-Longman.

Candlin, C. (1982). English as an international language: Intelligibility over interpretability. In C. Brumfit (Ed.), *English as an international language* (pp. 95-98). London: Pergamon Press.

Casteleiro, J., Meira, A., & Pascoal, J. (1988). *Nível limiar. Para o ensino/Aprendizagem do Português como lingua segunda/Lingua estrangeira* [The threshold level in Portuguese]. Strasbourg: Council of Europe.

Catford, J. (1950). Intelligibility. *English Language Teaching, 1,* 7-15.

Catford, J. (1969). J. R. Firth and British linguistics. In A. Hill (Ed.), *Linguistics* (pp. 247-257). Voice of America Forum Series. Washington, DC: United States Information Agency.

Census Report of India. (1961). Delhi: Manager of Publications, Government of India.

Chaturvedi, M., & Mohale, B. (1976). *Position of languages in school curriculum in India.* New Delhi: NCERT.

Chishimba, M. (1985). African varieties of English: Text in context (Doctoral dissertation, University of Illinois, Urbana, 1983). *Dissertation Abstracts International, 45,* 168A.

Chomsky, N. (1965). *Aspects of the theory of syntax.* Cambridge, MA: MIT Press.

Chomsky, N. (1977). *Language and responsibility.* New York: Pantheon Books.

Clyne, M. (1981). Cultural and discourse structure. *Journal of Pragmatics, 5,* 61-66.

Coste, D., Courtillon, J., Ferenczi, F., Martins-Baltar, M., & Papo, E. (1981). *Un niveau-seuil* [The threshold level in French]. Paris: Hatier.

Coulthard, M. (1977). *An introduction to discourse analysis*. London: Longman.

Daneš, F. (1964). A three level approach to syntax. *Travaux Linguistique de Prague, 1,* 225-240.

Davis, P. (1973). *Modern theories of language*. Englewood Cliffs, NJ: Prentice Hall.

Denison, N. (1981). English in Europe, with particular reference to the German-speaking area. In W. Pöckl (Ed.), *Europäische Mehrsprachigkeit* (pp. 2-18). Tübingen, West Germany: Max Niemeyer.

Deutsch Wird Aprilfrisch. (1983, February 3). *Süddeutsche Zeitung*.

Dixon, R. (1965). *What IS language? A new approach to linguistic description*. London: Longman.

Dubský, J. (1972). The Prague conception of functional style. In V. Fried (Ed.), *The Prague school of linguistics and language teaching* (pp. 112-127). London: Oxford University Press.

Edelhoff, C. (1981). Theme-oriented English teaching: Text varieties, media, skills and project-work. In C. Candlin (Ed. and Trans.), *Communicative teaching of English: Principles and an exercise typology* (pp. 49-62). London: Oxford University Press.

Edelhoff, C. (1983). The comprehensive school in the Federal Republic of Germany. In C. Edelhoff (Ed.), *The communicative teaching of English* (pp. 10-15). Report on 1981/1982 Danish/German Teachers' Conferences, Skarrildhus, Jutland. Grebenstein, West Germany: Sprogsam English Committee/Gesellschaft zur Förderung des Englischunterrichts an Gesamtschulen e.v. (GFE).

Ferguson, C. (1966). National sociolinguistic profile formulas. In W. Bright (Ed.), *Sociolinguistics: Proceedings of the UCLA Sociolinguistics Conference, 1964* (pp. 309-315). The Hague: Mouton.

Ferguson, C. (1982). Foreword. In B. Kachru (Ed.), *The other tongue: English across cultures* (pp. vii-xi). Urbana, IL: University of Illinois Press.

Finocchiaro, M., & Brumfit, C. (1983). *The functional-notional approach: From theory to practice*. Oxford: Oxford University Press.

Firbas, J. (1964). Comparative word order studies. *Brno Studies in English, 4,* 111-128.

Firbas, J. (1972). On the interplay of prosodic and non-prosodic means of functional sentence perspective. In V. Fried (Ed.), *The Prague school of linguistics and language teaching* (pp. 77-94). London: Oxford University Press.

Firth, J. R. (1930). *Speech*. London: Ernest Benn.

Firth, J. R. (1935). The technique of semantics. In J. R. Firth (1957b), pp. 7-33. (Reprinted from *Transactions of the Philological Society*, 36-72)

Firth, J. R. (1937). *Tongues of men*. London: Watts & Co. (Reissued 1964)

Firth, J. R. (1950). Personality and language in society. In J. R. Firth (1957b), pp. 177-189. (Reprinted from *The Sociological Review, 42,* 37-52)

Firth, J. R. (1955). Structural linguistics. In F. R. Palmer (Ed.) (1968), pp. 35-52. (Reprinted from *Transactions of the Philological Society*, 83-103)

Firth, J. R. (1957a). Synopsis of linguistic theory 1930-1955. In F. R. Palmer (Ed.) (1968), pp. 168-205. (Reprinted from *Studies in Linguistic Analysis* [Special volume of the Philological Society, Oxford], 1-31)

Firth, J. R. (1957b). *Papers in linguistics 1934-1951*. London: Oxford University Press.

Fisiak, J. (1986). The word formation of English loanwords in Polish. In W. Viereck and W. Bald (Eds.), *English in contact with other languages. Studies in honour of Broder Carstensen on the occasion of his 60th birthday* (pp. 253-263). Budapest: Akademiai Kiado.

Frake, C. O. (1964). How to ask for a drink in Subanun. *American Anthropologist, 66* (6), 127-132.

Frank, J. (1988). Miscommunication across cultures: The case of marketing in Indian English. *World Englishes, 7,* 25-36.

Fried, V. (Ed.). (1972). *The Prague school of linguistics and language teaching*. London: Oxford University Press.

Fukuzawa, Y. (1899). *The autobiography of Yukichi Fukuzawa*. New York: Schocken Books. (Reprinted 1972)

Galli dé Paratesi, N. (1981). *Livello soglia per l'insegnamento dell'italiano come lingua straniera* [The threshold level in Italian]. Strasbourg: Council of Europe.

Garvin, P. (1963). Linguistics in Eastern Europe: Czechoslovakia. In T. Sebeok (Ed.), *Current trends in linguistics I* (pp. 499-522). The Hague: Mouton.

Garvin, P. (1972). *On machine translation: Selected papers*. The Hague: Mouton.

Geiger, A. (1979). *Britischer kontextualismus und fremdsprachenunterricht*: [British contextualism and foreign language teaching]. Berlin: Cornelsen-Velhagen and Klasing.

Geiger, A. (1981). The application of "British contextualism" to foreign language teacher training. *English Language Teaching Journal, 35*, 209-215.

Ghosh, I., & Datta, S. (1983). *Teaching English as a second language for social purposes. Phase 1: A preliminary survey in Jhargram*. Jhargram Raj College, West Bengal.

Gimson, A. (1980). *An introduction to the pronunciation of English* (3rd ed.). London: Edward Arnold.

Gompf, G. (1986). The early start of English—Recent trends and new directions in the Federal Republic of Germany. *International Review of Education, 32*, 3-22.

Görlach, M., & Schröder, K. (1985). Good usage in an EFL context. In S. Greenbaum (Ed.), *The English language today* (pp. 227-232). Oxford: Pergamon Press.

Greenwood, J. (1985). Bangalore revisited: A reluctant complaint. *ELT Journal, 39*, 268-273.

Gregory, M., & Carroll, S. (1978). *Language and situation: Language varieties and their social contexts*. London: Routledge and Kegan Paul.

Grice, H. P. (1975). Logic and conversation. In P. Cole & J. Morgan (Eds.), *Syntax and semantics 3: Speech acts* (pp. 41-48). New York: Academic Press.

Gutschow, H. (1976, September 16). *Kommunikative kompetenz* [Communicative competence]. Remarks delivered at the 7. Arbeitstagung der Fachdidaktiker für Neue Sprachen, Giessen, West Germany.

Habermas, J. (1970). Toward a theory of communicative competence. *Inquiry, 13*, 360-375.

Habermas, J. (1971). Vorbereitende bemerkungen zu einer theorie der kommunikative kompetenz [Preliminary remarks on a theory of communicative competence]. In N. Lishman (Ed.), *Theorie der Gesellschaft oder Sozialtechnologie* [Theory of society or social technology] (pp. 101-141). Frankfurt: Suhrkamp.

Halliday, M. (1961). Categories of the theory of grammar. *Word, 17*, 241-292.

Halliday, M. (1967). Notes on transitivity and theme in English. Parts 1 and 2. *Journal of Linguistics, 3*, 37-81, 199-244.

Halliday, M. (1968). Notes on transitivity and theme in English. Part 3. *Journal of Linguistics, 4*, 179-215.

Halliday, M. (1970a, October). *The place of "functional sentence perspective" in the system of linguistic description*. Paper presented at the International Symposium on FSP, Marianske, Lazne. (Reprinted in G. Kress [Ed.], 1976, pp. 26-35)

Halliday, M. (1970b). Language structure and language function. In J. Lyons (Ed.), *New horizons in linguistics* (pp. 140-165). Harmondsworth, England: Penguin.

Halliday, M. (1973). *Explorations in the functions of language*. London: Edward Arnold.

Halliday, M. (1975). *Learning how to mean*. London: Edward Arnold.

Halliday, M. (1978). *Language as social semiotic: The social interpretation of language and meaning*. Baltimore, MD: Edward Arnold.

Halliday, M., & Hasan, R. (1976). *Cohesion in English*. London: Longman.

Halliday, M., & Hasan, R. (1985). *Language, context, and text: Aspects of language in a social semiotic perspective*. Geelong, Victoria, Australia: Deakin University Press.

Halliday, M., & Martin, J. (Eds). (1981). *Readings in systemic linguistics*. London: Batsford.

Halliday, M., McIntosh, A., & Strevens, P. (1964). *The linguistic sciences and language teaching.* London: Longman.

Helgesen, M. (1987). Playing in English: Games and the L2 classroom in Japan. In S. Savignon & M. Berns (Eds.), *Initiatives in communicative language teaching II.* (pp. 205-226). Reading, MA: Addison-Wesley.

Hessische Kultusminister. (1980). *Rahmenrichtlinien. Sekundarstufe I: Neue sprachen* [Curriculum Guidelines. Secondary Level I. Modern Languages]. Frankfurt: Diesterweg.

Huckin, T. (1980). Review of H. G. Widdowson, *Teaching language as communication. Language Learning, 30,* 209-227.

Hughes, A., & Trudgill, P. (1987). *English accents and dialects: An introduction to social and regional varieties of British English* (2nd ed.). London: Edward Arnold.

Hymes, D. (1971). Competence and performance in linguistic theory. In R. Huxley & E. Ingram (Eds.), *Language acquisition: Models and methods* (pp. 3-28). London: Academic Press.

Hymes, D. (1972). Editorial introduction. *Language in Society, 1,* 1-14.

Hymes, D. (Ed.). (1980). *Language in education: Ethnolinguistic essays.* Washington, DC: Center for Applied Linguistics.

Iyengar, K. (1962). *Indian writing in English.* London: Asia Publishing House.

Jakobovits, L. (1968). The physiology and psychology of second language learning. In E. Birkmaier (Ed.), *Britannica review of foreign language education* (Vol. 1, pp. 181-227). Chicago: Encyclopaedia Britannica.

Jessen, J. (1983). *Et taerskelniveau for dansk* [The threshold level in Danish]. Strasbourg: Council of Europe.

Jha, J. (1979). Attitudes of parents towards English medium and non-English medium schools. *Journal of Educational Research and Extension, 16,* 115-119.

Johnson, K. (1982). *Communicative syllabus design and methodology.* Oxford: Pergamon Press.

Jones, D. (1956). *The pronunciation of English* (4th ed.). Cambridge: Cambridge University Press.

Kachru, B. (1965). The *Indianness* in Indian English. *Word, 21,* 391-410.

Kachru, B. (1977). The new Englishes and old models. *English Teaching Forum, 15,* 29-35.

Kachru, B. (1981a). Socially realistic linguistics: The Firthian tradition. *International Journal of the Sociology of Language, 31,* 65-89.

Kachru, B. (1981b). The pragmatics of non-native varieties of English. In L. Smith (Ed.), *English for cross-cultural communication* (pp. 15-39). New York: St. Martin's Press.

Kachru, B. (1982a). Models for non-native Englishes. In B. Kachru (Ed.), *The other tongue: English across cultures* (pp. 31-57). Urbana, IL: University of Illinois Press.

Kachru, B. (Ed.). (1982b). *The other tongue: English across cultures.* Urbana, IL: University of Illinois Press.

Kachru, B. (1982c). Meaning in deviation: Toward understanding non-native English texts. In B. Kachru (Ed.), *The other tongue: English across cultures* (pp. 325-250). Urbana, IL: University of Illinois Press.

Kachru, B. (1983). *The Indianization of English: The English language in India.* Delhi: Oxford University Press.

Kachru, Y. (1983). Linguistics and written discourse in English and Hindi. In R. Kaplan (Ed.), *Annual review of applied linguistics, 1982* (pp. 50-77). Rowley, MA: Newbury House.

Kachru, Y. (1987). Cross-cultural texts, discourse strategies and text interpretation. In L. Smith (Ed.), *Discourse across cultures: Strategies in world Englishes* (pp. 87-100). New York: Prentice Hall.

Kaplan, R. (1966). Cultural thought patterns in inter-cultural education. *Language Learning, 16,* 1-20.

Kaplan, R. (Ed.). (1983). *Annual review of applied linguistics, 1982.* Rowley, MA: Newbury House.

King-ek, A., Artetxe, S., Astigarraga, M., Beloki, E., Gaminde, I., Goenaga, X., Ibero, I., Ithurssary,

I., Jiminez, E., Labiano, R., Piedra, G., & Urrutia, E. (1988). *Atalase Maila* [The threshold level in Catalan]. Strasbourg: Council of Europe.

Koike, I. (1978). English language teaching policies in Japan: Past, present, and future. In I. Koike *et al.* (Eds.), *The teaching of English in Japan* (pp. 3-14). Tokyo: Eichosha Publishing.

Koike, I., Matsuyama, M., Igarashi, Y., & Suzuki, K. (Eds.). (1978). *The teaching of English in Japan*. Tokyo: Eichosha Publishing.

Kress, G. (Ed.). (1976). *Halliday: System and function in language*. London: Oxford University Press.

Kuhn, T. (1970). *The structure of scientific revolutions* (2nd ed.). Chicago: University of Chicago Press.

Langendoen, D. (1968). *The London school of linguistics* (Research Monograph No. 46). Cambridge, MA: MIT Press.

Leech, G. (1983). *Principles of pragmatics*. London: Longman.

Lowenberg, P. (1985). English in the Malay archipelago: Nativization and its functions in a sociolinguistic area (Doctoral dissertation, University of Illinois, Urbana, 1984). *Dissertation Abstracts International, 45*, 3340A.

Lyons, J. (1970). *New horizons in linguistics*. Harmondsworth, England: Penguin.

Magura, B. (1985). Style and meaning in African English: A sociolinguistic analysis of South African and Zimbabwean English (Doctoral dissertation, University of Illinois, Urbana, 1984). *Dissertation Abstracts International, 45*, 3340A.

Malinowski, B. (1923). The problem of meaning in primitive language. In C. Ogden & I. Richards (Eds.), *The meaning of meaning* (pp. 296-336). London: Trubner and Co.

Malinowski, B. (1935). *Coral gardens and their magic I, II*. London: Allen and Unwin.

Malinowski, B. (1939). The present state of studies in culture contact: Some comments on an American approach. *Africa, 12*, 27-47.

Mathesius, V. (1928). On linguistic characterology with illustrations from modern English. In J. Vachek (Comp.) (1964), *A Prague school reader in linguistics* (pp. 59-67). Bloomington, IN: Indiana University.

Mathesius, V. (1961). *A functional analysis of present day English on a general linguistic basis*. Prague: Československá Akademie Věd.

Matsuyama, M. (1978). Entrance exams: College entrance examinations and English education in Japan. In I. Koike *et al.* (Eds.), *The teaching of English in Japan* (pp. 35-46). Tokyo: Eichosha Publishing.

Menšíková, A. (1972). Sentence patterns in the theory and practice of teaching the grammar of French as a foreign language. In V. Fried (Ed.), *The Prague school of linguistics and language teaching* (pp. 43-61). London: Oxford University Press.

Miller, R. (1967). *The Japanese language*. Chicago: University of Chicago Press.

Ministry of Education, Japan. (1972). *Suggested course of study* (2nd ed.). Tokyo, Japan: Ministry of Education.

Mitchell, T. (1957). The language of buying and selling in Cyrenaica: A situational statement. *Hesperis* (now *Hesperis-Tamuda*, University of Rabat). (Reprinted in Mitchell, 1975, 31-71)

Mitchell, T. (1975). *Principles of Firthian linguistics*. London: Longman.

Monaghan, J. (1979). *The neo-Firthian tradition and its contribution to general linguistics*. Tübingen, West Germany: Max Niemeyer.

Morrow, P. (1987). The users and uses of English in Japan. *World Englishes, 6* (1), 49-62.

Moser, H. (1974). Von den 80er Jahren der 19. Jahrhundert zur Gegenwart. *Deutsche Wortgeschichte* (3rd ed.) (pp. 529-646). Berlin: Walter de Gruyter.

Moynahan, B. (1983, March 27). Sprechen sie Germish? *Sunday Times*, p. 7.

Mulaisho, D. (1971). *Tongue of the dumb*. London: Heinemann.

Munby, J. (1978). *Communicative syllabus design*. Cambridge: Cambridge University Press.

Nelson, C. (1983, May). *Syntactic creativity and intelligibility.* Paper presented at the Annual South Asian Languages Association Roundtable, Urbana, IL.

Nelson, C. (1985). Intelligibility: The case of non-native varieties of English (Doctoral dissertation, University of Illinois, Urbana, 1984). *Dissertation Abstracts International, 45,* 172A.

Ohtani, T. (1978). Adult education: A brief history of teaching and study of business English in Japan. In I. Koike *et al.* (Eds.), *The teaching of English in Japan* (pp. 187-203). Tokyo: Eichosha Publishing.

Oller, J. (1978). Pragmatics and language testing. In B. Spolsky (Ed.), *Approaches to language testing.* Arlington, VA: Center for Applied Linguistics.

Olsson, M. (1978). Intelligibility: An evaluation of some features of English produced by Swedish 14-year-olds. *Gothenburg Studies in English* 40. Goteborg: Acta Universitatis Gothoburgensis.

Omura, K. (1978). Prewar (before 1945): From the Phaeton Incident up to the Pacific War. In I. Koike *et al.* (Eds.), *The teaching of English in Japan* (pp. 91-103). Tokyo: Eichosha Publishing.

Palmer, F. R. (Ed.). (1968). *Selected papers of J.R. Firth, 1952-1959.* Bloomington, IN, and London: Indiana University Press.

Palmer, H. (1920). *The principles of language study.* London: Oxford University Press. (Reprinted 1964)

Passin, H. (1980). *Japanese and the Japanese.* Tokyo: Kinseido.

Paulston, C. (1974). Linguistic and communicative competence. *TESOL Quarterly, 8,* 347-362.

Paulston, C. (1976). *Teaching English as a second language: Techniques and procedures.* Cambridge, MA: Winthrop.

Piepho, H. E. (1974). *Kommunikative kompetenz als übergeordnetes lernziel des Englischunterrichts* [Communicative competence as a general learning goal in English instruction]. Dornburg-Frickhofen, West Germany: Frankonius.

Piepho, H. E. (1979). *Kommunikative didaktik des Englischunterrichts* [Communicative English language teaching]. Limburg, West Germany: Frankonius.

Piepho, H. E. (1981). Establishing objectives in the teaching of English: Principles and an exercise typology. In C. Candlin (Ed. and Trans.), *Communicative teaching of English: Principles and an exercise typology* (pp. 8-23). London: Langenscheidt-Longman.

Piepho, H. E., & Bredella, L. (Eds.). (1976). *Contacts. Integriertes Englischlehrwerk für klassen 5-10* [Contacts. Integrated English series for grades 5-10]. Bochum, West Germany: Kamp.

Piepho, H. E., & Gerster, L. (1979). *Kommentar Contacts 6* [Instructor's manual *Contacts* 6]. Bochum, West Germany: Kamp.

Prabhu, N. S. (1980). Theoretical background to the Bangalore project. In RIE (1980a), (pp. 17-26).

Prabhu, N. S. (1987). *Second language pedagogy.* Oxford: Oxford University Press.

Prator, C. E. (1968). The British heresy in ESL. In J. Fishman, C. Ferguson, & J. Das Gupta (Eds.), *Language problems of developing nations* (pp. 459-476). New York: John Wiley and Sons.

Preston, D. (1981). Ethnography of TESOL. *TESOL Quarterly, 15,* 105-116.

Priebsch, R., & Collinson, W. (1966). *The German language* (6th ed.). London: Faber and Faber.

Pytelka, J. (1972). The Prague school and studies in the language of commerce. In V. Fried (Ed.), *The Prague school of linguistics and language teaching* (pp. 211-223). London: Oxford University Press.

Quirk, R. (1985). The English language in a global context. In R. Quirk & H. G. Widdowson (Eds.), *English in the world: Teaching and learning the language and literatures* (pp. 1-6). Cambridge: Cambridge University Press.

Ragan, P. (1987, April). *Text, context and language teaching: A systemic-functional perspective.* Paper presented at the International Meeting of TESOL, Miami, FL.

Raimes, A. (1983). Tradition and revolution in ESL teaching. *TESOL Quarterly, 17,* 535-552.

Rao, R. (1963). *Kanthapura.* New York: New Directions.

Reid, T. B. W. (1956). Linguistics, structuralism and philology. *Archivum Linguisticum*, *8*, 28-37.

RIE (1980a). Bulletin. No. 4(i). New approaches to teaching English: Report on "Bangalore Project," 1979-1980 [Report of seminar]. Regional Institute of English, South India, Bangalore.

RIE (1980b). Newsletter (Special Series). Vol. 1. No. 4. Teaching English as communication. Proposals for syllabus design, methodology, and evaluation. Regional Institute of English, South India, Bangalore.

RIE (1980c). Newsletter (Special Series). Vol. 2. No. 1. Teaching English through communication, Madras Group, Lesson Reports (1). Regional Institute of English, South India, Bangalore.

RIE (1980d). Newsletter (Special Series). Vol. 2. No. 2. Teaching English through communication, Bangalore Group, Lesson Reports (1). Regional Institute of English, South India, Bangalore.

Rivers, W. (1971). Talking off the tops of their heads. *TESOL Quarterly*, *5*, 71-81.

Rivers, W. (1973). From linguistic competence to communicative competence. *TESOL Quarterly*, *7*, 25-34.

Rivers, W. (1976). The natural and the normal in language learning. In H.D. Brown (Ed.), Papers in second language acquisition [Special issue]. *Language Learning*, *4*, 1-8.

Rivers, W. (1983). *Speaking in many tongues: Essays in foreign-language teaching* (3rd ed.). Cambridge: Cambridge University Press.

Ross, D. (1981). From theory to practice: Some critical comments on the communicative approach to language teaching. *Language Learning*, *31*, 223-242.

Rumelhart, D. (1980). Schemata: The building blocks of cognition. In R. Spiro, B. Bruce, & W. Brewer (Eds.), *Theoretical issues in reading comprehension* (pp. 33-35). Hillsdale, NJ: Lawrence Erlbaum Associates.

Sampson, G. (1980). *Schools of linguistics*. Stanford, CA: Stanford University Press.

Savignon, S. (1972). *Communicative competence: An experiment in foreign language teaching*. Philadelphia, PA: Center for Curriculum Development.

Savignon, S. (1983). *Communicative competence: Theory and classroom practice*. Reading, MA: Addison-Wesley.

Savignon, S., & Berns, M. (1983). *English around the world: Integrated EFL junior high series for Japan*. Unpublished manuscript.

Savignon, S., & Berns, M. (Eds.). (1984). *Initiatives in communicative language teaching*. Reading, MA: Addison-Wesley.

Savignon, S., & Berns, M. (Eds.). (1987). *Initiatives in communicative language teaching II*. Reading, MA: Addison-Wesley.

Scollon, R., & Scollon, S. (1983). Face in interethnic communication. In J. Richards & R. Schmidt (Eds.), *Language and communication* (pp. 156-190). London: Longman.

Sekimori, G. (1983). Business ELT. *JALT Newsletter*, *7*, 1-2, 4.

Sey, D. (1973). *Ghanian English: An exploratory survey*. London: Macmillan.

Shaw, D. (1977). Foreign-language syllabus development: Some recent approaches. *Language teaching and linguistics: Abstracts* (pp. 217-233).

Sibata, T. (1975). On some problems in Japanese sociolinguistics: Reflections and prospects. In C. Peng (Ed.), *Language in Japanese society* (pp. 159-174). Tokyo: University of Tokyo Press.

Sinclair, J. (1980). Some implications of discourse analysis for ESP methodology. *Applied Linguistics*, *1*, 253-261.

Slagter, P. (1980). *Un nivel umbral* [The threshold level in Spanish]. Strasbourg: Council of Europe.

Smith, E., & Luce, L. (Eds.). (1979). *Towards internationalism*. Rowley, MA: Newbury.

Smith, L. (Ed.). (1981). *English for cross-cultural communication*. New York: St. Martin's Press.

Smith, L. (Ed.). (1983). *Readings in English as an international language*. Oxford: Pergamon Press.

Smith, L. (Ed.). (1987). *Discourse across cultures: Strategies in world Englishes*. New York: Prentice Hall.

Smith, L., & Bisazza, J. (1982). The comprehensibility of three varieties of English for college students in seven countries. *Language Learning, 32,* 259-270.

Smith, L., & Nelson, C. (1985). International intelligibility of English: Directions and resources. *World Englishes, 4,* 333-342.

Smith, L., & Rafiqzad, K. (1979). English for cross-cultural communication: The question of intelligibility. *TESOL Quarterly, 13,* 371-380. (Reprinted in L. Smith [Ed.], 1983, pp. 49-58)

Smith, S. (1987). Second language teaching in the business world: Communicative English course content in West Germany. In S. Savignon & M. Berns (Eds.), *Initiatives in communicative language teaching II.* (pp. 107-124). Reading, MA: Addison-Wesley.

Sridhar, K. (1989). *English in Indian bilingualism.* Delhi: Manohar.

Sridhar, S. N. (1982). Non-native English literatures: Context and relevance. In B. Kachru (Ed.), *The other tongue: English across cultures* (pp. 291-306). Urbana, IL: University of Illinois Press.

Stanlaw, J. (1982). English in Japanese communicative strategies. In B. Kachru (Ed.), *The other tongue: English across cultures* (pp. 168-197). Urbana, IL: University of Illinois Press.

Stanlaw, J. (1987). Japanese and English: Borrowing and contact. World Englishes, 6, 93-109.

Statistisches Bundesamt, Wiesbaden. (1987). *Statistisches jahrbuch für die Bundesrepublik Deutschland.* Stuttgart/Mainz, West Germany: Kohlhammer.

Steiner, E. (1983). *Die entwicklung des Britischen kontextualismus.* Heidelberg: Julius Groos Verlag.

Strevens, P. (1977). *New orientations in the teaching of English.* London: Oxford University Press.

Strevens, P. (1978, August). *Functional Englishes (ESP): A British view.* Paper presented at Conference on Functional Englishes, University of Illinois, Urbana.

Strevens, P. (1980). *Teaching English as an international language: From practice to principle.* Oxford: Oxford University Press.

Svanes, B., Hagen, J., Manne, G., & Svindland, A. (1987). *Et terskelnivå for norsk* [The threshold level in Norwegian]. Strasbourg: Council of Europe.

Svoboda, A. (1968). The hierarchy of communicative units and fields as illustrated by English attributive constructions. *Brno Studies in English, 7,* 49-101.

Tanabe, Y. (1978). English as an international language: Qualifications, adaptation and perspective. In I. Koike *et al.* (Eds.), *The teaching of English in Japan* (pp. 47-57). Tokyo: Eichosha Publishing.

Taylor, D. (1988). The meaning and use of the term "competence" in linguistics and applied linguistics. *Applied Linguistics, 9,* 148-168.

Threadgold, T., Grosz, E., Kress, G., & Halliday, M. (Eds.). (1986). *Semiotics, idealogy, language* (Sydney Studies in society and culture, No. 3). Sydney, Australia: Sydney Association for Studies in Society and Culture.

Tongue, R. K. (1974). *The English of Singapore and Malaysia.* Singapore: Eastern Universities Press.

Trubetzkoy, N. (1939). *Grundzüge der Phonologie.* Travaux du Cercle Linguistique de Prague, 7.

Vachek, J. (Comp.) (1964). *A Prague school reader in linguistics.* Bloomington, IN: Indiana University Press.

Vachek, J. (1966). *The linguistic school of Prague.* Bloomington, IN: Indiana University Press.

Vachek, J. (1972). The linguistic theory of the Prague school. In V. Fried (Ed.), *The Prague school of linguistics and language teaching* (pp. 11-25). London: Oxford University Press.

Vachek, J. (1976). *Selected writings in English and general linguistics.* The Hague: Mouton.

Vackek, J. (1985). The 1929 Praguian "theses", internal speech and internal language. In U. Pieper and G. Stickel (Eds.), *Studia Linguistica Diachronia et Synchronica. Werner Winter. Sexagenario Anno MCMLXXXIII.* (pp. 851-847). Berlin: Mouton de Gruyter.

Valentine, T. (1985). Cross-sex conversation in Indian English fiction. *World Englishes, 4,* 319-332.

Van Dijk, T. (1972). *Some aspects of text grammars.* The Hague: Mouton.

Van Ek, J., & Alexander, L. (1980). *Threshold level English*. Oxford: Pergamon Press.

Ventola, E. (1983, March). *Orientation to social semiotics in language teaching*. Paper presented at the International Meeting of TESOL, Toronto, Canada.

Verma, S. K. (1987). Teaching English as a second language in India: Focus on objectives. In R. Steele & T. Threadgold (Eds.), *Language topics: Essays in honour of Michael Halliday Vol. I* (pp. 417-423). Amsterdam: John Benjamins.

Voegelin, C., & Harris, Z. (1951). Determining intelligibility among dialects. *Proceedings of the American Philological Society*, *95*, 322-329.

Wells, S. (1986). Jürgen Habermas, communicative competence, and the teaching of technical discourse. In C. Nelson (Ed.), *Theory in the classroom* (pp. 245-270). Urbana, IL: University of Illinois Press.

Widdowson, H. G. (1978). *Teaching language as communication*. Oxford: Oxford University Press.

Widdowson, H. G. (1979). *Explorations in applied linguistics*. Oxford: Oxford University Press.

Wilkins, D. (1976). *Notional syllabuses*. Oxford: Oxford University Press.

Wittman, H. (1981, April 19). Was der Sprachunterricht braucht - Kommunikationsfähigkeit und mehr nicht? *Frankfurter Allgemeine Zeitung*, p. 27.

Wolfson, N. (1984). Pretty is as pretty does: A speech act view of sex roles. *Applied Linguistics*, *5*, 236-244.

Wynants, A. (1985). *Drempelniveau. Nederlands als vreemde taal* [The threshold level in Dutch]. Strasbourg: Council of Europe.

Index